Flutter®

for **dummies**®
A Wiley Brand

Flutter®

by Barry Burd, PhD

A Wiley Brand

Flutter® For Dummies®

Published by: **John Wiley & Sons, Inc.**, 111 River Street, Hoboken, NJ 07030-5774, www.wiley.com

Copyright © 2020 by John Wiley & Sons, Inc., Hoboken, New Jersey

Published simultaneously in Canada

For general information on our other products and services, please contact our Customer Care Department within the U.S. at 877-762-2974, outside the U.S. at 317-572-3993, or fax 317-572-4002. For technical support, please visit https://hub.wiley.com/community/support/dummies.

Wiley publishes in a variety of print and electronic formats and by print-on-demand. Some material included with standard print versions of this book may not be included in e-books or in print-on-demand. If this book refers to media such as a CD or DVD that is not included in the version you purchased, you may download this material at http://booksupport.wiley.com. For more information about Wiley products, visit www.wiley.com.

Library of Congress Control Number: 2020935615

ISBN: 978-1-119-61258-2; 978-1-119-61261-2 (ebk); 978-1-119-61262-9 (ebk)

Manufactured in the United States of America

V10019548_063020

Contents at a Glance

Table of Contents

Introduction

On December 5, 2018, at an annual developers' event in London, Google announced the release of Flutter 1.0. Between December 5 and the end of December, the number of page visits to the official flutter.io website jumped from 2.3 million to 4.7 million. In the following year, the number of posts about Flutter on the Stack Overflow developers' website increased by 70 percent, exceeding the count of posts about React Native — the most popular alternative to Flutter.

Companies such as Capital One, Alibaba, Groupon, and Philips Hue use Flutter to develop mobile apps. The official app for the musical *Hamilton* is written using Flutter. Google's next mobile operating system, code-named Fuchsia, is based on Flutter. An estimated 200 million users run apps written in Flutter. More than 250,000 developers write Flutter code, and the Google Play Store has over 3,000 Flutter apps.

Are you interested in developing Flutter apps? If so, you're in good company.

How to Use This Book

You can attack this book in either of two ways: Go from cover to cover or poke around from one chapter to another. You can even do both. Start at the beginning and then jump to a section that particularly interests you. This book was designed so that the basic topics come first, and the more-involved topics follow them. But you may already be comfortable with some basics, or you may have specific goals that don't require you to know about certain topics.

In general, my advice is this:

>> If you already know something, don't bother reading about it.

>> If you're curious, don't be afraid to skip ahead. You can always sneak a peek at an earlier chapter, if you need to do so.

Conventions Used in This Book

Almost every technically themed book starts with a little typeface legend, and *Flutter For Dummies* is no exception. What follows is a brief explanation of the typefaces used in this book:

>> New terms are set in *italics*.

>> If you need to type something that's mixed in with the regular text, the characters you type appear in bold. For example: "Type **MyNewProject** in the text field."

>> You also see this computerese font. I use computerese for Flutter code, filenames, onscreen messages, and other such text. Also, if something you need to type is really long, it appears in computerese font on its own line (or lines).

>> You may need to change certain characters when you type them on your own computer keyboard. For instance, I may ask you to type

```
final String anyname;
```

which means that you type **final String**, and then a name that you make up on your own, and then a semicolon. Words you need to replace with your own words are set in `italicized computerese`.

What You Don't Have to Read

Pick the first chapter or section that has material you don't already know, and start reading there. Of course, you may hate making decisions as much as I do. If so, here are some guidelines you can follow:

>> **If you already know what kind of an animal Flutter is and you don't care what happens behind the scenes when a Flutter app runs:** Skip Chapter 1 and go straight to Chapter 2. Believe me — I won't mind.

>> **If you already know how to get a Flutter app running:** Skip Part 1 and start with Part 2.

>> **If you've already tinkered with some simple Flutter apps:** Skim over Chapter 1, and then go to Part 3. Chapter 1 pulls together the bits and pieces that you've read about Flutter, and Part 3 takes you beyond the very basics.

>> **If you have experience writing Flutter apps:** Come to my house and help me write *Flutter For Dummies*, 2nd Edition.

If you want to skip the sidebars and the paragraphs with Technical Stuff icons, please do. In fact, if you want to skip anything at all, feel free.

Foolish Assumptions

In this book, I make a few assumptions about you, the reader. If one of these assumptions is incorrect, you're probably okay. If all these assumptions are incorrect . . . well, buy the book anyway:

>> **I assume that you have access to a computer.** Access to a smartphone is helpful but not absolutely necessary. All the software you need in order to test Flutter apps on a laptop or desktop computer is freely available. You simply download, install, and get going.

>> **I assume that you can navigate your computer's common menus and dialog boxes.** You don't have to be a Windows or Macintosh power user, but you should be able to start a program, find a file, put a file into a certain directory — that sort of thing. Much of the time, when you follow the instructions in this book, you're typing code on the keyboard, not pointing-and-clicking the mouse.

    On those occasions when you need to drag-and-drop, cut-and-paste, or plug-and-play, I guide you carefully through the steps. But your computer may be configured in any of several billion ways, and my instructions may not quite fit your special situation. When you reach one of these platform-specific tasks, try following the steps in this book. If the steps don't quite fit, consult a book with instructions tailored to your system. If you can't find such a book, send me an email. (My address appears later in the introduction.)

>> **I assume that you can think logically.** That's all there is to application development — thinking logically. If you can think logically, you've got it made. If you don't believe that you can think logically, read on. You may be pleasantly surprised.

>> **I make very few assumptions about your computer programming experience (or your lack of such experience).** In writing this book, I've tried to do the impossible: make the book interesting for experienced programmers yet accessible to people with little or no programming experience. This means that I don't assume any particular programming background on your part. If you've never written any code, that's okay.

    On the other hand, if you've done some coding (maybe in Java, Python, or C++), you'll discover some interesting plot twists in Dart — the language that's used to develop Flutter apps. The creators of Dart took the best ideas from object-oriented programming and functional programming, streamlined them, reworked them, and reorganized them into a simple yet powerful way of thinking about problems. You'll enjoy programming in Dart.

How This Book Is Organized

This book is divided into subsections, which are grouped into sections, which come together to make chapters, which are lumped, finally, into four parts (like one of those Russian matryoshka dolls). The parts of the book are described here.

Part 1, "Getting Ready"

Part 1 covers all the nuts-and-bolts. It introduces you to the major ideas behind mobile app development and walks you through the installation of the necessary software products.

The instructions in these chapters cover both Windows and Macintosh computers. They cover many computer configurations with all kinds of software already installed. But adding new software is always tricky, and you might have a few hurdles to overcome. If you do, check the end of this chapter for ways to reach me (the author) and get some quick advice. (Yes, I answer emails, tweets, Facebook posts, and notes sent by carrier pigeons.)

Part 2, "Flutter: A Burd's-Eye View"

Chapters 3 and 4 cover Flutter's basic building blocks. These chapters describe some simple Flutter apps and introduce Dart programming language fundamentals.

If you've created apps specifically for Android or iOS, some of the material in Part 2 may be familiar to you. If so, you can skip sections or read this stuff quickly. But don't read too quickly. Flutter is different from most other development frameworks, and Flutter's differences are worth noting.

Part 3, "Details, Details"

If you've tasted some Flutter and want more, you can find what you need in Part 3 of this book. This part's chapters cover the building blocks of a solid, useful app — tasks like responding to user input, laying out your app's components, navigating from page to page, getting data from the Internet, and more.

Part 4, "The Part of Tens"

In The Part of Tens, which is a little Flutter candy store, you can find lists — lists of tips for avoiding mistakes, tracking down resources, and finding all kinds of interesting goodies.

More on the web!

You've read the *Flutter For Dummies* book, seen the *Flutter For Dummies* movie, worn the *Flutter For Dummies* T-shirt, and eaten the *Flutter For Dummies* candy. What more is there to do?

That's easy. Just visit this book's website: `www.allmycode.com/Flutter`. There, you can find updates, comments, additional information, and answers to commonly asked questions from readers. You can also find a small chat application for sending me quick questions when I'm online. (When I'm not online, you can contact me in other ways. See the end of this chapter for more info.)

Icons Used in This Book

If you could watch me write this book, you'd see me sitting at my computer, talking to myself. I say each sentence in my head. Most of the sentences I mutter several times. When I have an extra thought, a side comment, or something else that doesn't belong in the regular stream, I twist my head a little bit. That way, whoever's listening to me (usually, nobody) knows that I'm off on a momentary tangent.

Of course, in print, you can't see me twisting my head. I need some other way to set a side thought in a corner by itself. I do it with icons. When you see a Tip icon or a Remember icon, you know that I'm taking a quick detour.

Here's a list of icons that I use in this book:

TIP

A tip is an extra piece of information — helpful advice that the other books may forget to tell you.

WARNING

Everyone makes mistakes. Heaven knows that I've made a few in my time. Anyway, when I think people are especially prone to make a mistake, I mark the text with a Warning icon.

REMEMBER

You can think of the word *Remember* in two different contexts. One context is, "Remember to do this good thing in your code, and remember not to do that bad thing in your code." Another context is, "When you find yourself not doing this good thing or doing that bad thing, remember that you can read about it in the section containing this icon." Personally, I prefer the latter context because it recognizes that everyone forgets stuff. When you forget something, simply go back and look it up.

CROSS
REFERENCE

"If you don't remember what such-and-such means, see blah-blah-blah," or "For more information, read blahbity-blah-blah."

ON THE
WEB

This icon calls attention to useful material that you can find online. (You don't have to wait long to see one of these icons. I use one at the end of this introduction!)

TECHNICAL
STUFF

Occasionally, I run across a technical tidbit. The tidbit may help you understand what the people behind the scenes (the people who created Java) were thinking. You don't have to read it, but you may find it useful. You may also find the tidbit helpful if you plan to read other (geekier) books about Flutter.

Beyond the Book

In addition to what you're reading right now, this book comes with a free access-anywhere Cheat Sheet containing code that you can copy-and-paste into your own Flutter program. To get this Cheat Sheet, simply go to www.dummies.com and type **Flutter For Dummies Cheat Sheet** in the Search box.

Where to Go from Here

If you've gotten this far, you're ready to start reading about Flutter app development. Think of me (the author) as your guide, your host, your personal assistant. I do everything I can to keep things interesting and, most importantly, to help you understand.

ON THE
WEB

If you like what you read, send me a note. My email address, which I created just for comments and questions about this book, is flutter@allmycode.com. If email and chat aren't your favorites, you can reach me instead on Twitter (@allmycode) and on Facebook (/allmycode). And don't forget — for the latest updates, visit this book's website. The site's direct address is www.allmycode.com/flutter. Alternatively, you can visit www.allmycode.com and find links to all my books' web pages.

Enough with the introduction! Onward to Flutter. . . .

1

Getting Ready

Chapter **1**

What Is Flutter?

Several years ago, I won a smartphone in a raffle at an app developer conference. What a joy it was to win something! The experience made me feel that the entire cosmos favored me. Every time I used that phone, I felt like a big shot.

Eventually, the phone's battery became so weak that I had to charge it every hour. I didn't realize that the phone was still under warranty, so I tried to replace the phone's battery myself. I bought a new battery from an online vendor. The instructions told me how to take the case apart, unhook the circuit connections, and remove the old battery from its cradle.

Everything went nicely until the part about removing the old battery. The instructions said to pull on a little tab, but I couldn't find a tab. So, I tried for several minutes to get a grip on the battery.

The battery wasn't budging, so I found a little screwdriver and tried to pry the battery from its tight surroundings. That's when I heard a pop, smelled smoke, and realized that the phone's battery had caught fire.

Fast-forward to the next afternoon. I was wandering past an electronics shop, so I went in and asked whether the shopkeeper might be able to fix my phone. "Yes," he said. "Bring it in the next time you're in the neighborhood. I can fix any phone."

You should have seen the look on the shopkeeper's face when, later that day, I brought in the charred, bent-up, barely recognizable phone. I would have included a picture in this book but, alas, I couldn't take a picture. I had no phone.

I still remember this phone battery story from beginning to end. I remember the joy of winning a free phone, the shock of seeing it go up in flames, and the look of horror on the shopkeeper's face. But my most powerful memory comes from the moment I opened the phone's case: Inside that little case, I saw enough circuitry to make me dizzy. Having done some electrical work in my own home, I'd handled thick 10-gauge wires and hefty 220-volt connectors. I had replaced desktop computers' sound cards, laptop computers' hard drives, and the SSD inside a tightly packed MacBook Air. But this smartphone was amazing. The circuit board looked like a microchip in its own right. The connectors were so tiny that I wondered how signals could reliably squeeze through them.

No doubt about it: Mobile phones are complicated beasts. So how do they work? What makes them tick? What's going on inside each of those remarkable gadgets?

Hardware and Software (Things You May Already Know)

A mobile phone is really a small computer. And, like any computer, a mobile phone operates on several layers. Figure 1-1 shows you a few of those layers.

Hardware is the stuff you can touch. It's the bottom layer of the diagram in Figure 1-1. Hardware consists of items like circuitry, memory, and the battery.

Electrical signals that travel along the hardware's circuits make the hardware do what you want it to do. These signals encode instructions. Taken as a whole, these instructions are called *software*.

When people create software, they don't describe each electrical signal that travels through the hardware's circuitry. Instead, people write *source code* — instructions that look something like English-language instructions. One source code instruction can be shorthand for hundreds or thousands of electrical signals.

A collection of source code instructions that perform a particular task (word processing, web browsing, managing a smart thermostat, or whatever) is called a *program*. A person who writes these instructions is a *programmer* or — a fancier-sounding term — a *developer*. The person who runs a program on their own device is a *user*.

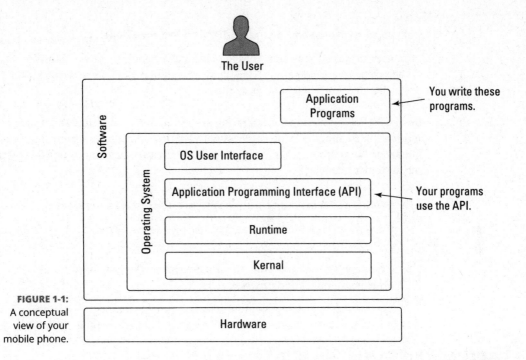

The User

Software

Operating System

Application Programs

You write these programs.

OS User Interface

Application Programming Interface (API)

Your programs use the API.

Runtime

Kernal

Hardware

FIGURE 1-1:
A conceptual view of your mobile phone.

Just as people communicate using many spoken languages, programmers write source code using many *programming languages*. If you create iPhone apps, you probably write code in either the Swift language or the Objective-C language. If you create Android apps, you're likely to write code in either Kotlin or Java.

When you create a Flutter app, you write code in the Dart programming language. Here's a complete Dart language program:

```
main() => print('Hello');
```

This program displays the word *Hello* on the screen. It's not very useful, but please be patient. This is only Chapter 1!

Figure 1-1 distinguishes between two kinds of software:

>> *Operating system* (OS) software runs whenever the device is turned on.

OS software manages the device and provides ways for the user to interact with the device. Devices made by Apple, such as iPhones and iPads, run the *iOS* operating system. Android phones and tablets run the *Android* operating system (of course).

>> *Application programs* do the work that users want done.

Apps to make phone calls, apps to read email, calendar apps, web browsers, and games are examples of application programs. As a Flutter developer, your job is to create application programs.

By one estimate, the popular operating system named Linux consists of nearly 28 million instructions. No one can deal with that much code, so operating systems are divided into layers of their own. Figure 1-1 shows only four of a typical operating system's many layers:

>> A *kernel* performs the operating system's most fundamental tasks.

The kernel schedules apps to be run, manages a device's memory and files, provides access to input and output, and does many other essential tasks.

>> A *runtime* is a bunch of code that does extra work in the background while your application program runs.

Runtimes come in many shapes and sizes. A runtime for the C programming language consists of a relatively small amount of code. In contrast, a Java language runtime (a *Java Virtual Machine,* or *JVM*) is a big piece of software with lots of moving parts.

When you run an iOS app, the app uses the *Objective-C runtime*. When you run an Android app, that app uses the *Android runtime*, also known as *ART*.

>> An *application programming interface* (API) is a bunch of code that app developers use over and over again.

For example, Android's API has something named `toUpperCase`. If you apply `toUpperCase` to `"Flutter For Dummies"`, you get `"FLUTTER FOR DUMMIES"`. You don't have to write your own code to change each of the letters. Android's API provides this functionality for you. All you have to do is tell Android's API to apply its `toUpperCase` feature, and then you're all set.

Here's some useful terminology: Rather than tell an API to "apply its `toUpperCase` feature," you *call* `toUpperCase`. This use of the word *call* dates back to the FORTRAN programming language of the 1950s.

Operating systems haven't cornered the market on APIs. All kinds of software come with APIs. Flutter and Dart have their own APIs.

Dart's API has general-purpose things, like `toUpperCase`, `isAtSameMomentAs`, and a bunch of others. Flutter's API has features that apply to visually oriented apps. For example, when you want to display a box where the user can type text, you don't have to describe every aspect of the box's appearance and behavior. Instead, you can call the API's `TextField` constructor and have Flutter do the hard work for you.

I sometimes refer to an API as a *library*. You borrow books from a public library, and you borrow existing code from the Dart and Flutter APIs.

In the Dart programming terminology, the word *library* has a slightly different meaning. You don't have to worry about that yet.

Throughout most of this book, I describe pieces of the Dart and Flutter APIs and then the way you use those pieces to create Flutter programs.

A typical API has thousands of pieces. No one memorizes all of them. When you want to add an image to your app, you open Flutter's documentation and search for the word `Image`. The documentation's `Image` page tells you how to display an image, how to size an image, how to tile an image, and how to do all kinds of other good stuff.

>> **The *OS user interface* is the area that includes the home screen, the launch icons, a file explorer, and any other stuff users see when they're not working with a particular application program.**

On your laptop computer, you probably have a *desktop* instead of a home screen. One way or another, the OS presents options to help users launch application programs and perform other maintenance tasks. These options are part of the OS user interface.

Each layer in Figure 1-1 contains a collection of related components. This helps programmers focus on the components that concern them the most — for example:

>> **The API has code to help developers write application programs.**

A developer who's creating an online purchasing app looks for components in the API.

>> **The Runtime layer has code to run programs efficiently.**

To make everyone's code run faster, engineers at Apple make improvements to the iOS Runtime layer.

In addition to separating parts of the code from one another, the layers form organized paths of communication among parts of the system. In general, a layer's code communicates only with the layers immediately above and below it. For example, a user taps a button belonging to a weather app. The app responds by calling on functionality provided by the API. Communication works its way down the diagram in Figure 1-1 until it reaches the hardware, which responds by changing the pixels on the device's screen. A user never communicates directly with the API, and application programs have no direct access to the operating system's kernel.

CODE YOU CAN USE

During the early 1980s, my cousin-in-law Chris worked for a computer software firm. The firm wrote code for word processing machines. (At the time, if you wanted to compose documents without a typewriter, you bought a "computer" that did nothing but word processing.) Chris complained about being asked to write the same old code over and over again. "First, I write a search-and-replace program. Then I write a spell checker. Then I write another search-and-replace program. Then a different kind of spell checker. And then a better search-and-replace program."

How did Chris manage to stay interested in his work? And how did Chris's employer manage to stay in business? Every few months, Chris had to reinvent the wheel — toss out the old search-and-replace program and write a new program from scratch. That's inefficient. What's worse, it's boring.

For years, computer professionals were seeking the holy grail — a way to write software so that it's easy to reuse. Don't write and rewrite your search-and-replace code. Just break the task into tiny pieces. One piece of code searches for a single character, another piece looks for blank spaces, and a third piece substitutes one letter for another. When you have all the pieces, just assemble these pieces to form a search-and-replace program. Later on, when you think of a new feature for your word processing software, you reassemble the pieces in a slightly different way. It's sensible, it's cost-efficient, and it's much more fun.

The late 1980s saw several advances in software development, and by the early 1990s, many large programming projects were being written from prefabricated components. For a particular project or a particular programming language, these prefab components formed a library of reusable code. This was the birth of the modern API.

When you create a Flutter app, you use the Dart programming language. Dart and Flutter have separate APIs:

- **Dart's API deals with the tasks that every programming language should be able to do, no matter what programmers want to do with that language.**

  For example, Dart's API helps programmers round a number, trim a string of characters, describe a time interval, reverse a list, and so on.

- **Flutter's API deals with the presentation of components and images on a device's screen.**

  One part of Flutter's API deals with buttons, text fields, check boxes, and the like. Another part handles a user's gestures. Yet another covers animation.

Every Dart program, even the simplest one, calls on code in the Dart API, and every Flutter app calls on both the Dart and Flutter APIs. These APIs are both useful and formidable. They're useful because of all the things you can do with the API code. They're formidable because both APIs are extensive. No one memorizes all the features made available by the Dart and Flutter APIs. Programmers remember the features that they use often and look up the features that they need in a pinch. They look up these features on a website called the *Flutter API reference documentation*.

The API documentation (see `https://.api.flutter.dev`) describes the features in both the Dart and Flutter APIs. As a Flutter developer, you consult this API documentation on a daily basis. You can bookmark the website and revisit the site whenever you need to look up something.

Where Does Flutter Fit In?

The heart of Flutter is an API for creating apps. Most Flutter apps run on mobile devices, but Flutter apps can run on laptop and desktop computers, too. Flutter certainly wasn't the first API for mobile devices, so why should anyone consider using Flutter to create apps?

Cross-platform development

My favorite burger joint advertised a new mobile ordering app. I needed the app so that I could quickly hop off a commuter train, grab a burger, and run to a nearby tech meeting. I did this several times each month. But I had a problem: The app ran only on iPhones, and I had an Android phone.

Behind the scenes, the burger joint's app developers were hard at work converting their iPhone app to an Android app. This was no minor task, because Android's API doesn't recognize the same commands as iPhone's API. Going from one API to the other isn't straightforward. It's not a matter of making routine code changes. To convert from one kind of phone to another, developers rewrite thousands (and maybe even millions) of lines of code. The process is time-consuming and expensive.

So I waited and waited for the restaurant to have an Android app. I was so desperate for a delicious cheeseburger that I finally broke down and bought a second phone. But that turned out to be a bad idea. As soon as my new iPhone arrived, the burger place released its shiny, new Android app.

The whole story comes down to things called platforms. People throw around the word *platform* as if the word means everything and nothing. But to my mind, a *platform* is a particular operating system along with the hardware the OS runs on.

What makes the Android platform different from its iOS counterpart? To create radio buttons in Android's API, you write code of the following kind:

```
<RadioGroup>

    <RadioButton
        android:id="@+id/radioButton1"
        android:text="Red"
        android:onClick="onRadioButtonClicked"/>


    <RadioButton
        android:id="@+id/radioButton2"
        android:text="Yellow"
        android:onClick="onRadioButtonClicked"/>


    <RadioButton
        android:id="@+id/radioButton3"
        android:text="Green"
        android:onClick="onRadioButtonClicked"/>

</RadioGroup>
```

Try converting that code to work on an iPhone. The iOS API doesn't have radio buttons, so, to adapt an Android app with radio buttons for iOS, you write code to make things that look like radio buttons. You also code rules for the radio buttons to follow — rules like "only one button at a time can be selected." If you don't want to create radio buttons from scratch, you can replace Android's radio buttons with an iOS picker component, a thing that looks like an old automobile odometer. One way or another, replacing an app's components takes time and costs money.

Some companies give up and create apps for only one platform — iPhone or Android. Other companies hire two teams of programmers — one for iPhone development and another for Android development. Still other companies have one team of programmers that work on both versions of the code. For the companies' managers, the problem is exasperating. Why spend nearly twice the money and create two apps that do almost the same things?

The developer community has names for this ugly situation:

» Software written for one platform isn't *compatible* with other platforms.

>> The mobile phone arena suffers from *fragmentation*: The market is divided between two different operating systems, and the Android half is divided among many vendors' phones.

A program that makes direct use of either the Android or iOS API is called *native code*, and native code written for Android can't run on an iOS device. In the same way, native code written for iOS is meaningless to an Android device. What's a developer to do?

A framework is a second-level API. What the heck does that mean? A *framework* is an API that serves as an intermediary between the developer and some other API. If direct use of the Android or iOS API is problematic, you switch to a framework's API. The framework's API deals head-on with Android's and iOS's problems.

Frameworks like Flutter offer an alternative to native app development. When you write a Flutter program, you don't write code specifically for Android or iOS. Instead, you write code that can be translated into either system's API calls. Here's how you create radio buttons in the Flutter framework:

```
Radio(
  value: TrafficLight.Red,
  groupValue: _trafficLightValue,
  onChanged: _updateTrafficLight,
),
Radio(
  value: TrafficLight.Yellow,
  groupValue: _trafficLightValue,
  onChanged: _updateTrafficLight,
),
Radio(
  value: TrafficLight.Green,
  groupValue: _trafficLightValue,
  onChanged: _updateTrafficLight,
)
```

Your computer translates code of this kind into either Android API calls or iOS API calls — or both. That's cool!

A quick-and-easy development cycle

You may have heard stories about the early days of computer programming. I worked for a few summers at the University of Pennsylvania Physics department. I wrote FORTRAN programs and typed them myself on a big deck of punch cards. A 600-line program weighed about 1400 grams (roughly 3 pounds).

A BRIEF HISTORY

130,000 years ago: Humans first walk the earth.

10,000 years ago: Humans begin farming.

1752: Ben Franklin discovers electricity.

1760: The Industrial Revolution begins.

March 10, 1876: Alexander Graham Bell makes the first telephone call.

April 3, 1973: Martin Cooper makes the first mobile phone call.

August 16, 1994: BellSouth Cellular releases IBM Simon — the first smartphone.

June 29, 2007: Apple releases the first iPhone.

November 5, 2007: Google releases the first public beta of Android.

Both the iOS and Android are native development technologies. With native development, the programmer makes calls directly to the system's API.

December 2007: Articles and blog posts about fragmentation in mobile phone technologies start appearing in large numbers.

March 13, 2009: Nitobi Software introduces a framework that uses HTML, CSS, and JavaScript to create mobile phone apps.

October 4, 2011: Adobe acquires Nitobi, rebrands its framework with the name PhoneGap, and spins off an open-source version that eventually becomes Apache Cordova.

Cordova and its cousins are hybrid app development frameworks. With *hybrid app development*, an app runs in a window that's essentially a web browser. Because web browser technology is standard across all platforms, a hybrid app can run on both Android and iOS devices, or even on a desktop computer.

What's "hybrid" about hybrid apps? The code to display text and images in a web browser doesn't vary much from one environment to another, so a browser page on an iPhone looks more or less like the same page on an Android phone. But communicating with hardware devices, such as the GPS receiver and vibration motor, is another story entirely.

Web pages aren't designed to talk directly to a device's hardware. In fact, you don't want to visit awfulwebsite.com and have the site's code quietly take pictures with your laptop's built-in camera. To make a hybrid app interact with hardware, you have to backpedal and make calls to the iPhone's API, the Android API, or whatever other API you can use. That's why frameworks like Apache Cordova have *plug-ins* — additional programs whose code is specific to either iOS or Android. The bottom line is, a typical hybrid app does some of its work in a web browser and the rest of its work with native API calls.

What's the downside with hybrid apps? Frameworks like Apache Cordova are like foreign language interpreters: While the app runs, the device must constantly translate web browser instructions into native code instructions. When you talk through an interpreter, the conversation can become sluggish. Hybrid apps aren't always as responsive as native apps. In addition, hybrid apps can't do all the things that native apps can do. It's the same when you talk through a foreign language interpreter. You can say most of the things you want to say, but some ideas simply can't be translated.

Returning to the history lesson . . .

Summer 2013: A hackathon for Facebook employees gives birth to *React Native* — a cross-platform framework based on the React.js JavaScript framework.

February 24, 2016: Microsoft acquires Xamarin — a cross-platform mobile development framework based indirectly on Microsoft's own .NET framework.

With a *cross-platform framework*, a programmer writes one program that targets neither iOS nor Android. When the programmer says, "Test this code," the framework translates the whole program into native code for either Android or iOS, whichever platform the programmer chooses. When the program is ready for public distribution, the framework translates it into two different native apps — one for iOS and the other for Android.

But why stop there? If you can translate code into both iOS and Android apps, you can translate the code into web pages and desktop apps. A developer can create one piece of code and have it run on all kinds of phones, tablets, PCs, Macs, watches, toasters, or whatever.

This brings me to the subject of my book:

December 4, 2018: Google announces Flutter 1.0 for cross-platform development.

(continued)

(continued)

Flutter differs from Xamarin and React Native in some significant ways. First and foremost, Xamarin isn't entirely free. Using Xamarin for professional projects costs between $300 and $1900 a year, depending on the size and scope of the projects under development.

In addition, Flutter's way of displaying components is different from the React Native and Xamarin way. When you run a React Native app on an iPhone, the app calls on the iOS API to create iOS buttons, text fields, and other visual components. The same is true for Android development. React Native gets the Android API to display Android-specific components. Components created by the iOS and Android APIs don't look alike. The two APIs use different shapes, different color palettes, and different navigation schemes. The differences can lead to unexpected results and can occasionally sabotage the whole cross-platform development effort.

Flutter doesn't call on the iOS or Android APIs to display an app's components. Instead, Flutter specifies all the tiny pixels required to draw a button or a text field and calls on the iOS or Android API to paint those pixels. If you want an app to look the same on both iOS and Android devices, Flutter is your natural choice.

What if you want your app to have that special, iPhone look when it runs on iOS devices? Can you do that with Flutter? Of course, you can. (I wouldn't pose the question if the answer were "No.") The Flutter framework has two special libraries — one for Android and another for iOS. Flutter's Material Design library draws things that look like Android components, and Flutter's Cupertino library makes objects look like iOS components. This book emphasizes the Material library, but almost everything in it has a Cupertino counterpart.

I end this sidebar with one more historical nougat:

May 10, 2239: Technology historian Alice Touge publishes a paper on the origin of the word *phone,* which is Latin for "sound." She explains that 23rd century phones came from devices whose original purpose was solely to transmit sound. This surprising fact goes viral on all the direct-to-mind streaming outlets.

I'd carry my program from the punch card machine to the computer operator's counter, where a permanently surly operator would tell me about the unusually long job-turnaround time.

Four hours later, I'd get back an inch-thick pile of paper with an error message somewhere in the middle of it. I'd go back to the punch card machine, make another card with an added comma in the 23rd column, and do the whole business again.

There's no doubt about it — a long and arduous development cycle hinders productivity. These days, shaving a few seconds off the turnaround time can make a huge difference.

Here's what happens when you create an app for mobile devices:

1. You write some code, or you modify some existing code.

    You don't write Android or iOS code on a phone of any kind. Phones aren't powerful enough for all the editing and other stuff you need to do. Instead, you create an app's code on a laptop or desktop computer. This laptop or desktop computer is called your *development computer*.

2. You issue a command for your development computer to build the code.

    Building the code takes place in several stages, one of which is called *compiling*. *Compiling* means automatically translating your program from the source code you wrote to detailed object code instructions. Think of object code as a bunch of zeros and ones. It's very detailed and extremely unintuitive. Humans hardly ever read or write object code but, at the heart of things, processors respond only to object code instructions.

    For a detailed look at compiling code, see this section's "What is a compiler?" sidebar.

    In addition to the translation step, the build process connects the program you wrote with additional code that your program needs in order to run. For example, if your program accesses the Internet, the build process integrates your code with existing network code.

    What happens next?

3. The development computer *deploys* your code to a target device.

    This so-called "device" may be a real phone connected to your computer or a picture of a phone on your computer's screen. One way or another, your program starts running.

4. You press buttons, type text, and otherwise test your app to find out whether it's doing the things you want it to do.

    Of course, it's not doing all those things. So you return to Step 1 and keep trying.

Steps 2 and 3 can be painfully slow. For some simple iPhone and Android apps, I've watched for several minutes as my computer prepares code for the program's next run. This sluggishness reduces my productivity considerably.

But along with Flutter comes some good news. Flutter uses the Dart programming language, and Dart comes with these two (count 'em — two) compilers:

>> **Ahead-of-time (AOT) compiler**

With an *AOT compiler*, your development computer translates an entire program and makes the translated code available for devices to run. No further translation takes place when the devices run your program. Each target device devotes its processing power to the efficient running of your code.

An app running on AOT-compiled code runs smoothly and efficiently.

>> **Just-in-time (JIT) compiler**

With a *JIT compiler*, your development computer translates enough code to start the app running. It feeds this code to a test device and continues translating while the test device runs the app. If the developer presses a button on the test device's screen, the JIT compiler hurries to translate that button's code.

An app running on a JIT compiler may appear to be sluggish because the compiler translates code while the app runs. But using a JIT compiler is a great way to test an app.

Here's what happens when you develop a Flutter app:

REMEMBER

1. You write some code.

2. You issue a command for your development computer to build the code.

   The first time around, building code can take some time.

3. The development computer deploys your code to a target device.

   Again, you face a noticeable time lag.

4. In testing your code, you find out that it's not doing all the things you want it to do.

5. You modify your existing code, and then . . .

6. You issue a command for your development computer to rebuild the code.

   Here's where Flutter's magic happens. Dart's JIT compiler recompiles only the part of the app that you've modified and sends the change straight to the target device. The modified code starts running in a fraction of a second. You save hours of time every day because you're not waiting for code changes to take effect.

WHAT IS A COMPILER?

You're a human being. (Sure, every rule has exceptions. But if you're reading this book, you're probably human.) Anyway, humans can write and comprehend the following Flutter source code:

```
import 'package:flutter/widgets.dart';

main() => runApp(SizedBox`());
```

When you paraphrase the source code in English, here's what you get:

Get some code (code from the Flutter API) named `widgets.dart`.

Run an application whose only component is a box widget.

If you don't see the similarities between the Flutter code and its English equivalent, don't worry. You're reading *Flutter For Dummies*, and, like most human beings, you can learn to read and write the Flutter code. In case you're wondering, this source code contains the world's simplest and most useless Flutter app. When the app runs, you see a completely black screen. It's not what you'd call a "killer app."

Source code is nice, but source code isn't for everyone and everything. The processors in computers and mobile devices aren't human beings. Processors don't follow source code instructions. Instead, they follow cryptic instructions of the following kind:

```
1100100 1100101 1111000 00001010 00110000 00110011 00110101 00000000 10000100
```

These zeros and ones are, in fact, the first few words in an Android phone's version of the Black Screen app's code. Here's the Black Screen app after a processor interprets the zeros and ones:

```
.class public com/allmycode/dexperiment/MainActivity
.super io/flutter/embedding/android/FlutterActivity
.source MainActivity.java


.method public <init>()V
.limit registers 1
; this: v0 (Lcom/allmycode/dexperiment/MainActivity;)
.line 8
    invoke-direct    {v0},io/flutter/embedding/android/FlutterActivity/<init>
    ; <init>()V
    return-void
.end method
```

(continued)

(continued)

```
.method public configureFlutterEngine(Lio/flutter/embedding/engine/
    FlutterEngine;)V
.limit registers 2
; this: v0 (Lcom/allmycode/dexperiment/MainActivity;)
; parameter[0] : v1 (Lio/flutter/embedding/engine/FlutterEngine;)
.line 11
    invoke-static    {v1},io/flutter/plugins/GeneratedPluginRegistrant/
    registerWith
    ; registerWith(Lio/flutter/embedding/engine/FlutterEngine;)V
.line 12
    return-void
.end method
```

What a mess! Humans don't want to read or write instructions of this kind. These instructions aren't Dart source code instructions. They're *Dalvik bytecode* instructions. When you write a Flutter program, you write Dart source code instructions. If you test your program on an Android device, your development computer translates the source code into bytecode. If you test your program on an iPhone, the computer translates your source code into something that's even more obscure than bytecode.

The tool that performs the translation is a compiler. The *compiler* takes code that you can write and understand and translates it into code that a processor has a fighting chance of carrying out.

You might put your source code in a file named main.dart. To run your app on Android devices, the compiler creates other files named MainActivity.dex and app. apk. Normally, you don't bother looking at these compiled files. You can't even examine .dex files or .apk files with an ordinary editor. If you try to open MainActivity.dex with Notepad, TextEdit, or even Microsoft Word, you'll see nothing but dots, squiggles, and other gobbledygook.

No one (except for a few crazy programmers in some isolated labs in faraway places) writes Dalvik bytecode or any other kind of code that processors actually understand. When you ask your development computer to run your code, the computer uses its own software (a compiler) to create processor-friendly instructions. The only reason to look at the bytecode in this sidebar is to understand what a hard worker your development computer is.

Flutter gives you two ways to apply changes to a running app:

>> With *hot restart*, the app begins its run anew, removing any data that you've entered during the most recent test, displaying the app as if you're running it for the first time.

» With *hot reload*, the app takes up from where it left off, with the data you last entered intact, if possible. The only changes are the ones dictated by your modifications to the code.

Flutter's hot restart and hot reload are both blazingly fast. They turn the app development cycle into a pleasure rather than a chore.

CROSS
REFERENCE

Chapter 2 tells you more about building, testing, and rerunning apps.

A great way to think about app development

The language you speak influences the way you think. If you don't believe me, look up the Sapir-Whorf hypothesis. You're bound to find it on your favorite linguistics website.

Spoken languages are neither good nor bad, but programming languages can have good qualities and bad qualities. Most hybrid apps are written in the JavaScript programming language. Yes, JavaScript is one of the world's most widely used languages. But, no, JavaScript doesn't encourage good software design. It's easy to write confusing code in JavaScript because its rules are quite permissive. You can write sloppy JavaScript code, and the code runs just fine. That is, it runs fine until someone enters unexpected input. When that happens, you have trouble figuring out how your code was working in the first place. Even when you're not busy fixing errors, adding new features to JavaScript code can be difficult and frustrating. JavaScript aficionados will argue with every word in this paragraph but, one way or another, JavaScript has its downsides.

Apple's iOS platform uses the Swift and Objective-C languages, whereas Android uses Kotlin and Java. Objective-C dates back to the early 1980s and, like me, it's showing its age. The other three languages fare pretty well on the scale of good language features, but none of them is as straightforward and intuitive as Dart.

On top of that, both iOS and Android divide an app's code into two separate parts:

» **Layout:** How the app looks.

» **Logic:** The sequence of instructions that the app performs.

The Android radio button example in this chapter's earlier section "Cross-platform development" is neither Kotlin nor Java code. It's XML code (a term that I don't bother to define here). It has a different format and lives in a different file from the code that responds to radio button choices.

In my Android books, I argue that separating layout from logic is a good thing. It puts distinct aspects of an app into different parts of the code. Developers can maintain each part independently. For an Android developer, that's a good thing.

But this isn't an Android book. It's a Flutter book. So, in this book, I claim that separating layout from logic is *not* optimal. Here's why:

You may have heard the all-encompassing mantra of Flutter app development:

> *In Flutter, almost everything is a widget.*

And what is a widget? In a mobile app, every button is one of the app's widgets. Every text field is a widget. The app itself is a widget. The positioning of buttons and text fields is a widget. The animating of objects from one part of the screen to another is a widget. When you create a Flutter app, you put widgets inside of other widgets, which in turn are inside even more widgets. Listing 1-1 has some fake code that illustrates the point:

LISTING 1-1: **Like a Wheel Within a Wheel**

```
// Don't fall for my trickery. This isn't real Flutter code!
Application(
  Background(
    CenterWhateverIsInsideThis(
      Button(
        onPressed: print("I've been clicked."),
        Padding(
          Text(
            "Click Me"
          ),
        ),
      ),
    ),
  ),
)
```

Listing 1-1 has a Text widget inside of a Padding widget, which is inside of a Button widget inside a CenterWhateverIsInsideThis widget. That Center WhateverIsInsideThis widget is inside a Background widget, which is inside an Application widget. When I created Listing 1-1, I modeled it after real Flutter code. The real Flutter code creates the app shown in Figure 1-2. When the user presses the Button in Figure 1-2, the words *I've been clicked* appear.

FIGURE 1-2:
An app with a
button.

ON THE
WEB

To see the real code that inspired this chapter's fake code, visit www.allmycode. com/flutter and look for the big download link. The real code is in a file named app0101.

Compare Figures 1-2 and 1-3. Figure 1-2 shows the app as the user sees it. Figure 1-3 shows the same app as the Flutter developer codes it.

```
Application
  Background
    CenterWhatsInside




          Button
            Padding
              Text
                Click Me
```

FIGURE 1-3:
Widgets within
widgets.

If you're not already a Flutter developer, the word *widget* might suggest a visible component, such as a button, a slider, an icon, or some other such thing. But in Flutter, things that aren't really visible are also widgets. For example, in Listing 1-1, `CenterWhateverIsInsideThis` is a widget. Having layout features like `CenterWhateverIsInsideThis` be widgets is a powerful idea. It means that Flutter developers can focus their attention on one overarching task — stuffing widgets inside other widgets. Flutter has a certain simplicity and elegance that other app development frameworks don't have.

TIP

Flutter has no built-in widget named `CenterWhateverIsInsideThis`. But don't be disappointed. Flutter's `Center` widget does what my fictitious `CenterWhateverIsInsideThis` widget is supposed to do.

Enough New Terminology! What's Next?

You may have read this chapter from start to finish but not one word in the chapter prompted you to touch your computer keyboard. What a shame! If you'll read the next chapter, I can rectify that awful omission.

IN THIS CHAPTER

» Installing Dart and Flutter

» Installing a development environment

» Mimicking mobile devices on your laptop computer

Chapter **2**

Setting Up Your Computer for Mobile App Development

A rchimedes lived in ancient Greece during the second century BCE. His work in the early development of mathematics was groundbreaking. In the peace and quiet of his own bathtub, he chanced upon an important formula — a formula to describe the relationship between his weight and the amount of water his body displaced. Upon making this discovery, he yelled "Eureka!" and jumped out of the tub to tell everyone in his city. Tunic or no tunic, Archimedes wanted all Greeks to share in his joy.

Jump forward roughly 2200 years. I'm 12 years old. In a conversation about moving some furniture, my father quotes Archimedes: "Give me a big enough lever, and I can move the world." I try to picture this. Here's Earth, hanging out in space, and there's a long, long stick with a curl at the bottom. The curl reaches under the big planet and nudges it to a new position.

Stinker that I was, I saw three problems with this scenario. First, how would you anchor the bottom of the lever at a fixed point in empty space? Second, how would you keep the lever from digging an enormous hole into some soft part of the Earth? And finally, how would the people of Earth take to having their planet knocked out of orbit? As you can see, I was an ornery kid.

But the idea of leverage stuck in my mind. The longer the lever, the more benefit you get from it. You can't lift a big boulder on your own without a lever, but you can move the boulder with a humongous lever. A lever is a tool, and tools are wonderful things.

Tools don't directly do the things you want done. You can't eat a tool, read a good tool, hear a tool's happy song, or dance the jig with a tool. But you can use tools to make food, books, musical instruments, and dance floors.

This chapter is all about tools — the tools you use to make great mobile apps.

The Stuff You Need

This book tells you how to create apps using Flutter. Before you can create apps, you need some software tools. Here's a list of the tools you need:

>> **The Flutter Software Development Kit (SDK)**

The Flutter SDK includes lots and lots of prewritten, reusable Flutter code and a bunch of software tools for running and testing Flutter apps. The SDK has the official Flutter code libraries, Dart code libraries, documentation, and even some sample apps.

>> **An integrated development environment**

You can create Flutter apps by using geeky, keyboard-only tools, but eventually you'll tire of typing and retyping commands. An *integrated development environment (IDE),* on the other hand, is a little like a word processor: A word processor helps you compose documents (memos, poems, and other works of fine literature); in contrast, an IDE helps you compose instructions for processors.

For composing Flutter apps, I recommend the Android Studio IDE. Don't be fooled by the word *Android* in the IDE's name. Using Android Studio, you can create iPhone apps, web apps, and other kinds of apps.

>> **Some sample Flutter apps, to help you get started**

All examples in this book are available for download here:

```
www.allmycode.com/Flutter
```

>> A device for testing your Flutter code

You write some code, and then you run it to see whether it works correctly. Usually, it doesn't work correctly until you make some changes. Most often, it doesn't work correctly until you make *lots* of changes.

In this book, I emphasize the creation of apps for iPhones and Android phones. You can run your code on your own phone, but you can also run it on your computer. To run a mobile app on your computer, you need software that displays a phone on your screen and runs your app within that display.

In the iPhone world, this type of software is called a *simulator*, and Android calls its software an *emulator*. Simulators and emulators are examples of *virtual devices*. In contrast, an actual iPhone or Android phone is called a *physical device*.

TIP

Another name for a physical device is a *real device*. For emphasis, I sometimes write *real, physical device*. I suppose I could be more emphatic and write *real, actual, hard-core, physical device, you betcha!*

TECHNICAL STUFF

An emulator isn't quite the same thing as a simulator. An emulator is software that behaves, to a large extent, like the hardware of a real, physical phone. A simulator is software that runs a phone's apps without really behaving too much like the phone's hardware. Fortunately, when you run this book's apps, you can ignore this subtle difference.

All these tools run on the *development computer* — the laptop or desktop computer you use to develop Flutter apps. Later, when you publish your app, users run the app on their *target devices* — physical devices such as iPhones, Android phones, and (someday soon) smart toasters.

Here's good news: You can download for free all the software you need to run this book's examples. The software is separated into four downloads:

>> When you visit `https://flutter.dev/docs/get-started/install`, you can click a button to install the Flutter SDK.

>> A button at the page `http://developer.android.com/studio` gives you the Android Studio IDE download. Along with this download comes the Android emulator.

>> This book's website (`www.allmycode.com/Flutter`) has a link to all of the book's code.

>> The iPhone simulator, as well as all the code you need for generating iPhone apps, comes with the installation of Xcode on your Mac. Xcode is available from the Macintosh App Store. (Unfortunately, you can't develop for iPhone on a Windows PC.)

WARNING

In the world of mobile app development, things change very quickly. The instructions I write on Tuesday can be out-of-date by Thursday morning. The creators of Flutter are always creating new features and new tools. The old tools stop working, and the old instructions no longer apply. If you see something on your screen that doesn't look like one of my screen shots, don't despair. It might be something very new, or you might have reached a corner of the software that I don't describe in this book. One way or another, send me an email, a tweet, or some other form of communication. (Don't try sending a carrier pigeon. My cat will get to it before I find the note.) My contact info is in this book's introduction.

What to Do

It's an old, familiar refrain. First you get some software. Then you run the software.

Getting and installing the stuff

1. **Visit** www.allmycode.com/Flutter **and download a file containing all the program examples in this book.**

The downloaded file is a .zip archive file. (Refer to the later sidebars "Those pesky filename extensions" and "Compressed archive files.")

TIP

Most web browsers save files to the Downloads directory on the computer's hard drive. But your browser may be configured a bit differently. One way or another, make note of the folder containing the downloaded file FlutterForDummies_Listings.zip.

2. **Extract the contents of the downloaded file to a place on your computer's hard drive.**

3. **Visit** https://flutter.dev/docs/get-started/install **and download the Flutter SDK.**

Choose a version of the software that matches your operating system (Windows, Macintosh, or whatever).

4. **Extract the contents of the downloaded file to a place on your computer's hard drive.**

The aforementioned *contents* is actually a directory full of stuff. The directory's name is flutter. Put your new flutter directory in a place that isn't protected with special privileges. For example, if you try extracting the flutter directory inside the c:\program files directory, Windows displays its User

Account Control dialog box and asks for confirmation. Don't put the `flutter` directory inside a place like that.

You say "folder." I say "directory." To not-quite-quote Gershwin, let's call the whole thing off because, in this book, I use these two words interchangeably.

Personally, I like to put the `flutter` directory inside my home directory. My computer has a directory named `Users`, and inside that `Users` directory is a directory named `barryburd`. That `barryburd` directory is my home directory. This *home directory* contains my `Documents` directory, my `Downloads` directory, and lots of other stuff. After I extract the downloaded file's content, my `barryburd` home directory has a brand-new `flutter` directory.

You don't have to extract the `flutter` directory right inside your home directory, but it's the simplest, most reliable thing I can think of doing.

5. **Make a note of the place on your hard drive where the new `flutter` directory lives.**

   For example, if you copied the `.zip` file's contents to your `/Users/janeqreader` directory, make a note of the `/Users/janeqreader/flutter` directory. That's your *Flutter SDK path*.

   To make sure that you've extracted the downloaded file's contents correctly, look inside the `flutter` directory for a subdirectory named `bin`. My flutter directory has other subdirectories, named `dev`, `examples`, and `packages`. Your mileage may vary, depending on when you download the Flutter SDK.

6. **Visit** `http://developer.android.com/studio` **and download the Android Studio IDE.**

   The download is an `.exe` file, a `.dmg` file, or maybe something else.

7. **Install the software that you downloaded in Step 6.**

   During the installation, a dialog box may offer the option of installing an Android virtual device (AVD)**.** If so, accept the option.

   For other details about installing Android Studio, see this chapter's later section "On Installing Android Studio."

   Android Studio isn't the only IDE that has features for creating Flutter apps. Some developers prefer Virtual Studio Code (known affectionately as VS Code), which is available for Windows, Macintosh, and Linux. And if you enjoy roughing it, you can do without an IDE and use the command line along with your favorite text editor — Emacs, vi, or Notepad. In this book, I focus on Android Studio, but you can find plenty of alternatives.

   To learn more about Visual Studio Code, visit `https://code.visualstudio.com`.

THOSE PESKY FILENAME EXTENSIONS

The filenames displayed in File Explorer or in a Finder window can be misleading. You may browse a directory and see the name android-studio-ide or flutter_windows. The file's real name might be android-studio-ide.exe, flutter_windows.zip, or plain old flutter_windows. Filename endings such as .zip, .exe, .dmg, .app, and .dart are *filename extensions*.

The ugly truth is that, by default, Windows and the Mac hide many filename extensions. This awful feature tends to confuse people. If you don't want to be confused, change your computer's system-wide settings. Here's how to do it:

- **In Windows 7:** Choose Start ➪ Control Panel ➪ Appearance and Personalization ➪ Folder Options. Then skip to the third bullet.

- **In Windows 8:** On the Charms bar, choose Settings ➪ Control Panel. In the Control Panel, choose Appearance and Personalization ➪ Folder Options. Then proceed to the following bullet.

- **In Windows 7 or 8:** Follow the instructions in one of the preceding bullets. Then, in the Folder Options dialog box, click the View tab. Look for the Hide File Extensions for Known File Types option. Make sure that this check box is *not* selected.

- **In Windows 10:** On the File Explorer's main menu, select View. On the ribbon that appears, put a check mark next to File Name Extensions.

- **In macOS:** On the Finder application's menu, select Preferences. In the resulting dialog box, select the Advanced tab and look for the Show All File Extensions option. Make sure that this check box *is* selected.

TIP

While you're visiting any software download site, check the requirements for downloading, installing, and running that software. Make sure you have enough memory and an operating system that's sufficiently up to date.

For Mac users only

If you have a Mac and you want to create iPhone apps, follow these steps:

1. **Select App Store from the Apple menu.**

2. **In the store's search field, type** Xcode **and then press Enter.**

   The App Store's search finds dozens of apps, but only one has the simple name Xcode.

COMPRESSED ARCHIVE FILES

When you visit www.allmycode.com/Flutter and download this book's examples, you download a file named FlutterForDummies_Listings.zip. A zip file is a single file that encodes a bunch of smaller files. The FlutterForDummies_Listings.zip file encodes files with names such as App0301.dart, App0302.dart, and App0401.dart. The App0301.dart file contains the code in Listing 3-1 — the first listing in Chapter 3. Likewise, App0302.dart and App0401.dart have the code in Listings 3-2 and 4-1.

The FlutterForDummies_Listings.zip file also encodes a folder named assets. This folder contains copies of the images that appear in the book's apps.

A .zip file is an example of a *compressed archive* file. Other examples of compressed archives include .tar.gz files, .rar files, and .sparsebundle files. When you *uncompress* a file, you extract the original files and folders stored inside the larger archive file. (For a .zip file, another word for uncompressing is *unzipping*.)

When you download FlutterForDummies_Listings.zip, the web browser may uncompress the file automatically for you. If not, you can get your computer to uncompress the file. Here's how:

- **On a Windows computer,** double-click the .zip file's icon. When you do this, Windows File Explorer shows you the files and folders inside the compressed .zip archive. Drag all these files and folders to another place on your computer's hard drive (a place that's not inside the archive file).

- **On a Mac,** double-click the .zip file's icon. When you do this, the Mac extracts the contents of the archive file and shows you the extracted contents in a Finder window.

3. **Click the Xcode app's Get button.**

   As a result, the App Store installs Xcode on your computer.

4. **Launch the Xcode application.**

   The first time you run Xcode, your Mac installs some additional components. If you want your apps to run on Apple devices, you need those additional components.

Configuring Android Studio

Android Studio doesn't come automatically with Flutter support, meaning you have to add Flutter support the first time you run the IDE. Here's what you do.

1. **Launch the Android Studio application.**

   The first time you run a fresh, new copy of Android Studio, you see the Welcome screen.

2. **Select Configure ⇨ Plugins on the Welcome screen.**

   You'll find the Configure drop-down menu in the lower right corner of the Welcome screen. (See Figure 2-1.)

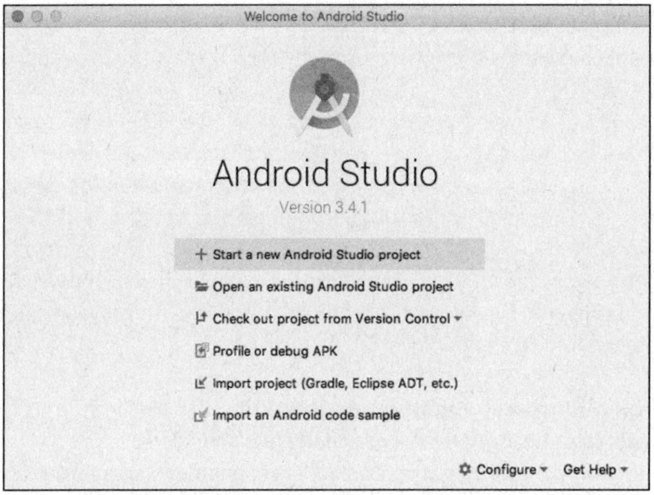

FIGURE 2-1:
Android Studio's default Welcome screen.

3. **Search for a plugin named Flutter. Install that plugin.**

   If Android Studio offers the option of installing Dart as well, accept the option.

   After installing the plugin, Android Studio may want to be restarted. Of course, you should restart it. When you do, you see the Welcome screen again. Now the Welcome screen includes the Start a New Flutter Project option. (See Figure 2-2.)

   For other details about configuring Android Studio, see the section "On installing Android Studio's Flutter plugin," later in this chapter.

Running your first app

You've installed Android Studio, added Android Studio's Flutter plugin, and then restarted Android Studio. Now you're staring at Android Studio's Welcome screen. What do you do next?

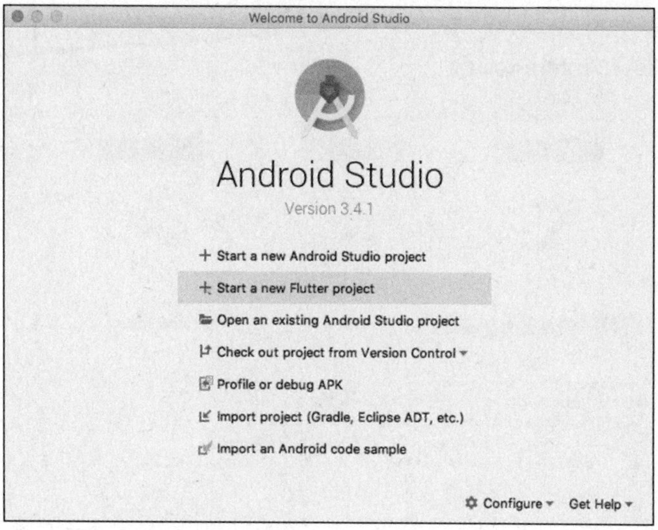

Figure shows the "Welcome to Android Studio" window with the following options:

Android Studio
Version 3.4.1

+ Start a new Android Studio project
+ Start a new Flutter project
📂 Open an existing Android Studio project
↳ Check out project from Version Control ▾
🔲 Profile or debug APK
📥 Import project (Gradle, Eclipse ADT, etc.)
📄 Import an Android code sample

⚙ Configure ▾   Get Help ▾

FIGURE 2-2:
You've installed
the Flutter plugin.

1. **Connect to the Internet.**

   During the run of your very first app, Android Studio downloads some additional software.

2. **Select the Start a New Flutter Project option. (Refer to Figure 2-2.)**

   On your phone, an app is an app, and that's all there is to it. But on your development computer, all your work is divided into projects. For professional purposes, you're not absolutely correct if you think of one app as equaling one project. But, for the examples in this book, the "one project equals one app" model works just fine.

   TIP

   If you don't see the Start a New Flutter Project option, you may not have installed the Flutter plugin correctly. I recommend double-checking the instructions in the "Configuring Android Studio" section, earlier in this chapter. If that doesn't help, or if you get stuck somewhere else in this chapter, send me an email. My email address is in the book's introduction.

   Having selected Start a New Flutter Project, you'll see three dialog boxes, one after another. The first asks what kind of Flutter project you want to create, the second asks for the new app's name and other details, and the third creates something called a package.

3. **In the first dialog box, select Flutter Application and then click Next. (See Figure 2-3.)**

   The second dialog box has four fields: Project Name, Flutter SDK Path, Project Location, and Description. (See Figure 2-4.)

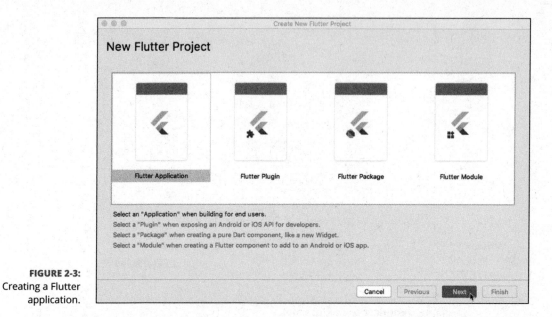

FIGURE 2-3:
Creating a Flutter
application.

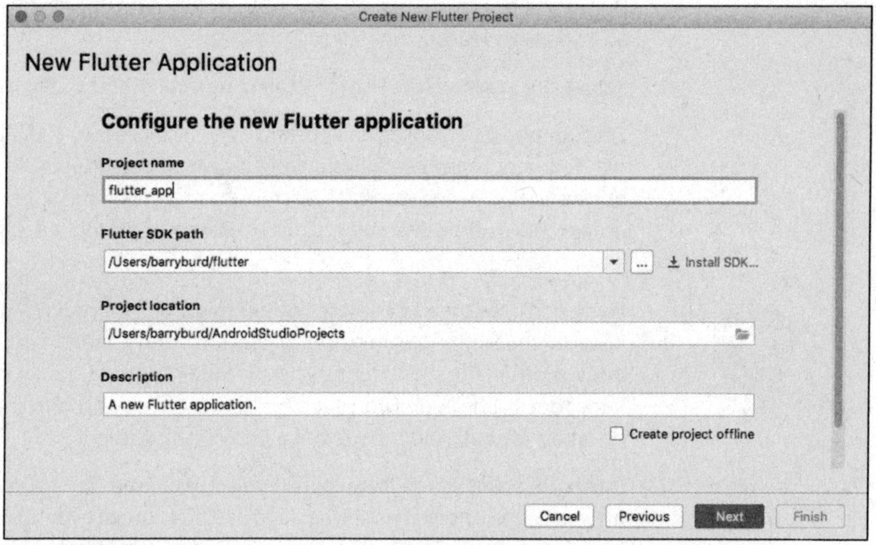

FIGURE 2-4:
Details about
your new app.

4. **Select a name that has only lowercase letters and, if you want, under-score (_) characters.**

REMEMBER

Flutter project names cannot contain uppercase letters, blank spaces, or punctuation characters other than the underscore.

TIP

If you create many apps, keeping track of them all can drive you crazy. So, it helps if you decide on a formula for naming your apps and then stick to that formula as closely as you can. Later on, when you start marketing your apps, you can abandon the formula, and use clever names that attract peoples' attention.

5. For the Flutter SDK path, supply your Flutter SDK path.

You copied down the Flutter SDK path when you followed Step 5 in the earlier section "Getting and installing the stuff," didn't you? If you forgot, search your hard drive for a folder named `flutter`. It's bound to be there somewhere.

6. Don't change the Project Location option, unless you have a specific reason for doing so.

You don't have to specify a new directory for each of your projects. Android Studio does that for you automatically with this project location as the starting point.

7. For the description, type something that's silly and off the wall.

Do it now, while you still can. When you create apps professionally, you have to be more serious.

After you click Next, Android Studio displays its Set the Package Name dialog box. (See Figure 2-5.)

```
●○○                          Create New Flutter Project

New Flutter Application

    Set the package name
    Applications and plugins need to generate platform-specific code

    Company domain
    ┌──────────────────────────────────────────────────────────────┐
    │ allmycode.com                                                  │
    └──────────────────────────────────────────────────────────────┘

    Package name
    com.allmycode.flutterapp                              [ Edit ]

    Sample Application
    ☐ generate sample content:  AppBar                    ▾

    Platform channel language
    ☐ Include Kotlin support for Android code
    ☐ Include Swift support for iOS code

    ─────────────────────────────────────────────────────────────────
                              [ Cancel ]  [ Previous ]  [ Next ]  [ Finish ]
```

FIGURE 2-5:
The finishing touches.

8. **If your company has a domain name, or if you have your own domain name, type it in the Company Domain field. If not, type anything at all or leave the default text alone.**

A *package* is a collection of closely related pieces of code, and each Flutter app belongs to its own package. In the Flutter world, it's customary to start a package's name with the reverse of a domain name. For example, my company's domain name is allmycode.com. So, when I create a Flutter app, the app is usually in a package named com.allmycode.*somethingorother*. The *somethingorother* part is unique to each of my apps.

When you create your first project, the Company Name field's default text is probably example.com. Several years ago, the Internet Corporation for Assigned Names and Numbers (ICANN) set this name aside for anyone to use. Immediately below that, the dialog box supplies the package name example.com.*whateveryounamedyourapp*. This default package name is just fine when you're creating your very first Flutter apps.

This dialog box may have check boxes labeled Generate Sample Content, Include Kotlin Support for Android Code, and Include Swift Support for iOS Code. Don't worry about these check boxes. Check them, or don't check them. For your first Flutter app, it doesn't matter.

9. **Click Finish.**

As if by magic, Android Studio's main window appears. (See Figure 2-6.) The main window has all the tools you need for developing top-notch Flutter applications. It even has a sample starter application, which you run in the next few steps.

CROSS REFERENCE

Android Studio's main window may look overwhelming at first. To help you become underwhelmed (or maybe just average-whelmed), I describe the main window's parts in this chapter's "Using Android Studio" section, later in this chapter.

In Figure 2-7, notice two important items near the top of Android Studio's main window:

- The *Target Selector* displays the text ‹no devices›.

- The *Run icon* is a little right-pointing green arrow.

What you do next depends on your development computer and your development goals.

10. **If you have a Mac, and you want to run an iPhone simulator, select Open iOS Simulator in the Target Selector drop-down list.**

If you don't have a Mac, or if you want to run an Android emulator, select Tools ➪ AVD Manager on Android Studio's main menu bar. In the resulting dialog box, look for a Green Arrow icon on the right side of the dialog box. Click that Green Arrow icon. (See Figure 2-8.)

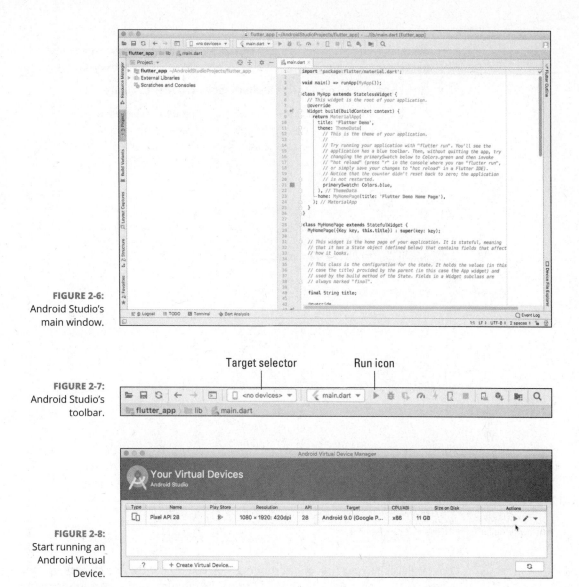

FIGURE 2-6:
Android Studio's
main window.

Target selector   Run icon

FIGURE 2-7:
Android Studio's
toolbar.

FIGURE 2-8:
Start running an
Android Virtual
Device.

**CROSS
REFERENCE**

If the AVD manager is empty — that is to say, if it's not like the manager shown in Figure 2-8, which shows a virtual device labeled Pixel API 28 — you have to create an Android Virtual Device. See the section "Running apps on an Android device," later in this chapter, for details.

WARNING

Android Virtual Devices don't always start quickly. On my computer with 16 gigabytes of RAM, the start-up time may be two to three minutes. On a computer with only 4 gigabytes of RAM, the AVD might never start up. Apple's iPhone simulator tends to be a bit snappier, but you never know. I've devoted two later sections of this chapter to Android emulator and iPhone simulator tricks — "On adding virtual devices" and "Divisiveness Among Devices."

When your virtual device's home screen appears on the screen, you're ready to run the sample Flutter app.

11. **Click the Run icon on Android Studio's toolbar. (Refer to Figure 2-7.)**

As a result, Android Studio's Run tool window appears in the lower portion of the main window. A few messages appear while you wait impatiently for the app to start running. When the app starts running, the virtual device (the simulator or emulator) sports a handsome display. (See Figure 2-9.)

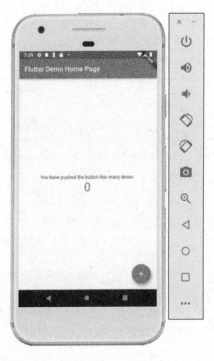

FIGURE 2-9: Isn't it wonderful?

Congratulations! Your first app is running. You can try out the app by clicking the mouse on the app's floating action button (the circular item in the lower right corner of the virtual device's screen). The message in the middle tells you how many times you've clicked the button. It's not the world's most useful app, but it's a good start.

For details about any of these steps, see the next several sections.

Dealing with the Devil's Details

Several decades ago, I bought a book about databases from the deep-discount table at my local supermarket. When I got the book home, I got hopelessly stuck in Chapter 1. I couldn't figure out how to run the software correctly. I struggled for several hours and then gave up. I've never touched the book since that day.

Why do I write about this nasty experience? I write about it to assure you that I've scraped my knuckles trying to get software running. It's the problem that most readers ask about when they send an email to me. It's natural to get stuck and need help.

In earlier sections, I present the basic steps for setting up your computer and running your first Flutter app. Basic steps are nice, but they don't work for everyone. That's why, in this section, I delve a bit deeper.

WARNING

In the world of mobile app development, things change very quickly. The instructions that I write on Tuesday can be out-of-date by Thursday morning. The creators of Flutter are always creating new features and new tools. The old tools stop working, and the old instructions no longer apply. If you see something on your screen that doesn't look like one of my screen shots, don't despair. It might be something very new, or you might have reached a corner of the software that I don't describe in this book. One way or another, send me an email or a tweet or some other form of communication. (Don't send a carrier pigeon. My cat will get to it before I find the note.) My contact info is in this book's introduction.

On installing Android Studio

What you do to install Android Studio depends on your operating system:

>> **In Windows:** The downloaded file is probably an .exe file. Double-click the .exe file's icon.

   When you double-click the .exe file's icon, a wizard guides you through the installation.

>> **On a Mac:** The downloaded file is probably a .dmg file. Double-click the .dmg file's icon.

   When you double-click the .dmg file's icon, you see the Android Studio icon (also known as the Android Studio.app icon). Drag the Android Studio icon to your Applications folder.

About .exe files and .dmg files, I make no guarantees. The downloaded file might be a .zip archive or maybe some other exotic kind of archive file. If you can't figure out what to do, send me an email.

CROSS REFERENCE

For more information on topics like .exe and .dmg, refer to the earlier sidebar "Those pesky filename extensions." And, if you need help with .zip files, see the earlier sidebar "Compressed archive files."

On launching Android Studio for the first time

Is it time to launch Android Studio? This section has a few small details.

>> **In Windows:** Click the Start button and look for the Android Studio entry.

>> **On a Mac:** Press Command-space to make the Spotlight appear. In the Spotlight's search field, start typing *Android Studio*. When your Mac makes the full name *Android Studio* appear in the Spotlight's search field, press Enter.

TIP

If your Mac complains that Android Studio is from an unidentified developer, look for the Android Studio icon in your Applications folder. Ctrl-click the Android Studio icon and select Open. When another "unidentified developer" box appears, click the box's Open button.

When you launch Android Studio for the first time, you might see a dialog box offering to import settings from a previous Android Studio installation. Chances are, you don't have a previous Android Studio installation, so you should firmly but politely decline this offer.

When the dust settles, Android Studio displays the Welcome screen. The Welcome screen has options such as Start a New Android Studio Project, Open an Existing Android Studio Project, Configure, and Get Help. (Refer to Figures 2-1 and 2-2.)

You see this Welcome screen again and again. Stated informally, the Welcome screen says, "At the moment, you're not working on any particular project (any particular Flutter app). So, what do you want to do next?"

On installing Android Studio's Flutter plugin

When you first launch Android Studio, you should definitely install Android Studio's plugin for developing Flutter apps. Here's a closer, more detailed look at how you do it:

1. **On Android Studio's Welcome screen, select Configure ⇨ Plugins. (See Figure 2-10.)**

   A Plugins dialog box with three tabs appears on the screen. The tabs are labeled Marketplace, Installed, and Updates (see Figure 2-11).

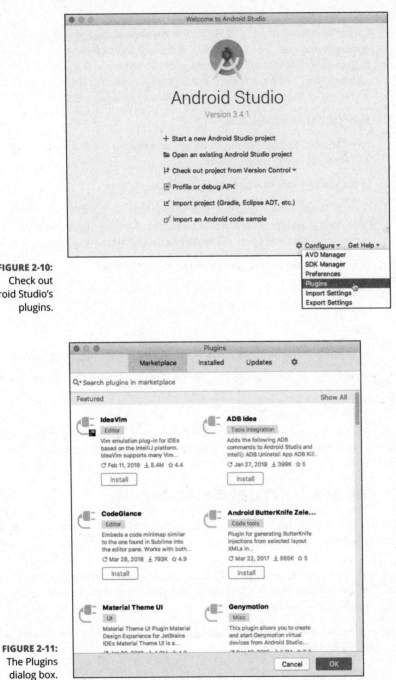

FIGURE 2-10:
Check out
Android Studio's
plugins.

FIGURE 2-11:
The Plugins
dialog box.

On some versions of Android Studio, the Welcome screen has no Configure option. In that case, select the Welcome screen's Start a New Android Studio Project option. Accept all the defaults until you see Android Studio's main window. Then, in the main menu bar, select File ⇨ Settings ⇨ Plugins (on Windows) or Android Studio ⇨ Preferences ⇨ Plugins (on a Mac).

2. **Select the Marketplace tab.**

When you do, Android Studio shows you an extensive list of available plugins. You'll want to narrow down this list.

3. **In the dialog box's search field, type the word** Flutter.

Android Studio shows you a bunch of plugins with the word *Flutter* in their titles. Each plugin has its own Install button. Look for the plugin named *Flutter* — not *Flutter Snippets*, *flutter_json_format*, or anything like that.

4. **Select the Install button for the plugin named Flutter.**

After showing you a dialog box that Google's lawyers created, Android Studio asks whether you want to install the Dart plugin.

5. **Select Yes.**

You definitely want to install the Dart plugin. (To find out why, refer to Chapter 1.)

When the plugin installations are finished, Android Studio offers to restart itself.

6. **Restart Android Studio.**

After the restart, Android Studio's Welcome screen has a new option, with the label Start a New Flutter Project. (Refer to Figure 2-2.) You're all set.

On adding virtual devices

When it comes to installing virtual devices, the stories for iPhone and Android are a bit different.

>> With an Apple, Windows, or Linux computer, you can download Android Studio and get the Android emulator that comes with it. You might have to do a bit of work to install an Android Virtual Device (AVD), but that's not a big deal.

>> If you have an Apple computer, you get an iPhone simulator by downloading Apple's Xcode software.

If you don't have an Apple computer, you can find third-party simulators by searching the Web, but keep in mind that creating iPhone apps on anything other than a Mac is difficult. Depending on the way you do it, the process might even be illegal.

Android makes a distinction between an emulator and an Android Virtual Device (AVD). Here's the scoop:

>> When you install Android Studio, you get the Android phone emulator automatically. This emulator can bridge the gap between your development computer's hardware and a mock-up of a phone's hardware. But which phone's hardware is it mocking? Is it a Samsung Galaxy or a Sony Xperia? How big is the phone's screen? What kind of camera does the phone have?

MIMICKING AN ANDROID PHYSICAL DEVICE

Android's emulated device is really three pieces of software rolled into one:

- **A *system image* is a copy of one version of the Android operating system.**

  For example, a particular system image might be for Android Pie (API Level 28) running on an Intel x86_64 processor.

- **An *emulator* bridges the gap between the system image and the processor on your development computer.**

  You might have a system image for an Atom_64 processor, but your development computer runs a Core i5 processor. The emulator translates instructions for the Atom_64 processor into instructions that the Core i5 processor can execute.

- **An Android Virtual Device (AVD) is a piece of software that describes a device's hardware.**

  An AVD contains a bunch of settings, telling the emulator all the details about the device to be emulated. What's the screen resolution of the device? Does the device have a physical keyboard? Does it have a camera? How much memory does it have? Does it have an SD card? All these choices belong to a particular AVD.

Android Studio's menus and dialog boxes make it easy to confuse these three items. When you create a new AVD, you create a new system image to go with that AVD. But Android Studio's dialog boxes blur the distinction between the AVD and the system image. You also see the word *emulator,* when the correct term is *AVD.* If the subtle differences between system images, emulators, and AVDs don't bother you, don't worry about them.

A seasoned Android developer typically has several system images and several AVDs on the development computer, but only one Android emulator program.

>> An *Android Virtual Device* is a description of a phone's hardware. The emulator doesn't work unless you create an AVD for the emulator to emulate. When you install Android Studio, you may or may not see an option to install an AVD. If you do, accept the option. If you don't, that's okay. You'll be able to create a bunch of AVDs when you get Android Studio running.

When you install Android Studio, the installer may offer you the option to create an AVD for you to use. If you weren't offered this option, or if you skipped the option, you can create an AVD using the AVD Manager tool. In fact, you can create several additional AVDs and use several different AVDs to run and test your Flutter apps on Android's emulator.

To open the AVD Manager, go to Android Studio's main menu bar and choose Tools ⇨ AVD Manager. Figures 2-12 through 2-15 show the dialog boxes that you might find in the AVD Manager.

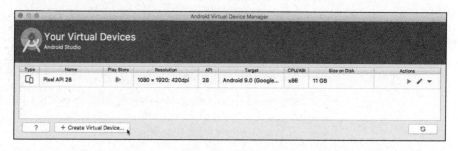

FIGURE 2-12: The opening page of the AVD Manager.

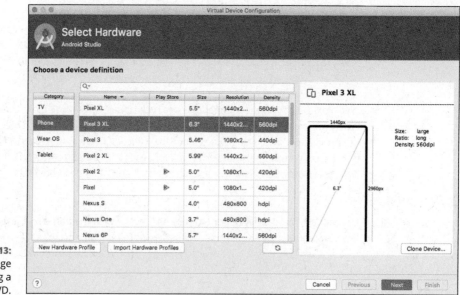

FIGURE 2-13: The first page in creating a new AVD.

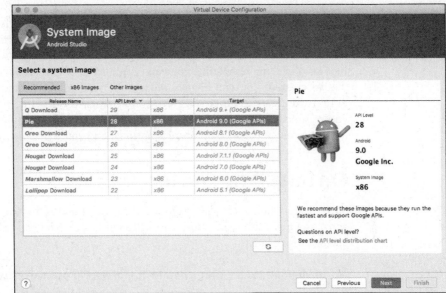

I'm reluctant to list instructions for using the AVD Manager, because the look of the AVD Manager tool is constantly in flux. Chances are, what you see on your computer's screen doesn't look much like the mid-2019 screen shots in Figures 2-12 through 2-15.

Instead of giving you explicit instructions, my general advice when creating a new AVD is to select the newer phones or tablets and the higher-numbered API levels, and to accept defaults whenever you're tempted to play eeny-meeny-miny-moe. Just keep clicking Next until you can click Finish. If you don't like the AVD that you've created, you can always reopen the AVD Manager and select different options to create another AVD. When you reach the level of proficiency where you're finicky about your AVD's characteristics, you'll probably know your way around many of the AVD Manager's options, and you'll be able to choose wisely.

On installing Flutter

Sometimes, when I feel sick, I go to the doctor. If you're having trouble running apps, and you think your Flutter installation is sick, you can take Flutter to the doctor. Here's how:

1. **In Android Studio, start a new Flutter project or open an existing project.**

   For help with that, refer to this chapter's "Running your first app" section.

2. **In Android Studio's main menu bar, select Tools ⇨ Flutter ⇨ Flutter Doctor.**

   As a result, the computer reports to you on the health of your Flutter installation.

The report from Flutter Doctor isn't always helpful. Some of the report's findings may be false alarms. Others may be difficult to interpret. If you see something that looks like a useful diagnosis, give it a try. Many of the doctor's hints involve opening up a Terminal or Command Prompt window. You'll find advice about that in the "Your friend, the command line" sidebar.

YOUR FRIEND, THE COMMAND LINE

In ancient times, the only way to communicate with a computer was at the command line. You had to know exactly what to type and, if you got it wrong, either nothing happened or something bad happened. These days, you issue most commands through a *graphical user interface* (GUI). You click here, drag-and-drop there, and do all kinds of things in a windowed environment.

But, alas, command line interfaces haven't gone away. Some tasks still require long, cryptic typewritten commands, and some people prefer typing commands over clicking buttons.

Most of the instructions in this book require pointing and clicking. But, here and there, you have to do things the old-fashioned way. To help you survive the unimaginable misery of typing error-prone, enigmatic commands, I provide a few tips:

- You can't type commands just anywhere. To communicate directly with your computer, you must first open your computer's Terminal (as it's known in the Mac world) or Command Prompt (as it's known to Windows users).

  If Android Studio is running, you can open Mac's Terminal or the Windows Command Prompt by clicking the little Terminal tool button near the bottom of Android Studio's window.

- On a Mac, you can always open Mac's Terminal by pressing Command+space, typing **Terminal**, and then pressing Enter.

  On Windows, you can always open the Command Prompt by pressing Start, typing **cmd**, and then pressing Enter.

- At any moment, a Terminal or Command Prompt window has a *working directory*. For example, if the working directory is /Users/isaacnewton/Documents, and you type more myfile.txt, the computer looks in the /Users/isaacnewton/Documents directory for a file named myfile.txt. If the /Users/isaacnewton/Documents directory has a file named myfile.txt, the computer displays the contents of myfile.txt in page-size chunks.

  (On Windows): To find out which directory is the working directory, look at the prompt or type **cd**. To change the working directory, type **cd** followed by the new directory's name.

  ```
  c:\Users\isaacnewton\Documents>cd
  c:\Users\isaacnewton\Documents

  c:\Users\isaacnewton\Documents>cd c:\Users\isaacnewton

  c:\Users\isaacnewton>cd
  c:\Users\isaacnewton
  ```

- **(On a Mac):** To find out which directory is the working directory, type pwd. To change the working directory, type **cd** followed by the new directory's name.

  ```
  Isaacs-Air:Documents isaacnewton$ pwd
  /Users/isaacnewton/Documents

  Isaacs-Air:Documents isaacnewton$ cd /Users/isaacnewton

  Isaacs-Air:~ isaacnewton$ pwd
  /Users/isaacnewton
  ```

WARNING

The content provided by `flutter doctor` is not intended to serve as a substitute for professional medical advice. Seek the advice of your Flutter physician with any questions you may have regarding a medical condition. Never disregard professional medical advice because of something you have read in the output of `flutter doctor`.

Divisiveness Among Devices

If your development computer has enough horsepower, you can run a few Android Virtual Devices simultaneously. On a Mac, you can run an iPhone simulator while your Android Virtual Devices are running. But using your virtual and physical devices can be tricky. This section gives you some tips.

Running apps on an Android device

A reader from Minnesota writes:

> Dear Barry,
>
> I've followed all your instructions. Things go well until I try to run an app. The Android emulator doesn't work. What should I do?
>
> Signed,
>
>
>
> Still Freezing in Minneapolis

Well, Ms. Freezing, the emulator that comes with Android Studio swallows up lots of resources on your development computer. If you're like me and you don't always have the latest, most powerful hardware, you may have trouble running apps in the emulator. Maybe you don't see Android's home screen or you don't see your app running five minutes or so after the emulator starts running. If so, here are several things you can try:

>> **Lather, rinse, repeat.**

Close the emulator and launch your application again. Sometimes, the second or third time's a charm. On rare occasions, my first three attempts fail, but my fourth attempt succeeds.

- **If you have access to a computer with more RAM, try running your app on it.**

  Horsepower matters.

- **If you don't have access to a computer with more RAM, close all non-essential programs on your development computer, and try running your app again.**

- **Try a different AVD.**

  The "On adding virtual devices" section, earlier in this chapter, tells you how to add a new AVD to your system. An AVD with an x86 system image is better than an AVD with an armeabi image. (Fortunately, when a dialog box lets you choose between x86 and armeabi, you don't have to know what *x86* or armeabi means.)

- **Wrestle with virtualization technology.**

  You might not want to start down this rabbit hole.

  When it runs on an Intel x86 processor, Android's emulator tries to use something called Intel Virtualization Technology (VT) with the Intel Hardware Accelerated Execution Manager (HAXM). If your computer isn't completely comfortable with a VT-and-HAXM configuration, you're likely to have trouble using Android's emulator.

  Don't despair! Try installing an armeabi system image.

  Finally, if your computer can use VT and HAXM, and if you want to adjust these items on your computer, go right ahead. Just don't blame me if, a month later, you suddenly remember that your goal was to learn about Flutter.

The previous bulleted list describes a few remedies for problems with Android Studio's emulator. Unfortunately, none of the bullets in this list is a silver bullet. If you've tried these tricks, and you're still having trouble, you might try abandoning the emulator that comes with Android Studio and running apps on a "real" device.

Testing apps on a physical device

You can bypass virtual devices and test your apps on a physical phone, a tablet device, or maybe even a smart coffee pot. To do so, you have to prepare the physical device, prepare your development computer, and then hook together the two. It's quite a chore, but after you do it the first time, it becomes much easier. This section describes an outline of the steps you must follow.

ON THE WEB

For more details, visit these pages:

```
https://flutter.dev/docs/get-started/install/macos - deploy-to-ios-devices
https://flutter.dev/docs/get-started/install/windows - set-up-your-android-device
```

Preparing to test on an Android physical device

To test your app on an Android device, follow these steps:

1. **On your Android device, enable Developer Options.**

   On many Android devices, you do this by choosing Settings ⇨ About. In the About list, tap the Build Number item seven times. (Yes, seven times.) Then press the Back button to return to the Settings list. In the Settings list, tap System ⇨ Developer Options.

TIP

   Some people have reported that, after tapping the Build Number item seven times, it helps to twirl a rabbit's foot over their head three times. So far, I haven't been able to replicate these results.

2. **In the Developer Options list, turn on USB debugging.**

   Here's what one of my devices displays when I mess with this setting:

```
USB debugging is intended for development purposes.
Use it to copy data between your computer and your device,

install apps on your device without notification, and read log data.
```

   The stewards of Android are warning me that the USB Debugging option can expose my device to malware.

   On my device, I keep USB debugging on all the time. But if you're nervous about security, turn off USB debugging when you're not using the device to develop apps.

3. **(For Windows users only) Visit** https://developer.android.com/studio/run/oem-usb.html **to download your Android device's Windows USB driver. Install the driver on your Windows development computer.**

   While you follow the next step, keep an eye on your Android device's screen.

4. **With a USB cable, connect the device to the development computer.**

TIP

Not all USB cables are created equal. Some cables, called *data cables*, have wires and metal in places where other cables, called *charging cables*, have nothing except plastic. Try to use whatever USB cable came with your device. If, like me, you can't find the cable that came with your device or you don't know which cable came with your device, try more than one cable. When you find a cable that works, label that able cable. (If the cable *always* works, label it "stable able cable.")

When you plug in the cable, you see a pop-up dialog box on the Android device's screen. The pop-up asks whether you want to allow USB debugging.

5. **Yes, allow USB debugging.**

If you're not looking for it, you can miss the pop-up to allow USB debugging. Be sure to look for this pop-up when you plug in your device. If you definitely don't see the pop-up, you might be okay anyway. But if the message appears and you don't respond to it, you definitely won't be okay.

CHECKING THE CONNECTION AND BREAKING THE CONNECTION

To find out whether your Android phone is properly connected to your development computer, follow these steps:

1. **Open the Terminal on a Mac, or the Command Prompt on Windows.**

For details, refer to the earlier sidebar "Your friend, the command line."

2. **Use the** cd **command to navigate to Android's** platform-tools **directory.**

I'm a rootin'-tootin', two-fisted computer user. On my PC, I type

```
cd %HOMEDRIVE%%HOMEPATH%\AppData\Local\Android\Sdk\platform-tools
```

On my Mac, I type

```
cd ~/Library/Android/sdk/platform-tools/
```

(continued)

(continued)

3. **Type** adb devices. **(On a Mac, type** ./adb devices.**)**

   If your computer's response includes a very long hexadecimal number (such as 2885046445FF097), that number represents your connected device. For example, with one particular phone connected, my computer's response is

   ```
   emulator-5554 device
   emulator-5556 device
   2885046445FF097 device
   ```

   If you see the word *unauthorized* next to the long hexadecimal number, you probably didn't answer OK to the question "Allow USB debugging?" in Step 5 of the earlier section "Preparing to test on an Android physical device."

   If your computer's response doesn't include a long hexadecimal number, you might have missed the boat on one of the other steps in that earlier section.

Eventually, you'll want to disconnect your device from the development computer. Look for some reference to the device in File Explorer or the Finder.

- If you don't see a reference, you can probably yank the device's USB cable from your computer.

- If you see a reference, try to eject the device.

If you try to eject the device, and you see the dreaded Not Safe to Remove Device message, start by following Steps 1 and 2 in this sidebar. Then do one of the following:

- On a Mac, type

   ```
   ./adb kill-server
   ```

and then press Enter.

- On Windows, type

   ```
   adb kill-server
   ```

and then press Enter.

After that, you see the friendly Safe to Remove Hardware message.

Preparing to test on an iPhone

To test your app on an iPhone (or even an iPad), you must be using an Apple computer. If you have a Mac, follow these steps:

1. **Visit** `https://brew.sh` **and follow the instructions to install Homebrew on your computer.**

Homebrew is a third-party software package manager for macOS and Linux. You can use it to install all kinds of software, not just iPhone development tools.

2. **Open your Mac's Terminal application.**

3. **In the Terminal application window, type the following commands, one after another:**

```
brew update
brew install --HEAD usbmuxd
brew link usbmuxd
brew install --HEAD libimobiledevice
brew install ideviceinstaller ios-deploy cocoapods
pod setup
```

Wasn't that fun? It takes a long time to get responses, and you probably see scary warning messages along the way.

WARNING

The instructions in this step are current as of August 23, 2019 at 10:05 AM, Eastern Daylight Time. After that moment, I make no promises. If you get stuck, consult the web or send me an email.

4. **Visit** `developer.apple.com`, **and sign up for free membership in Apple's developer program.**

After these three steps, your development computer is ready to go. Follow these steps whenever you want to test a new Flutter app on a physical iPhone:

1. **Connect the physical phone to your development computer using a USB data cable.**

REMEMBER

Not all cables are alike. Apple puts a proprietary chip in each of its iPhone cables. If you buy your cable from a third-party vendor, you might not be able to use it to transfer an app to your phone.

2. **In Android Studio, open your new Flutter project.**

3. **Look for the Project tool window — the panel displaying a tree of files and folders.**

You find the Project tool window along the left side of Android Studio's main window. If you have trouble finding it, skip ahead to the section entitled "The Project tool window" in this chapter.

4. **Expand one of the tree's topmost branches to find a subbranch named iOS.**

5. **Right-click the iOS subbranch. In the resulting context menu, select Flutter ⇨ Open iOS Module in Xcode.**

   As a result, Xcode starts up. There's a tree of files and folders on the left side of the Xcode window.

6. **In the tree of files and folders, select Runner. (See Figure 2-16.)**

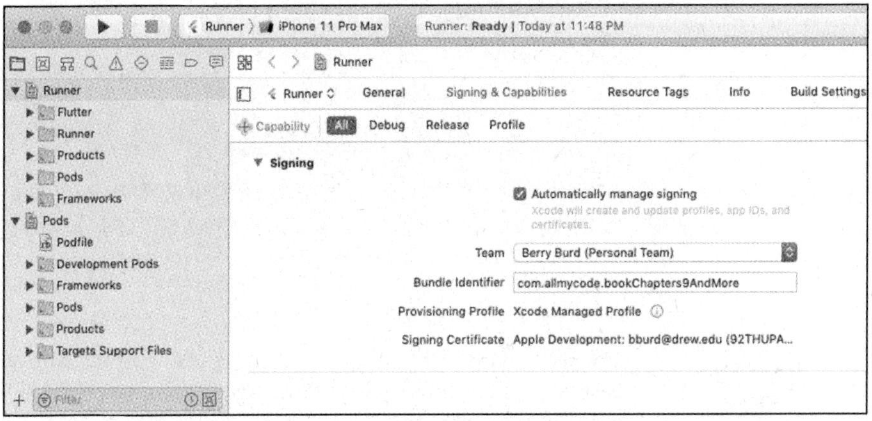

FIGURE 2-16:
Who's Berry
Burd?

7. **Select the Signing & Capabilities tab near the top of the Xcode window. (Again, refer to Figure 2-16.)**

   The Signing & Capabilities tab has a Team dropdown list.

8. **In the Team drop-down list, select Add an Account.**

   As a result, an Accounts dialog box appears. With your Apple ID, you automatically belong to a team of developers — your personal team with you as its only member.

9. **Do whatever you have to do in the Accounts dialog box, and then dismiss the dialog box.**

   As a result, you return to the Signing & Capabilities tab.

10. **In the Team drop-down list, select your very own team.**

11. **Close Xcode.**

    You're good to go.

Testing on any physical device (Android or iPhone)

When you're ready to test your app on a physical device, and you've connected the device to your development computer, look at the Target Selector drop-down list on Android Studio's toolbar. When your development computer is communicating properly with the physical device, the device's name appears as one of this drop-down list's items. (See Figure 2-17.) Select this item and then click the Run icon.

FIGURE 2-17:
My iPhone is
connected!

Using Android Studio

Android Studio is a customized version of IntelliJ IDEA — a general-purpose IDE with tools for Java development, C/C++ development, PHP development, modeling, project management, testing, debugging, and much more.

In this section, you get an overview of Android Studio's main window. I focus on the most useful features that help you build Flutter apps, but keep in mind that Android Studio has hundreds of features and many ways to access each feature.

Starting up

Each Flutter app belongs to a project. You can have dozens of projects on your computer's hard drive. When you run Android Studio, each of your projects is either open or closed. An *open* project appears in a window (its own window) on your computer screen. A *closed* project doesn't appear in a window.

Several of your projects can be open at the same time. You can switch between projects by moving from window to window.

TECHNICAL
STUFF

I often refer to an open project's window as Android Studio's *main window*. This can be slightly misleading because, with several projects open at a time, you have several main windows open at a time. In a way, none of these windows is more "main" than the others. When I write *main window*, I'm referring to the window whose Flutter project you're working on at that moment.

If Android Studio is running and no projects are open, Android Studio displays its Welcome screen. (Refer to Figure 2-2.) The Welcome screen may display some recently closed projects. If so, you can open a project by clicking its name on the Welcome screen. For an existing app that's not on the Recent Projects list, you can click the Welcome screen's Open an Existing Android Studio Project option.

If you have any open projects, Android Studio doesn't display the Welcome screen. In that case, you can open another project by choosing File ➪ Open or File ➪ Open Recent in an open project's window. To close a project, you can choose File ➪ Close Project, or you can do whatever you normally do to close one of the windows on your computer. (On a PC, click the X in the window's upper right corner. On a Mac, click the little red button in the window's upper left corner.)

TIP

Android Studio remembers which projects were open from one run to the next. If any projects are open when you quit Android Studio, those projects open again (with their main windows showing) the next time you launch Android Studio. You can override this behavior (so that only the Welcome screen appears each time you launch Android Studio). In Android Studio on a Windows computer, start by choosing File ➪ Settings ➪ Appearance and Behavior ➪ System Settings. In Android Studio on a Mac, choose Android Studio ➪ Preferences ➪ Appearance and Behavior ➪ System Settings. In either case, uncheck the Reopen Last Project on Startup check box.

The main window

Android Studio's main window is divided into several areas. Some of these areas can appear and disappear on your command. What comes next is a description of the areas in Figure 2-18, moving from the top of the main window to the bottom.

FIGURE 2-18:
The main window has several areas.

The areas that you see on your computer screen may be different from the areas in Figure 2-18. Usually, that's okay. You can make areas come and go by choosing certain menu options, including the View option on Android Studio's main menu bar. You can also click the little tool buttons on the edges of the main window.

The top of the main window

The topmost area contains the toolbar and the navigation bar.

>> **The *toolbar* contains action buttons, such as Open and Save All. It also contains the Target Selector and the Run icon.**

The Target Selector is the dropdown list whose default option is <no devices>. In Figure 2-18, the Target Selector displays the name *iPhone XR*.

The Run icon is the thing that looks like a green Play button.

You can read more about these items earlier, in this chapter's "Running your first app" section.

>> **The navigation bar displays the path to one of the files in your Flutter project.**

A Flutter project contains many files, and, at any particular moment, you work on one of these files. The navigation bar points to that file.

The Project tool window

Below the main menu and the toolbars, you see two different areas. The area on the left contains the *Project tool window*, which you use to navigate from one file to another within your Android app.

At any given moment, the Project tool window displays one of several possible views. For example, back in Figure 2-18, the Project tool window displays its *Project view*. In Figure 2-19, I click the drop-down list and select Packages view (instead of Project view).

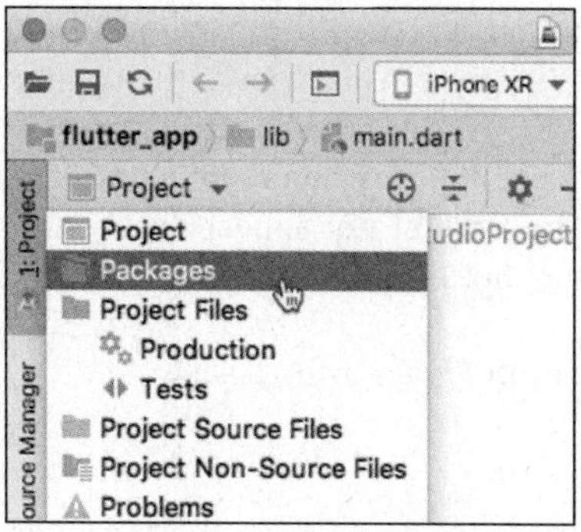

FIGURE 2-19:
Selecting
Packages view.

Packages view displays many of the same files as Project view, but in Packages view, the files are grouped differently. For most of this book's instructions, I assume that the Project tool window is in its default view; namely, Project view.

If Android Studio doesn't display the Project tool window, look for the Project tool button — the little button displaying the word *Project* on the left edge of the main window. Click that Project tool button. (But wait! What if you can't find the little Project button? In that case, go to Android Studio's main menu and select Window ⇨ Restore Default Layout.)

The Editor area

The area to the right of the Project tool window is the *Editor area*. When you edit a Dart program file, the editor displays the file's text. (Refer to Figure 2-18.) You can type, cut, copy, and paste text as you would in other text editors.

The Editor area can have several tabs. Each tab contains a file that's open for editing. To open a file for editing, double-click the file's branch in the Project tool window. To close the file, click the little x next to the file's name on the Editor tab.

The lower area

Below the Project tool window and the Editor area is another area that contains several tool windows. When you're not using any of these tool windows, you might not see this lower area.

In the lower area, the tool window that I use most often is the Run tool window. (Refer to the lower portion of Figure 2-18.) The Run tool window appears automatically when you click the Run icon. This tool window displays information about the run of a Flutter app. If your app isn't running correctly, the Run tool window may contain useful diagnostic information.

You can force other tool windows to appear in the lower area by clicking tool buttons near the bottom of the Android Studio window. For example, when you click the Terminal tool button, Android Studio displays the Windows Command Prompt, the Mac Terminal app, or another text-based command screen that you specify. For details, refer to the earlier sidebar "Your friend, the command line."

A particular tool button might not appear when there's nothing you can do with it. For example, the Run tool button might not appear until you press the Run icon. Don't worry about that. The tool button shows up whenever you need it.

Finishing your tour of the areas in Figure 2-18. . . .

The status bar

The status bar is at the bottom of Android Studio's window.

The status bar tells you what's happening now. For example, if the cursor is on the 37th character of the 11th line in the editor, you see 11:37 somewhere on the status line. When you tell Android Studio to run your app, the status bar contains the Run tool window's most recent message.

The kitchen sink

In addition to the areas that I mention in this section, other areas might pop up as the need arises. You can dismiss an area by clicking the area's Hide icon. (See Figure 2-20.)

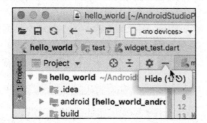

FIGURE 2-20:
Hiding the Project tool window area.

Running This Book's Sample Programs

This book has dozens of sample Flutter apps, and they're all available for download from the book's website: https://allmycode.com/Flutter. You can run any of these programs as part of an Android Studio Flutter app. This section has all the details.

REMEMBER

1. **Launch Android Studio.**

   For the run of your first app, you need an Internet connection.

   What you do next depends on what you see when you launch Android Studio.

2. **If you see Android Studio's Welcome screen (refer to Figure 2-2), select Start a New Flutter Project.**

   If you see another Android Studio window with a File option on the main menu bar, choose File ⇨ New ⇨ New Flutter Project on the main menu bar.

   Either way, the first dialog box for creating a new Flutter project appears.

3. **Create a new Flutter project by following Steps 3 through 9 in this chapter's earlier section "Running your first app."**

4. **In Android Studio's Project tool window, look for a folder named** `lib`.

    If you need help finding that tool window, refer to the "Project tool window" section earlier in this chapter.

    The Project tool window contains a tree of folders and files. Expand one of the tree's topmost branches to find the `lib` folder. This `lib` folder contains your project's Dart code.

5. **Right-click the tree's** `main.dart` **branch, and then select Delete.**

    If Android Studio prompts you for confirmation, click OK. One way or another, give `main.dart` the old heave-ho.

TIP

    Throughout this book, I write *right-click* as though everyone has a mouse with two or more buttons. If you're a Mac user and your mouse has only one button, Control+click wherever you see the term *right-click*.

6. **Make sure that you've uncompressed the** `FlutterForDummies_Listings.zip` **file.**

    For details, refer to the earlier sidebar "Compressed archive files."

TIP

    If you're unsure where to find the `FlutterForDummies_Listings.zip` file, look first in a folder named `Downloads`. Most web browsers put stuff inside `Downloads` by default.

CROSS REFERENCE

    Safari on a Mac generally uncompresses `.zip` archives automatically, and Windows browsers (Internet Explorer, Firefox, Chrome, and others) do not uncompress `.zip` archives automatically. For the complete scoop on archive files, see the earlier sidebar "Compressed archive files."

7. **In File Explorer or the Finder, navigate to the uncompressed** `FlutterForDummies_Listings` **folder. Inside that folder, look for the example that you want to run.**

    If you look inside the uncompressed download, you notice files named `App0301.dart`, `App0302.dart`, and so on. With a few exceptions, the numbers in these file names are chapter numbers followed by listing numbers. For example, in the name `App0602.dart`, the `06` stands for Chapter 6, and the `02` stands for the second code listing in that chapter.

    For this experiment, I suggest that you look for the `App0201.dart` file. (No code is listed anywhere in this chapter. So, in this unusual case, `0201` doesn't refer to a project whose code is in Listing 2-1.)

8. **Right-click the chosen** `App####.dart` **file. Then, in the resulting context menu, select Copy.**

9. **Right-click the new project's empty** `lib` **folder. On the resulting context menu, select Paste.**

   If Android Studio displays a dialog box offering to paste to a particular directory, check to make sure that the directory's full name ends in `lib`. Then, press OK.

   Now you're ready to run one of this book's examples. Go for it!

WARNING

On occasion, you may have more than one file in your project's `lib` folder and more than one app in your project. If you do, pressing the Run icon might not run the app that appears in Android Studio's editor area. To run the app that's showing in the editor area, look for that app's tab along the top of the editor area. When you right-click that tab, you see an option such as Run 'App0201.dart'. Select that option and watch the program run.

Enjoying reruns

The second time you run a particular example from this book, you don't have to follow all the steps in the previous section. It's easy to run an example over and over again. You can make changes to the code and then click the Run icon again. That's all you have to do.

If you've closed a project and you want to run it again, simply reopen the project in Android Studio and click the Run icon. For details, refer to this chapter's "Starting up" section.

If you're finicky . . .

After following the steps in the previous section, you may see some error markers (squiggly, red underlines) in the Project tool window. Android Studio's sample Flutter project describes something named MyApp, but the code that you copied into the `lib` folder makes no mention of MyApp. You can run this project over and over again without fixing the squiggly, red underlines. But if you want to fix them, simply follow these steps:

1. **In the Project tool window, expand the branch labeled** test.

   Inside that branch, you find a file named widget_test.dart.

2. **Delete the** `widget_test.dart` **file.**

   The squiggly, red underlines are gone. Problem solved!

The apps in this book are practice apps. No one runs these apps to get real work done. (This includes Doris, whom you meet in Chapter 7.) When you develop a real app, you must never ignore code in the `test` folder. Testing is an essential part of the software development process. Thorough testing is what makes programs work reliably.

Another way to get rid of the squiggly, red underlines is to jump into a time machine and redo instructions in the "Running This Book's Sample Programs" section. If you disregard Step 5 and don't delete `main.dart`, you won't get those red underlines. But you may have to deal with two other issues. The Run icon's behavior may become a bit confusing. In addition, you may create a rift in the space-time continuum and become your own grandparent.

Were These Setup Steps Fun or What?

I always dread any software setup that isn't completely trivial. Everybody's computer is different, and the instructions for an app's installation can't possibly cover every possible scenario. But, after getting the software up and running, I feel exhilarated. I can finally start using the software and enjoying the payoff from having labored through the setup steps.

If all the jibber-jabber in this chapter got you to the point where you're ready to learn Flutter, great! But if you're still struggling to get the software working, drop me a line. My contact info is in the book's introduction. I'll be happy to help.

2

Flutter: A Burd's-Eye View

Chapter **3**

"Hello" from Flutter

♪ *"Hello, I Must Be Going"* ♪

BERT KALMAR AND HARRY RUBY, SUNG BY GROUCHO MARX,
IN *ANIMAL CRACKERS*, 1930

The word *hello* is a relative newcomer in the English language. Its first known use in print was in the Norwich, Connecticut, *Courier* in 1826. Alexander Graham Bell, the inventor of the telephone, believed that phone calls should start with the term *Ahoy!* but, apparently, Thomas Edison preferred *Hello*, and early telephone books recommended Edison's choice.

According to legend, the first computer program to print nothing but "Hello world!" was written by Brian Kernighan, as part of the BCPL programming language documentation. The first public appearance of such a program was in Kernighan and Ritchie's 1972 book, *The C Programming Language*. Nowadays, the term *Hello world program*, or simply *Hello program*, applies to any dirt-simple code for someone's first exposure to a new language or new framework.

This chapter features a simple "Hello world" Flutter program and several embellishments. You can run the code, dissect it, change it, and have fun with it.

First Things First

Listing 3-1 contains your first Flutter app.

LISTING 3-1: **Ahoy, Maties!**

```
import 'package:flutter/material.dart';

main() => runApp(App0301());

class App0301 extends StatelessWidget {
  Widget build(BuildContext context) {
    return MaterialApp(
      home: Material(
        child: Text("Hello world!"),
      ),
    );
  }
}
```

You can download this app's code (and the code for every other listing in this book) from my website. The URL is https://allmycode.com/Flutter. You can find detailed instructions for running the code in Chapter 2.

If you prefer to type the code yourself, follow these steps:

1. **Create a new Flutter project.**

   Refer to Chapter 2.

   As usual, Android Studio creates a file full of Dart code for you. The file's name is main.dart.

2. **Make sure that the main.dart code appears in Android Studio's editor.**

   If it doesn't, expand the tree in the Project tool window on the left side of Android Studio's main window. Look for lib branch and, within the lib branch, the main.dart branch. Double-click that main.dart branch.

3. **In Android Studio's editor, delete all the main.dart code.**

   How liberating!

4. **In Android Studio's editor, type the code that you see in Listing 3-1.**

WARNING

   tHE dART PROGRAMMING LANGUAGE IS cASe-sEnsITiVE. If you change a lowercase letter in a word to an UpperCase letter, you can change the word's meaning. cHANGING the case can make the entire word go from being meaningful to being meaningless. In the first line of Listing 3-1, you can't replace import with Import. iF YOU DO, THE WHOLE PROGRAM STOPS WORKING. Try it and see for yourself!

   Figure 3-1 shows you the finished product.

```
main.dart ×
1    import 'package:flutter/material.dart';
2
3    main() => runApp(App0301());
4
5    class App0301 extends StatelessWidget {
6      Widget build(BuildContext context) {
7        return MaterialApp(
8          home: Material(
9            child: Text("Hello world!"),
10          ),
11        );
12      }
13    }
14
```

FIGURE 3-1:
A Flutter app is
ready to run.

5. **Run your new app.**

   For detailed instructions about initiating a run, refer to Chapter 2.

Figure 3-2 shows you what you see when you run the Flutter app in Listing 3-1. The app looks pretty bad, but at least you can see the little *Hello world!* in the upper left corner of the screen. I'll tend to the app's cosmetic aspects later in this chapter.

FIGURE 3-2:
Running the code
in Listing 3-1.

You may see red markers in Android Studio's editor. If you do, hover over a marker and read the explanation that appears. Some explanations are easy to understand; others aren't. The more practice you have in interpreting these messages, the more skilled you become at fixing the problems.

Another thing you can try is to select the Dart Analysis tab at the bottom of Android Studio's main window. This tab lists many of the spots in your project that contain questionable code. For any item in the list, a red icon indicates an error — something that must be fixed. (If you don't fix it, your app can't run.) Any other color icon indicates a warning — something that won't prevent your code from running but might be worth considering.

In the next several sections, I take apart the code in Listing 3-1. I explore the code from many points of view. I explain what the code does, why it does what it does, and what it might do differently.

What's it all about?

When you look at Listing 3-1, you may see words, punctuation, and indentation, but that's not what experienced Flutter developers see. They see the broad outline. They see big ideas in complete sentences. Figure 3-3 shows you what Listing 3-1 looks like to an experienced developer.

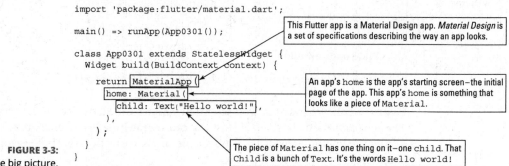

```
import 'package:flutter/material.dart';

main() => runApp(App0301());

class App0301 extends StatelessWidget {
  Widget build(BuildContext context) {
    return MaterialApp (
      home: Material(
        child: Text("Hello world!"),
      ),
    );
  }
}
```

This Flutter app is a Material Design app. *Material Design* is a set of specifications describing the way an app looks.

An app's home is the app's starting screen—the initial page of the app. This app's home is something that looks like a piece of Material.

The piece of Material has one thing on it—one child. That Child is a bunch of Text. It's the words Hello world!

FIGURE 3-3:
The big picture.

A Flutter program is like a set of Russian matryoshka dolls. It's a thing within a thing within another thing, and so on, until you reach an endpoint. (See Figure 3-4.)

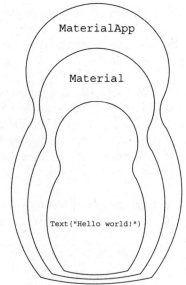

FIGURE 3-4:
The layered look.

Listing 3-1 has some `Text` inside a piece of `Material` which is, in turn, inside a `MaterialApp`. The words `Text`, `Material`, and `MaterialApp` begin commands to construct things. In Dart language terminology, the words `Text`, `Material`, and `MaterialApp` are the names of *constructor calls*. Here's the inside story:

>> The code

```
Text("Hello world!")
```

is a *constructor call*. When Flutter executes this code, it constructs a `Text` object. That `Text` object contains the words `Hello world!`

>> The code

```
Material(
    child: Text("Hello world!"),
)
```

is another constructor call. When Flutter executes this code, it constructs a `Material` object. That `Material` object contains the aforementioned `Text` object. (See Figure 3-5.)

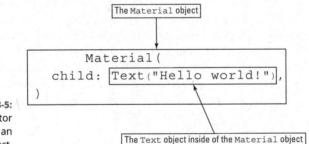

FIGURE 3-5: Each constructor call creates an object.

A `Material` object has some of the characteristics that physical material, such as a piece of fabric, might have. It has a certain shape. It may be elevated from the surface below it. You can move it or pinch it. Granted, the background in Figure 3-2 doesn't look much like a piece of fabric. But imitating the texture of cloth isn't Material Design's goal. The point of Material Design is to create a language for describing the status of the components on a user's screen, and to describe how these components relate to one another.

For the scoop on Material Design, visit `https://material.io/`.

CROSS REFERENCE

>> The code

```
MaterialApp(
  home: Material(
    child: Text("Hello world!"),
  ),
)
```

is yet another constructor call. When Flutter executes this code, it constructs a MaterialApp whose starting screen is the Material object. (Refer to Figure 3-3.)

Here's a way to sum it all up:

In Listing 3-1, the MaterialApp object **has a** Material object, and the Material object **has a** Text object.

In that sentence, the seemingly innocent use of the words "has a" is important. For more details, see the later section "A brief treatise on within-ness'."

TIP

To understand the code in Listing 3-1, you have to know where pairs of parentheses begin and end. But finding the matches between open and close parentheses isn't always easy. To help with this problem, Android Studio has a few tricks up its virtual sleeve. If you place the cursor near a parenthesis character, Android Studio highlights the matching parenthesis. In addition, you can visit Android Studio's Settings or Preferences dialog box. (On Windows, select File⇨Settings. On a Mac, select Android Studio⇨Preferences.) In that dialog box, select Editor⇨General⇨Appearance and put a check mark in the Show Closing Labels in Dart Source Code check box. After you dismiss the dialog box, Android Studio displays comments marking the ends of many constructor calls. (Notice the labels // Material and // MaterialApp in Figure 3-6.)

FIGURE 3-6:
Helpful closing labels.

A constructor's parameters

Every constructor call has a list of *parameters* (usually called a *parameter list*). In Listing 3-1, each constructor's parameter list has only one parameter in it. (See Figure 3-7.)

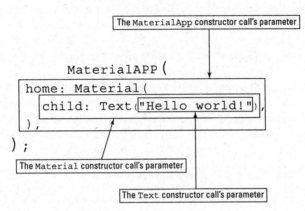

FIGURE 3-7:
Constructor calls have parameters.

Constructor calls can have many parameters, or have no parameters. Take, for example, the Text call in Listing 3-1. In that code, the parameter "Hello world!" supplies information to Dart — information that's specific to the Text widget that Dart is constructing. Try changing Text("Hello world!") to Text("Hello world!", textScaleFactor: 4.0). When you save the new code, Android Studio does a hot restart that changes the look of the app in your emulator. (See Figure 3-8.)

FIGURE 3-8:
An ugly app to illustrate the textScaleFactor parameter's effect.

Chapter 1 describes the difference between Flutter's hot restart and hot reload features. Both features apply updates to an app while the app is running. To do a hot restart, simply save your code. To do a hot reload, press the Run icon near the top of Android Studio's main window.

TIP

The constructor call

```
Text("Hello world!", textScaleFactor: 4.0)
```

contains two kinds of parameters:

>> `"Hello world!"` **is a positional parameter.**

A *positional parameter* is a parameter whose meaning depends on its position in the parameter list. When you create a new `Text` object, the characters to be displayed must always come first in the list. You can see this for yourself by changing the constructor call to the following, invalid code:

```
Text(textScaleFactor: 4.0, "Hello world!")  // Bad code!!
```

In this code, the positional `"Hello world!"` parameter doesn't come first in the list. So, if you type this line in Android Studio's editor, the editor marks this line with an ugly red error indicator. Quick! Change it back so that the `"Hello world!"` parameter comes first! You don't want Android Studio to form a bad impression of you!

>> `textScaleFactor: 4.0` **is a named parameter.**

A *named parameter* is a parameter whose meaning depends on the word before the colon. A `Text` constructor call can have many different named parameters, such as `textScaleFactor`, `style`, and `maxLines`. You can write the named parameters in any order as long as they come after any of the positional parameters.

When you supply a `textScaleFactor` parameter, the parameter tells Flutter how large the text should be. (Refer to Figure 3-8.) When you don't supply a `textScaleFactor` parameter, Flutter uses the default 1.0 factor.

TECHNICAL STUFF

The size of the text depends on a few things, such as the `textScaleFactor` and a `style` parameter's font size. For example, the following code makes `Hello world!` twice as large as it is in Figure 3-8.

```
Text("Hello world!", textScaleFactor: 4.0,
    style: TextStyle(fontSize: 28.0))
```

The app shown in Figure 3-8 already has `textScaleFactor` 4.0. But it has the default font size, which is 14.0. Because 28.0 is two times 14.0, the `fontSize: 28.0` parameter doubles the size of the text.

A note about punctuation

In Dart, you use commas to separate a constructor's parameters from one another. And, for all but the simplest parameter lists, you end the list with a *trailing comma*.

```
return MaterialApp(
  home: Material(
    child: Text("Hello world!"), // Trailing comma after the child parameter
  ),                             // Trailing comma after the home parameter
);
```

Without trailing commas, your code runs as expected. But the next section tells you how you can get Android Studio to make your code look good. And, without trailing commas, Android Studio doesn't do its best.

A pair of slashes (//) has a special meaning in Dart. To find out what it is, see Chapter 4.

CROSS
REFERENCE

Don't relent — simply indent

Take another look at Listing 3-1, and notice how some of the lines are indented. As a general rule, if one thing is subordinate to some other thing, its line of code is indented more than that other thing. For example, in Listing 3-1, the MaterialApp object contains the Material object, so the home: Material line is indented more than the return MaterialApp line.

Here are two facts to keep in mind:

>> In a Dart program, indentation *isn't* necessary.

>> In a Dart program, indentation *is* necessary.

Wait! What are those two facts again?

If you change the indentation in a Dart program, the program still runs. Here's a valid reworking of the code in Listing 3-1.

```
// Don't do this. It's poorly indented code.
  import 'package:flutter/material.dart';

main() => runApp(App0301());

class App0301 extends StatelessWidget {
Widget build(BuildContext context) {
return MaterialApp(
home: Material(
```

```
  child: Text("Hello world!"),
    ),
      );
      }
        }
```

When you ask Android Studio to run this poorly indented code, it works. Android Studio dutifully runs the code on your virtual or physical device. But having this code run isn't good enough. *This poorly indented code is hideous. It's almost impossible to read.* The indentation, or lack thereof, gives you no indication of the program's structure. You have to wade through the words to discover that the `Material` widget is inside the `MateralApp` widget. Instead of showing you the app's structure at a glance, this code makes your eyes wander aimlessly in a sea of seemingly unrelated commands.

The good news is, you don't have to learn how to indent your code. Android Studio can do the indentation for you. Here's how:

1. **Open Android Studio's Settings or Preferences dialog box.**

   On Windows, select File ⇨ Settings.

   On a Mac, select Android Studio ⇨ Preferences.

2. **In that dialog box, select Languages & Frameworks ⇨ Flutter and then put a check mark in the Format Code on Save check box.**

   The check mark tells Android Studio to fix your code's indentation whenever you save your work.

   While you're at it, you might as well put a check mark in the next check box — the Organize Imports on Save check box.

3. **Select OK to dismiss the dialog box.**

   Hazzah! When you run the code — or simply save the code — Android Studio fixes the code's indentation.

If you want more control over Android Studio's behavior, don't fiddle with the Settings or Preferences dialog box. Instead, whenever you want indentation to be fixed, put the cursor in the Editor panel, and then choose Code ⇨ Reformat Code from Android Studio's main menu.

One way or another, please indent your code properly.

Classes, Objects, and Widgets

Dart is an object-oriented language, so Dart has things called objects and classes. Listing 3-1 contains the names of many classes, such as App0301, Stateless Widget, Widget, BuildContext, MaterialApp, Material, and Text. It's fair to say that almost every word in Listing 3-1 that starts with an uppercase letter is the name of a class.

You don't have to know a lot about object-oriented programming to understand the role of these words in Listing 3-1, but it helps to keep a few facts in mind:

>> **An object is a thing of some kind. Each object belongs to a particular class of things.**

The word Text is the name of a class of things — things that contain characters to be displayed on the screen. On its own, a class doesn't do much. The fact that Flutter has a Text class doesn't mean anything for an app that displays images and no characters. You can talk about the class of all unicorns, but I've never seen a unicorn in my front yard.

In contrast, the constructor call Text("Hello world!") constructs an actual object. That object appears on the user's screen. For example, a Text object containing the words Hello world! appears in Figure 3-2. You can refer to that object as an *instance* of the Text class.

In any particular app, you can construct no Text instances, one Text instance, or many Text instances. The same is true of classes such as Widget and Material and almost every other class.

>> **Being an instance of one class might make you automatically be an instance of a bigger class.**

Every instance of the Cat class is, by definition, an instance of the Animal class. (If that weren't true, millions of YouTube videos wouldn't exist.) And what about the Animal class? Every instance of the Animal class is an instance of the LivingThing class. (See Figure 3-9.)

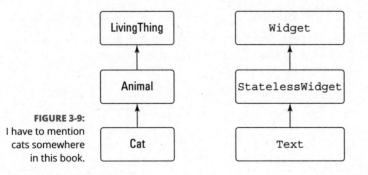

FIGURE 3-9:
I have to mention cats somewhere in this book.

In the same way, every instance of Flutter's Text class is, by definition, an instance of Flutter's StatelessWidget class. And, in turn, every instance of the StatelessWidget class is an instance of Flutter's Widget class. So every Text instance is also a Widget instance. (Refer to Figure 3-9.)

» **In Flutter, almost every object is, in one way or another, an instance of the** Widget **class.**

Informally, a widget is a component on a user's screen. Flutter takes this idea to another level, with each part of the user interface (the Text instance, the Material instance, and even the MaterialApp instance) being a widget in its own right.

In Listing 3-1, App0301 is the name of a class. In the line

```
main() => runApp(App0301());
```

the term App0301() is yet another constructor call. This call constructs an instance of the App0301 class.

The line

```
class App0301 extends StatelessWidget
```

and all the code below it is the *declaration* of the App0301 class. The declaration tells Dart what kind of class it is and what kinds of things you can do with the class. In particular, the word extends in that first line makes any instance of the App0301 class be an instance of the StatelessWidget class. That's all you have to do to make App0301 instances be instances of the StatelessWidget class.

Now you have several terms with subtly different meanings — *class*, *object*, *instance*, and *widget*. In Listing 3-1, the code Text("Hello world!") constructs something, but exactly what kind of thing does that code construct?

» **From the Dart language's point of view,** Text("Hello world!") **constructs an object.**

In Dart terminology, you call it an instance of the Text class.

» **From the Flutter point of view,** Text("Hello world!") **creates a widget.**

It's an instance of the Text class and therefore (. . . guilt by association . . .) an instance of the StatelessWidget class and an instance of the Widget class.

For more of my babble about objects, classes, and widgets, see Chapter 7.

CROSS
REFERENCE

A brief treatise on "within-ness"

In a Dart program, you can find widgets within other widgets. (Refer to Figure 3-4.) In the same Dart program, you find classes within other classes. (Refer to Figure 3-9.) These two kinds of "within-ness" aren't the same. In fact, these two kinds of "within-ness" have little to do with one another.

In Figure 3-3, a `Text` widget is the child of a `Material` widget. This *doesn't* mean that a `Text` instance is also an instance of the `Material` class. To understand the difference, think about two kinds of relationships: "is a" relationships and "has a" relationships.

>> **The relationships that I describe in the "What's it all about?" section are "has a" relationships.**

   In Listing 3-1, the `MaterialApp` object has a `Material` object inside of it, and the `Material` object has a `Text` object inside of it.

   There's nothing special about "has a" relationships. There can be "has a" relationships in a barnyard. A Cat has a Mouse, and the Mouse has a PieceOfCheese.

>> **The relationships that I describe in the earlier "Classes, Objects, and Widgets" section are "is a" relationships.**

   In every Flutter program, each `Text` object is a `StatelessWidget` object and, in turn, each `StatelessWidget` object is a `Widget` object.

   In a barnyard, each Cat is an Animal and, in turn, each Animal is a LivingThing.

It wouldn't make sense to say that a Cat is a Mouse, or that a `Material` object is a `Text` object. In the same way, it's not correct to say that every Cat has an Animal, or that every `Text` object has a `StatelessWidget` object. The two kinds of relationships — "has a" and "is a" — are quite different.

TECHNICAL STUFF

If you're hungering for terminology that's more formal than "has a" and "is a," I have some for you:

>> **A chain of things connected by the "has a" relationship is called a *composition hierarchy*.**

   Frivolous as it may be, the diagram in Figure 3-4 illustrates a composition hierarchy.

>> **The chain of things connected by the "is a" relationship is called the *inheritance hierarchy*.**

   The diagrams in Figure 3-9 are part of Flutter's class hierarchy.

Don't you feel better now that you have these fancy terms to fling around?

REMEMBER

In Flutter, almost everything is called a "widget." Many classes are widgets. When a class is a widget, the class's instances (any objects constructed from that class) are also called widgets.

The documentation is your friend

You may be asking yourself how you're going to memorize all these names: Text, StatelessWidget, MaterialApp, and probably thousands more. Sorry to say, you're asking the wrong question. You don't memorize anything. When you use a name often enough, you remember it naturally. When you don't remember a name, you look it up in the online Flutter docs. (Sometimes, you're not sure where to look for the name you want. In that case, you have to poke around a bit.)

To see what I mean, point your web browser to https://api.flutter.dev/ flutter/widgets/Text-class.html. When you do, you see a page with information about the Text class, some sample code, and some other stuff. (See Figure 3-10.)

Text class

A run of text with a single style.

The Text widget displays a string of text with single style. The string might break across multiple lines or might all be displayed on the same line depending on the layout constraints.

The style argument is optional. When omitted, the text will use the style from the closest enclosing DefaultTextStyle. If the given style's TextStyle.inherit property is true (the default), the given style will be merged with the closest enclosing DefaultTextStyle. This merging behavior is useful, for example, to make the text bold while using the default font family and size.

Sample

```
Text(
  'Hello, $_name! How are you?',
  textAlign: TextAlign.center,
```

CONSTRUCTORS
Text
rich

PROPERTIES
data
locale
maxLines
overflow
semanticsLabel
softWrap
strutStyle
style
textAlign
textDirection

FIGURE 3-10:
Useful info about the Text class.

In the page's upper right corner, you find a list of Text constructors. In Figure 3-10, there are two possibilities: Text and rich. If you select the Text link, you see a page describing the Text constructor call. (See Figure 3-11.)

This page lists the parameters in the constructor call and provides other helpful information.

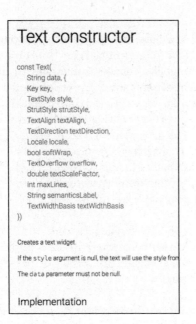

```
Text constructor

const Text(
    String data, {
    Key key,
    TextStyle style,
    StrutStyle strutStyle,
    TextAlign textAlign,
    TextDirection textDirection,
    Locale locale,
    bool softWrap,
    TextOverflow overflow,
    double textScaleFactor,
    int maxLines,
    String semanticsLabel,
    TextWidthBasis textWidthBasis
})


Creates a text widget.

If the style argument is null, the text will use the style from

The data parameter must not be null.


Implementation
```

FIGURE 3-11:
The Text
constructor call.

TIP

On the page in Figure 3-11, notice how all but one of the constructor's parameters are enclosed in a pair of curly braces. The parameter that's not in curly braces (namely, String data) is the constructor's one and only positional parameter. Each of the parameters inside the curly braces (including double textScaleFactor) is a named parameter.

REMEMBER

You can always count on Flutter's documentation to tell you what kinds of objects you can and cannot put inside of other objects. For example, the following code is doomed to failure:

```
return MaterialApp(
  child: Text("Hello world!"), // Don't do this!
);
```

It's doomed because, according to the Flutter docs, the MaterialApp constructor has no parameter named child.

Making Things Look Nicer

The app shown in Figure 3-2 looks pretty bad. The words *Hello world!* are tucked up against the screen's upper left corner. Fortunately, Flutter offers an easy way to fix this: You surround the Text widget with a Center widget. As its name suggests, the Center widget centers whatever is inside of it.

The word Center is the name of a class, so any object constructed from that class is called an instance of that class. In a term such as "Center widget," the word *widget* suggests that something like Center (something to help manage the screen's layout) is a component of some kind. A piece of Text on the screen is a component, a piece of Material on the screen is a component, and a Center object is also a component. Even though a Center widget doesn't light up somewhere on the screen, a Center widget is still a component. Part of Flutter's great strength is that Flutter treats all things the same way. When so many things are widgets, so many things can serve as parameters in the constructors of other things. The people who make up names for programming features call this the *composability* feature, and composability is a very nice feature to have.

You have a few ways to surround a Text widget's code with a Center widget's code. One way is to poke the cursor somewhere inside Android Studio's editor, start typing, and hope that you navigate the thicket of parentheses correctly. A better way is to do the following:

1. **Place the cursor on the word** Text **in the editor.**

2. **Press Alt+Enter.**

    As a result, a dropdown list appears.

3. **In the dropdown list, select Center Widget.**

    Listing 3-2 shows you what you get.

LISTING 3-2: **Centering the Text**

```
import 'package:flutter/material.dart';

main() => runApp(App0302());

class App0302 extends StatelessWidget {
  Widget build(BuildContext context) {
    return MaterialApp(
      home: Material(
        child: Center(
          child: Text("Hello world!"),
        ),
      ),
    );
  }
}
```

In Listing 3-2, the Material widget has a Center widget child, which, in turn, has a Text widget child. You can think of the Text widget as the grandchild of the Material widget.

Flutter supports hot restarting. After adding the Center code to the program in Android Studio's editor, save the changes by pressing Ctrl+S (on Windows) or Cmd+S (on a Mac). If the program from Listing 3-1 was already running, Flutter applies your changes and updates the emulator screen almost immediately.

WARNING

In some situations, hot restart doesn't work. Instead of updating your app, Android Studio displays an error message. If that happens, try a hot reload. (Press the Run icon near the top of Android Studio's main window.) And what if hot reload fails? In that case, press the Stop icon — the red square icon that's in the same row as the Run icon. When you press the Stop icon, the run of your app ends completely. Pressing the Run icon to start afresh may fix the problem.

Figure 3-12 shows what you get when you run the code in Listing 3-2.

FIGURE 3-12:
Yes, you've centered the text.

Creating a scaffold

The Text widget in Figure 3-12 looks so lonely. Let's add some fanfare to the basic app. Listing 3-3 has the code; Figures 3-13 and 3-14 show you the new screen.

LISTING 3-3: **Using a Scaffold**

```
import 'package:flutter/material.dart';

main() => runApp(App0303());

class App0303 extends StatelessWidget {
  Widget build(BuildContext context) {
    return MaterialApp(
      home: Scaffold(
        appBar: AppBar(
          title: Text("My First Scaffold"),
        ),
        body: Center(
          child: Text("Hello world!"),
        ),
        drawer: Drawer(
          child: Center(
            child: Text("I'm a drawer."),
          ),
        ),
      ),
    );
  }
}
```

FIGURE 3-13: Behold! A scaffold!

FIGURE 3-14:
Pulling out a
drawer.

The home for a MaterialApp doesn't have to be a Material widget. In Listing 3-3, the home is a Scaffold. When companies build skyscrapers, they create scaffolds — temporary wooden structures to support workers in high places. In programming, a *scaffold* is a structure that provides basic, often-used functionality.

The Scaffold constructor in Listing 3-3 has three parameters — an appBar, a body, and a drawer. In Figures 3-13 and 3-14, the appBar is the dark region at the top of the screen. The body is the large white region containing the Center with its Text widget. In Figure 3-14, the drawer is the big white area that appears when the user swipes from the left edge of the screen. The drawer also appears when the user presses the "hamburger" icon — three horizontal lines near the screen's top left corner.

The body is nothing special. It's very much like the entire screen in the earlier examples. But the appBar and drawer are new. The appBar and drawer are two of the things you can have when you create a Scaffold. Other things made available by Scaffold widgets include navigation bars, floating buttons, bottom sheets, footer buttons, and more.

WARNING

In this chapter, Listings 3-1 and 3-2 have Material widgets, and Listing 3-3 has a Scaffold. These widgets form the backgrounds for their respective apps. If you remove the Material widget from Listing 3-1 or 3-2, your app's screen becomes an ugly mess. You get large red letters with yellow underlines against a black background. The same thing happens when you remove the Scaffold from Listing 3-3. There are other widgets that can provide backgrounds for your apps, but Material and Scaffold are the most commonly used.

Adding visual tweaks

Try this experiment: Change the appBar parameter from Listing 3-3 to the code snippet in Listing 3-4.

LISTING 3-4: **A Slight Change for the Code from Listing 3-3**

```
appBar: AppBar(
  title: Text("My First Scaffold"),
  elevation: 100,
  brightness: Brightness.light,
)
```

In Figure 3-15, I try to show the effect of adding the elevation and brightness parameters to the AppBar constructor call. I might not succeed because the effect of the elevation parameter is subtle.

FIGURE 3-15:
A slight change from the screen in Figure 3-13.

In Google's Material Design language, you imagine that the background rests on some flat surface, and that other components are elevated off the background by some number of pixels. For an AppBar, the default elevation is 4, but you can change a bar's elevation with . . . wait for it . . . the elevation parameter.

A component's elevation affects several aspects of the component's appearance. But in this section, the most obvious change is probably the shadow beneath the AppBar. You might not be able to see the difference between the shadows in Figures 3-13 and 3-15, but when you run the code on a virtual or physical device, an AppBar with elevation: 100 casts quite a large shadow.

You may be wondering what the 100 in elevation: 100 means. Is it millimeters, pixels, points, or light-years? In truth, it means "100 density-independent pixels" — or "100 dps," for short. No matter what screen the user has, one dp is 1/160 of an inch. So elevation: 100 means 100/160 of an inch (better known as five-eighths of an inch).

For all the details about Material Design's elevation property, visit https:// material.io/design/environment/elevation.html.

An AppBar widget's brightness parameter is yet another matter. The effect of adding brightness: Brightness.light is to tell Flutter that, because the AppBar is light, the text and icons at the top of the AppBar should be dark. (Compare Figures 3-13 and 3-15.) The dark text and icons are easy to see against what is considered to be a light AppBar.

Dart's enum feature

An interesting feature of the Dart programming language is hiding inside Listing 3-4. The word Brightness refers to something called an enum (pronounced "ee-noom"). The word enum is short for *enumeration*. An enum is a bunch of values, like Brightness.light and Brightness.dark.

In Listing 3-4, notice how you refer to an enum's value. You don't use a constructor call. Instead, you use the name of the enum (such as Brightness), followed by a period, followed by the unique part of the value's name (such as light or dark).

Flutter has many other built-in enums. For example, the Orientation enum has values Orientation.portrait and Orientation.landscape. The Animation Status enum has values AnimationStatus.forward, AnimationStatus.reverse, AnimationStatus.completed, and AnimationStatus.dismissed.

To find out how to create a new enum, see 7.

Hello from sunny California!

Google announced Material Design at its developer conference in 2014. The first version of this design language dealt mostly with Android devices, but Version 2 embraced custom branding for iPhones and other iOS devices. Flutter's Material widget runs on iPhones with automatic platform-specific adaptations.

You can run any of this book's MaterialApp examples on iPhones as well as Android phones, but if you want an iPhone-first design strategy, you can use Flutter's Cupertino widget collection. Listing 3-5 has an example.

LISTING 3-5: **How to Look Like an iPhone App**

```
import 'package:flutter/cupertino.dart';

void main() => runApp(App0305());

class App0305 extends StatelessWidget {
  Widget build(BuildContext context) {
    return CupertinoApp(
      home: CupertinoPageScaffold(
        navigationBar: CupertinoNavigationBar(),
        child: Center(
          child: Text("Hello world!"),
        ),
      ),
    );
  }
}
```

Listing 3-5 is very much like its Material Design cousin, Listing 3-3. But instead of having MaterialApp, Scaffold and AppBar widgets, Listing 3-5 has the CupertinoApp, CupertinoPageScaffold, and CupertinoNavigationBar widgets. Instead of importing 'package:flutter/material.dart', Listing 3-5 imports 'package:flutter/cupertino.dart'. (This import declaration makes Flutter's Cupertino widget library available for use by the rest of the listing's code.)

WARNING

Flutter's Material Design and Cupertino widgets aren't completely parallel with one another. For example, the Scaffold constructor call in Listing 3-3 has a body parameter. In place of that parameter, the CupertinoPageScaffold constructor call in Listing 3-5 has a child parameter. When in doubt, check the official Flutter documentation pages to find out which parameter names belong to which widgets' constructor calls.

TECHNICAL STUFF

You can mix and match Material Design and Cupertino widgets in the same app. You can even tailor your app's design style for different kinds of phones. You can even put code of the following kind in your app:

```
if (Platform.isAndroid) {
  // Do Android-specific stuff
}
if (Platform.isIOS) {
  // Do iOS-specific stuff
}
```

For more information, visit https://pub.dev/packages/device_info.

Adding another widget

When you run out of things to talk about, you can ask people about their families. Sometimes you learn interesting facts, at other times you hear lists of complaints, and sometimes you get a long, boring monologue. One way or another, it fills in any awkward silences.

When it comes to understanding familial relationships, I'm a slow learner. Someone tells me about their second cousin's wife's mother-in-law, and I have to pause the conversation to draw a mental diagram. Otherwise, I'm just plain confused.

My own family tree is rather simple. It was Mom, Dad, and me. People ask me if I was lonely being an only child. "Heck, no!" I say. "As an only child, I didn't have to share things."

This discussion about families is my dubious lead-in to the subject of `Column` widgets. In the previous examples, the `Text` widget was an only child. But eventually, the `Text` widget must learn to share. (Otherwise, the `Text` widget becomes spoiled, like me.)

How do you put two children on a scaffold's body? You might be tempted to try this:

```
// DON'T DO THIS:
body: Center(
  child: Text("Hello world!"),
  child: AnotherWidget(...)
)
```

But a constructor call can't have two parameters with the same name. So, what can you do?

Flutter has a `Column` widget. The `Column` widget's constructor has a `children` parameter. The column widget's children line up, one under another, on the screen. That sounds promising! Listing 3-6 has some code, and Figure 3-16 has the resulting display.

LISTING 3-6: **More Widgets, Please!**

```
import 'package:flutter/material.dart';

main() => runApp(App0306());

class App0306 extends StatelessWidget {
```

(continued)

LISTING 3-6:   *(continued)*

```
Widget build(BuildContext context) {
  return MaterialApp(
    home: Scaffold(
      appBar: AppBar(
        title: Text("Adding Widgets"),
      ),
      body: Column(
        children: [
          Text(
            "Hello world!",
            textScaleFactor: 2.0,
          ),
          Text("It's lonely for me inside this phone.")
        ],
      ),
    ),
  );
}
}
```

FIGURE 3-16:
I wonder who's
in there!

A Column constructor call has a children parameter, and the children parameter's value is a list. In the Dart programming language, a *list* is a bunch of objects. Each object's position in the list is called an *index*. The index values start from 0 and work their way upward.

One way to create a list is to enclose objects in square brackets. For example, Listing 3-6 contains a list with two objects. (See Figure 3-17.)

A list's indices don't begin with 1. They begin with 0.

REMEMBER

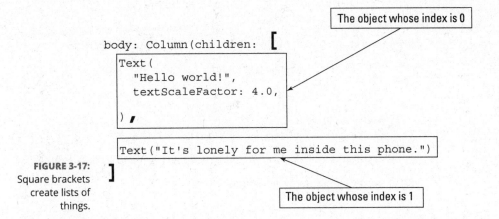

FIGURE 3-17:
Square brackets
create lists of
things.

STRING THINGS

In the Dart programming language, the stuff that you surround with quotation marks (as in `"Hello world!"`) is called a *string*. It's a bunch of characters, one after another. Here are some handy facts about strings:

- **To create a string, you can use double quotation marks or single quotation marks.**

  In other words, `'Hello world!'` is the same as `"Hello world!"`.

- **It's easy to put a single quotation mark inside a double quoted string.**

  Refer to the string

  ```
  "It's lonely for me inside this phone."
  ```

  in Listing 3-6.

- **It's easy to put a double quotation mark inside a single quoted string.**

  For example, the following is a valid string:

  ```
  '"Yikes!" she said.'
  ```

- **Using backslash characters (\), you can put either kind of quotation mark inside either kind of string.**

  Here are two examples:

  ```
  'It\'s lonely for me inside this phone.'
  "\"Yikes!\" she said."
  ```

(continued)

(continued)

- **A string can straddle several lines if you use triple quotation marks.**

  Both of these examples are valid Dart code:

  ```
  '''And the winner is ...
                    Charles Van Doren!'''
  """And the winner is ...
                    Charles Van Doren!"""
  ```

- **To paste strings one after another, use a plus sign (+) or some blank spaces.**

  Both of these examples are valid Dart code:

  ```
  "Hello" + " world!"

  "Hello" " world!"
  ```

For some other things you can do with strings, see Chapter 4.

Centering the text (Part 1)

Figure 3-16 looks strange because the words are tucked up against the upper left corner. In this section, I walk you through some steps to diagnose this problem, and to fix it.

1. While the app in Listing 3-6 runs, look on the right edge of Android Studio's window for a toolbar button with the words *Flutter Inspector* on it. Click that toolbar button.

   As a result, the Flutter Inspector appears. (See Figure 3-18.)

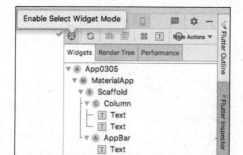

FIGURE 3-18: The Flutter Inspector.

2. In the upper left corner of the Flutter Inspector, look for the Enable Select Widget Mode icon. (Refer to Figure 3-18.) Click that icon.

3. Select the Flutter Inspector's Widgets tab. (Once again, refer to Figure 3-18.)

4. **In the tree of widgets, select Column. (See Figure 3-19.)**

   As a result, the device that's running your app adds highlighting and a little label to the Column widget on the screen. (See Figure 3-20.)

5. **Just for fun, select a few other branches in the Flutter Inspector's tree of widgets.**

   You can determine the boundaries of almost any of your widgets by using this technique.

The highlighting in Figure 3-20 tells you that the Column widget isn't centered inside of its parent Scaffold widget, and it's not wide enough to fill the entire Scaffold widget. To fix this, put the Column widget inside of a Center widget. Put the cursor on the word Column in Android Studio's editor, and then follow the instructions at the start of the earlier "Making Things Look Nicer" section. Listing 3-7 shows you what you get.

LISTING 3-7: **Centering the Column Widget**

```
import 'package:flutter/material.dart';

main() => runApp(App0307());

class App0307 extends StatelessWidget {
  Widget build(BuildContext context) {
    return MaterialApp(
      home: Scaffold(
        appBar: AppBar(
          title: Text("Adding Widgets"),
        ),
        body: Center(
          child: Column(
            children: [
              Text(
                "Hello world!",
                textScaleFactor: 2.0,
              ),
              Text("It's lonely for me inside this phone.")
            ],
          ),
        ),
      ),
    );
  }
}
```

When you save your changes, Android Studio does a hot restart and you see the new-and-improved display in Figure 3-21.

FIGURE 3-21:
The Column widget is centered.

Centering the text (Part 2)

The Text widgets in Figure 3-21 are centered horizontally, but they're not centered vertically. To center them vertically, you can fiddle with Flutter's Center widget, but there's a much easier way.

1. **In Android Studio's Flutter Inspector, select the** Column **widget.**

   The Flutter Inspector's lower panel displays all the properties of whatever widget you've selected.

   Wait! What's a "property"? Every object has *properties*, and each property of each object has a *value*. For example, every instance of Flutter's Text class has a textScaleFactor property. In Listing 3-7, a constructor call sets a Text instance's textScaleFactor property to the value 2.0.

   Constructor calls aren't the only way of setting the properties of objects. In Figure 3-22, the Flutter Inspector's lower panel shows the values of the Column widget's direction property, its mainAxisAlignment property, and many other properties. In addition, the two Text children appear in the Flutter Inspector's lower panel.

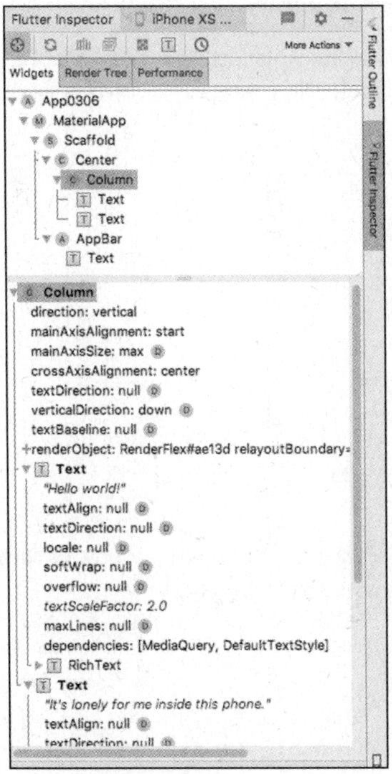

FIGURE 3-22: Properties of the Column (the Column widget that's constructed in Listing 3-7).

2. **In the lower panel, hover over the** Column **widget's** mainAxisAlignment **property.**

   When you do, Android Studio displays a pop-up explaining the mainAxisAlignment property's meaning. (See Figure 3-23.) The text in this pop-up comes automatically from Flutter's official documentation.

   A column's *main axis* is an invisible line going from the column's top to its bottom.

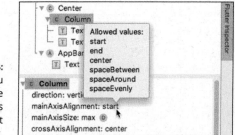

3. **Again in the lower panel, hover over the word** start **in the** Column **widget's** mainAxisAlignment **property.**

   The new pop-up says that you can replace start with any of the values end, center, spaceBetween, spaceAround, or spaceEvenly. (See Figure 3-24.)

4. **In Android Studio's editor, add a** mainAxisAlignment **parameter to the** Column **widget's constructor. (See Listing 3-8.)**

LISTING 3-8: **Time for an Alignment**

```
import 'package:flutter/material.dart';

main() => runApp(App0308());

class App0308 extends StatelessWidget {
  Widget build(BuildContext context) {
    return MaterialApp(
      home: Scaffold(
        appBar: AppBar(
          title: Text("Adding Widgets"),
        ),
        body: Center(
          child:
            Column(mainAxisAlignment:
            MainAxisAlignment.center, children: [
              Text(
                "Hello world!",
                textScaleFactor: 2.0,
              ),
              Text("It's lonely for me inside this phone.")
            ],
          ),
        ),
      ),
    );
  }
}
```

In Listing 3-8, `mainAxisAlignment` is the name of a parameter, `MainAxisAlignment` is the name of an enum, and `MainAxisAlignment.center` is one of the enum's values.

**CROSS
REFERENCE**

For another look at Dart's enum feature, refer to the "Dart's enum feature" section earlier in this chapter. And if you hunger for even more, see Chapter 7.

5. **Save your editor changes to do a hot restart.**

    On the device that's running your app, the `Text` widgets are centered horizontally and vertically. (See Figure 3-25.)

This section's example illustrates aspects of Flutter's `Column` widget, which displays things from top to bottom. It should come as no surprise that Flutter has a `Row` widget, which displays things from side to side. Most facts about the `Column` widget are also true of the `Row` widget. (Well, they're true when you're lying down instead of sitting upright.)

FIGURE 3-25:
How lovely!

In addition, Flutter has a ListView widget. The ListView widget displays things either way — from top to bottom or from side to side. In addition, the ListView widget has its own scrolling feature. You can put 100 items on a ListView even though only 20 items fit on the screen. When the user scrolls the screen, items move off the screen while other items move on.

**CROSS
REFERENCE**

To read about Flutter's ListView widget, see Chapter 8.

Displaying an image

Words are nice, but pictures are prettier. In this section, you put an image on your Flutter app screen.

1. **In Android Studio, start a new Flutter project.**

   I named my project app0308, but you don't have to use that name.

2. **In Android Studio's Project Tool window, right-click the project's name.**

   As a result, a contextual menu appears. (See Figure 3-26.)

FIGURE 3-26:
Right-clicking the
app0308 branch.

3. On the contextual menu, choose New ⇨ Directory. (Refer to Figure 3-26.)

As a result, the New Directory dialog box appears. How convenient!

4. In the dialog box, type the name assets, **and then press Enter.**

To be honest, you can name this new directory almost anything you want. But if you don't name it assets, you'll confuse other Flutter developers.

5. Check the Project Tool window to make sure that the project tree has a new assets **branch. (See Figure 3-27.)**

TECHNICAL
STUFF

Seasoned Flutter developers create an images subdirectory of the new assets directory. I won't bother with that right now.

FIGURE 3-27:
The assets
directory is a
subdirectory of
the app0308
directory.

6. Find an image file.

Search your development computer's hard drive for an image file. Look for filenames ending in .png, .jpg, .jpeg, or .gif.

CROSS
REFERENCE

If your File Explorer or Finder doesn't show filename extensions (such as .png, .jpg, .jpeg, or .gif for image files), refer to the sidebar in Chapter 2 that talks about those pesky filename extensions.

7. In your development computer's File Explorer or Finder, copy the image file.

That is, right-click the image file's name. On the contextual menu that appears, select Copy.

8. Using Android Studio's Project Tool window, paste the image file into the assets **directory.**

That is, right-click the assets branch. On the resulting contextual menu, choose Paste. In the resulting dialog box, type a name for your image file, and then press Enter.

When I did all this, I named the file MyImage.png, but you don't have to use that name.

9. **Open your project's** pubspec.yaml **file.**

   More specifically, double-click the pubspec.yaml branch in the Project Tool window's tree.

   Here's a fun fact: The extension .yaml stands for Yet Another Markup Language.

10. **In the** pubspec.yaml **file, look for advice about adding assets to your project.**

    The advice might look something like this:

    ```
    # To add assets to your application,
    # add an assets section, like this:
    # assets:
    #   - images/a_dot_burr.jpeg
    #   - images/a_dot_ham.jpeg
    ```

    (In case you're wondering, the file names a_dot_burr.jpeg and a_dot_ham.jpeg refer to Aaron Burr and Alexander Hamilton. These file names occur many times in Flutter's official documentation. Flutter is the technology behind the mobile app for the Broadway musical *Hamilton*.)

    In a .yaml file, a hashtag (#) tells the computer to ignore everything on the rest of the line. So, in this part of the .yaml file, none of the lines has any effect.

11. **Delete the hashtags on two of the lines. On the second line, change the name of the image file to the name you chose in Step 8.**

    When I do this, my pubspec.yaml file contains the following text:

    ```
    # To add assets to your application,
    # add an assets section, like this:
    assets:
      - MyImage.png
    #   - images/a_dot_ham.jpeg
    ```

    I use the name MyImage.png instead of images/MyImage.png because, in Step 5, I didn't create an images directory.

REMEMBER

I often forget to make the necessary changes in the pubspec.yaml file. Try not to forget this step. When you do forget (and almost everyone does), go back and edit the project's pubspec.yaml file.

12. **Replace all the code in the** `main.dart` **file with the code in Listing 3-9.**

Use your own class name and filename instead of my `App0309` and `MyImage.png` names.

LISTING 3-9:

Displaying an Image

```
import 'package:flutter/material.dart';

main() => runApp(App0309());

class App0309 extends StatelessWidget {
  Widget build(BuildContext context) {
    return MaterialApp(
      home: Scaffold(
        appBar: AppBar(
          title: Text("My First Image"),
        ),
        body: Center(
          child: Image.asset('MyImage.png'),
        ),
      ),
    );
  }
}
```

13. **Let 'er rip.**

That is, run the code on a virtual or physical device. The display on the device's screen looks something like the result in Figure 3-28.

At this point, I want to make one thing perfectly clear: I'm not a narcissist. The reason I use this book's cover image in Figure 3-28 is that I'm fascinated by recursion. I like having a reference to this book inside of this book.

(Besides, I'm a bit of a narcissist.)

Flutter has an `Image` class, and the `Image` class has several different constructors. The `Image.asset` constructor in Listing 3-9 grabs a file from a place inside your Flutter project's directory. To grab an image off the Internet, you call a different constructor — the `Image.network` constructor. To get an image from somewhere on your hard drive (somewhere outside of your Flutter project's directory), you can call the `Image.file` constructor. Each of these constructors is called a *named constructor*. In each case, the stuff after the dot (`.asset`, `.network`, and `.file`) is that particular constructor's *name*.

FIGURE 3-28:
To find Figure 3-28, look inside that *Flutter For Dummies* book.

Hey, Wait a Minute . . .

This chapter covers some fundamental ideas in Dart and Flutter app development. You start with a Hello World program and make several changes to it. While you do all that, you build up a vocabulary of useful concepts — concepts like classes, constructors, enums, and widgets.

You've done all that while I cleverly diverted your attention from several lines in the Hello World program. What do the first four lines of the Hello World program do? Why do you return something when you construct a MaterialApp?

The answers to these questions, and others like them, are in the next chapter. What are you waiting for? Read on!

♪ *"Happy trails to you / Until we meet again"* ♪

WRITTEN BY *DALE EVANS*, SUNG BY ROY ROGERS AND DALE EVANS ON "THE ROY ROGERS SHOW," 1944–1957

Chapter 4

Hello Again

♪ *"Hello, hello again, sh-boom and hopin' we'll meet again."* ♪
— JAMES KEYES, CLAUDE FEASTER, CARL FEASTER, FLOYD F. MCRAE, AND
JAMES EDWARDS, SUNG BY THE CHORDS, THE CREW-CUTS,
STAN FREBERG, AND OTHERS, 1954

hapter 3 is all about a simple Hello world program. For convenience, I copy one version of the code here, in Listing 4-1.

LISTING 4-1: | **Yet Another Look at the First Hello Program**

```
import 'package:flutter/material.dart';

main() => runApp(App0401());

class App0401 extends StatelessWidget {
  Widget build(BuildContext context) {
    return MaterialApp(
      home: Material(
        child: Center(child: Text("Hello world!")),
      ),
    );
  }
}
```

In Chapter 3, I have you concentrate on the middle of the program — the `MaterialApp` and all the stuff inside it. I let you gleefully ignore the other parts of the program. In particular, I let you ignore anything having to do with things called "functions." This chapter continues the tour of a Hello World program and sets its sites on those "function" things.

Creating and Using a Function

Here's an experiment: Run the app whose code is shown in Listing 4-2.

LISTING 4-2: **Words, Words, Words**

```
import 'package:flutter/material.dart';

main() => runApp(App0402());

class App0402 extends StatelessWidget {
  Widget build(BuildContext context) {
    return MaterialApp(
      home: Material(
        child: Center(child: Text(highlight("Look at me"))),
      ),
    );
  }
}

highlight(words) {
  return "*** " + words + " ***";
}
```

REMEMBER

You can download this app's code (and the code for every other listing in this book) from my website. The URL is `https://allmycode.com/Flutter`.

Figure 4-1 shows you the output of the app in Listing 4-2.

FIGURE 4-1:
Another exciting
Flutter app.

Listing 4-2 contains a function declaration and a function call. (See Figure 4-2.)

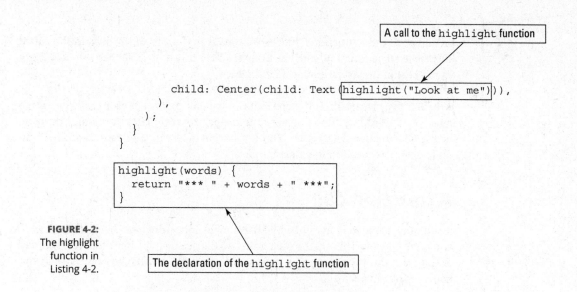

```
        child: Center(child: Text (highlight("Look at me"))),
      ),
    );
  }
}

highlight(words) {
   return "*** " + words + " ***";
}
```

A call to the highlight function

The declaration of the highlight function

FIGURE 4-2:
The highlight
function in
Listing 4-2.

The function declaration

Think about a recipe — a set of instructions for preparing a particular meal. A function declaration is like a recipe: It's a set of instructions for performing a particular task. In Listing 4-2, this set of instructions says, "Form the string containing asterisks followed by some words followed by more asterisks, and return that string somewhere."

Most recipes have names, like Macaroni and Cheese or Triple Chocolate Cake. The function at the bottom of Listing 4-2 also has a name: Its name is highlight. (See Figure 4-3.) There's nothing special about the name highlight. I made up the name highlight all by myself.

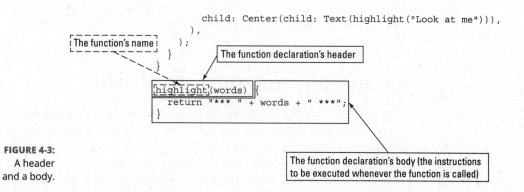

```
        child: Center(child: Text(highlight("Look at me"))),
      ),
    );
  }
}

highlight(words) {
   return "*** " + words + " ***";
}
```

The function's name

The function declaration's header

The function declaration's body (the instructions to be executed whenever the function is called)

FIGURE 4-3:
A header
and a body.

TIP

In Figure 4-3, the function name `highlight` is in the part of the declaration called the *header*. The function's instructions (`return "*** " + words + " ***"`) are in the part of the declaration called the *body*.

A recipe for macaroni and cheese sits in a book or on a web page. The recipe doesn't do anything. If no one uses the recipe, the recipe lies dormant. The same is true of a function declaration. The declaration in Listing 4-2 doesn't do anything on its own. The declaration just sits there.

A function call

Eventually, somebody might say, "Please make macaroni and cheese for dinner," and then someone follows the Macaroni and Cheese recipe's instructions. One way or another, the process begins when someone says (or maybe only thinks) the name of the recipe.

A *function call* is code that says, "Please execute a particular function declaration's instructions." Imagine a phone or another device that's running the code in Listing 4-2. When the phone encounters the function call `highlight("Look at me")`, the phone is diverted from its primary task — the task of constructing an app with its `Material`, `Center`, and `Text` widgets. The phone takes a detour to execute the instructions in the `highlight` function's body. After figuring out that it should create "*** Look at me ***", the phone returns to its primary task, adding the `Text` widget with "*** Look at me ***" to the `Center` widget, adding the `Center` widget to the `Material` widget, and so on.

A function call consists of a function's name (such as the name `highlight` in Listing 4-2), followed by some last-minute information (such as "Look at me" in Listing 4-2).

Wait! In the previous sentence, what does *some last-minute information* mean? Read on.

Parameters and the return value

Suppose that your recipe for macaroni and cheese serves one person and calls for two ounces of uncooked elbow macaroni. You've invited 100 people to your intimate evening gathering. In that case, you need 200 ounces of uncooked elbow macaroni. In a way, the recipe says the following: "To find the number of ounces of uncooked elbow macaroni that you need, multiply the number of servings by 2." That number of servings is last-minute information. The person who wrote the recipe doesn't know how many people you'll be serving. You provide a number of servings when you start preparing the mac-and-cheese. All the recipe says is to multiply that number by 2.

In a similar way, the `highlight` function declaration in Listing 4-2 says, "To find the value that this function returns, combine asterisks followed by the `words` that you want to be highlighted followed by more asterisks."

A function declaration is like a black box. You give it some values. The function does something with those values to calculate a new value. Then the function returns that new value. (See Figures 4-4 and 4-5.)

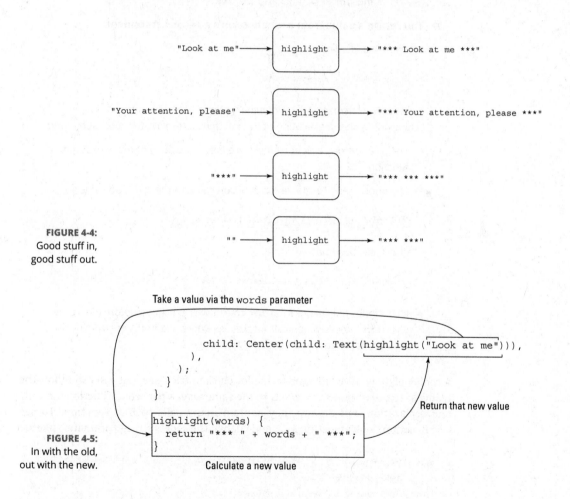

FIGURE 4-4:
Good stuff in,
good stuff out.

FIGURE 4-5:
In with the old,
out with the new.

Figures 4-4 and 4-5 show what it means to give values to a function, and for a function to return a value.

>> **You give values to a function with the function's parameter list.**

Like any constructor call, every function call has a parameter list. Each parameter feeds a piece of information for the function to use. In Figure 4-5, the function call highlight("Look at me") passes the value "Look at me" to the highlight function's declaration. Inside the function declaration, the name words stands for "Look at me", so the expression "*** " + words + " ***" stands for "*** Look at me ***".

>> **You return a value from a function with a return statement.**

In Listing 4-2, the line

```
return "*** " + words + " ***";
```

is a *return statement*. Again, imagine a phone that's running the code in Listing 4-2. With the execution of this return statement, this is what happens:

- The phone stops executing any code inside the body of the highlight function.

- The phone replaces the entire function call with the returned value so that

```
Center(child: Text(highlight("Look at me")))
```

effectively becomes

```
Center(child: Text("*** Look at me ***"))
```

- It continues to execute whatever code it was executing before it became diverted by the function call. It takes up where it left off, constructing the Center, Material, and MaterialApp widgets.

A cookbook may have only one recipe for chicken fricassee, but you can follow the recipe as many times as you want. In the same way, a particular function has only one declaration, but an app may contain many calls to that function. To see this in action, look at Listing 4-2, and change the code's child parameter, like so:

```
child: Column(mainAxisAlignment: MainAxisAlignment.center, children: [
  Text(highlight("Look at me")),
  Text(highlight("Your attention, please"))
])
```

The new child contains two calls to the highlight function, each with its own parameter value. The resulting app is what you see in Figure 4-6.

FIGURE 4-6:
Two Text widgets.

SAVING THE PLANET

In Chapter 3, I advise you to end each parameter list with a trailing comma. It's good advice in most cases. But, for printed books, page counts matter a lot. To keep this book to a reasonable size, I've omitted some trailing commas here and there.

For example, an excerpt from the code in Listing 4-2 looks like this:

```
home: Material(
  child: Center(child: Text(highlight("Look at me"))),
)
```

When you select Code ➪ Reformat Code, Android Studio formats your code according to official Dart guidelines. (Dart uses a tool named *Dartfmt*.) When Android Studio formats the excerpt from Listing 4-2, the excerpt has only three lines. The middle line ends with three close parentheses.

But, instead of having three parentheses in a row, I can separate the close parentheses with commas. When I do that, Android Studio formats the code this way:

```
home: Material(
  child: Center(
    child: Text(
      highlight("Look at me"),
    ),
  ),
)
```

The Dartfmt tool interprets a comma as a signal to start a new line of code. This doubles the number of lines in the code excerpt. I feel guilty for including so many lines in this sidebar!

So, do as I say, not as I do. Remember that many examples in this book omit trailing commas. The examples run correctly, but the code's style is out of whack. Add trailing commas to adhere to Dart's rigorous guidelines.

A `return` statement is only one of several kinds of statements in the Dart programming language. For more about this topic, see the section "Statements and declarations," later in this chapter.

In this chapter, I'm careful to distinguish between a function declaration and a function call. In many other chapters, I become sloppy and refer to either the declaration, the call, or both as a plain, old *function*. I'm not alone in this practice. Most programmers do the same thing.

Programming in Dart: The Small Stuff

"Dart is boring." That's what Faisal Abid said during a presentation at DevFest NYC 2017. He wasn't talking trash about Dart. He was merely explaining that Dart is much like many other programming languages. If you've written some programs in Java, C++, or JavaScript, you find Dart's features to be quite familiar. You encounter a few surprises, but not too many. When you're learning to create Flutter apps, you don't want a new, complicated programming language to get in your way. So, a boring language like Dart is just what you need.

This section presents some unexciting facts about the Dart programming language. Try not to fall asleep while you read it.

Statements and declarations

A *statement* is a piece of code that commands Dart to do something. If you think this definition is vague, that's okay for now. Anyway, in Listing 4-2, the line

```
return "*** " + words + " ***";
```

is a statement because it commands Dart to return a value from the execution of the `highlight` function.

Unlike a statement, a *declaration's* primary purpose is to define something. For example, the `highlight` function declaration in Listing 4-2 defines what should happen if and when the `highlight` function is called.

Statements and declarations aren't completely separate from one another. In Listing 4-2, the `highlight` function declaration contains one statement — a `return` statement. A function declaration may contain several statements. For example, the following declaration contains three statements:

```
highlight2(words) {
  print("Wha' da' ya' know!");
  print("You've just called the highlight2 function!");
  return "*** " + words + " ***";
}
```

The first two statements (calls to Dart's print function) send text to Android Studio's Run tool window. The third statement (the return statement) makes highlight("Look at me") have the value "*** Look at me ***".

REMEMBER

Use Dart's print function *only* for testing your code. Remove all calls to print before publishing an app. If you don't, you might face some trouble. At best, the calls serve no purpose and can slow down the run of your app. At worst, you may print sensitive data and show it to malicious hackers.

Dart's typing feature

What does "five" mean? You can have five children, but you can also be five feet tall. With five children, you know exactly how many kids you have. (Unlike the average American family, you can't have 2.5 kids.) But if you're five feet tall, you might really be five feet and half an inch tall. Or you might be four feet eleven-and-three-quarter inches tall, and no one would argue about it.

What else can "five" mean? Nuclear power plants can undergo fire-induced vulnerability evaluation, also known as *five*. In this case, "five" has nothing to do with a number. It's just f-i-v-e.

A value's meaning depends on the value's *type.* Consider three of the Dart language's built-in types: int, double, and String.

>> **An int is a whole number, with no digits to the right of the decimal point.**

If you write

```
int howManyChildren = 5;
```

in a Dart program, the 5 means "exactly five."

>> **A double is a fractional number, with digits to the right of the decimal point.**

If you write

```
double height = 5;
```

in a Dart program, the 5 means "as close to five as you care to measure."

>> A `String` **is a bunch of characters.**

If you use single quotes (or double quotes) and write

```
String keystroke = '5';
```

in a Dart program, the '5' means "the character that looks like an uppercase letter *S* but whose upper half has pointy turns."

A value's type determines what you can do with that value. Consider the values 86 and "86".

>> **The first one,** 86, **is a number. You can add another number to it.**

86 + 1 is 87

>> **The second one,** "86", **is a string. You can't add a number to it, but you can add another string to it.**

"86" + "1" is "861"

REMEMBER

In some languages, you can combine any value with any other value and produce some kind of a result. You can't do that in Dart. The Dart programming language is *type safe*.

Literals, variables, and expressions

The Dart language has literals and variables. The value of a *literal* is the same in every Dart program. For example, 1.5 is a literal because 1.5 means "one-and-a-half" in every Dart program. Likewise, "Hello world!" in Listing 4-1 is a literal because "Hello world!" stands for the same string of 12 characters in every Dart program. (Yes, the blank space counts as one of the characters.)

TECHNICAL STUFF

Fun fact: In early versions of FORTRAN (circa 1956), you could change the meaning of the literal 5 so that it stood for something else, like the number 6. Talk about confusing!

The value of a *variable* is not the same in every Dart program. In fact, the value of a variable may not be the same from one part of a Dart program to another. Take, for example, the following line of code:

```
int howManyChildren = 5;
```

This line is called a *variable declaration*. The line defines a variable named how-ManyChildren whose type is int. The line *initializes* that variable with the value 5. When Dart encounters this line, howManyChildren stands for the number 5.

Later, in the same program, Dart may execute the following line:

```
howManyChildren = 6;
```

This line is called an *assignment statement*. The line makes howManyChildren refer to 6 instead of 5. Congratulations on the birth of a new child! Is it a girl or a boy?

An *expression* is a part of a Dart program that stands for a value. Imagine that your code contains the following variable declarations:

```
int numberOfApples = 7;
int numberOfOranges = 10;
```

If you start with these two declarations, each entry in the left column of Table 4-1 is an expression.

TABLE 4-1 **Fruitful Expressions**

Expression	Value	Type	Notes
7	7	int	
7.1	7.1	double	
7.0	7.0	double	Even with .0, you get a double.
7.1 + 8	15.1	double	A double plus an int is a double.
0.1 + 0.1 + 0.1	0.30000000000000004	double	Arithmetic on double values isn't always accurate.
numberOfApples	7	int	
numberOfOranges	10	int	
numberOfApples + numberOfOranges	17	int	Who says you can't add apples and oranges?
8 + numberOfApples	15	int	
numberOfOranges * 10	100		An asterisk (*) stands for multiplication.

(continued)

TABLE 4-1 *(continued)*

Expression	Value	Type	Notes
`20 / 7`	`2.857142857142857`	`double`	A slash (/) performs division and produces a double.
`20.0 ~/ 7.0`	`2`	`int`	The ~/ combination performs division and produces an `int`. It *always* rounds down.
`(20 / 7).round()`	`3`	`int`	This is how you round up or down to the nearest `int` value.
`20 % 7`	`6`	`int`	When you divide 20 by 7, you get 2 with a remainder of 6.
`highlight("Look at me")`	`"*** Look at me ***"`	`String`	Assuming that you've declared `highlight` as in Listing 4-2, the function returns a `String`.
`'9' + numberOfApples.toString()`	`'97'`	`String`	`numberOfApples.toString()` is a `String`. Its value is `'7'`.

In the last row of Table 4-1, do you really need the `toString()` part? Yes, you do. If you write `'9' + numberOfApples`, you get an error message because `'9'` is a `String` and `numberOfApples` is an `int`. You can't add an `int` value to a `String` value.

REMEMBER

The Dart language has statements and expressions. A *statement* is a command to do something; an *expression* is code that has a value. For example, the statement `print("Hello");` does something. (It displays `Hello` in Android Studio's Run tool window.) The expression `3 + 7 * 21` has a value. (Its value is 150.)

You can apply Dart's `toString` to any expression. For some examples, see Chapter 7.

TIP

Dart provides a quick way to determine the type of a particular expression. To see this, change the `highlight` function declaration in Listing 4-2 as follows:

```
highlight(words) {
  print(20 / 7);
  print((20 / 7).runtimeType);
  return "*** " + words + " ***";
}
```

When you run the app, the following lines appear in Android Studio's Run tool window:

```
flutter: 2.857142857142857
flutter: double
```

The value of 20 /7 is 2.857142857142857, and the value of (20 / 7).runtime Type is double.

Two for the price of one

In Dart, some statements do double duty as both statements and expressions. As an experiment, change the highlight function in Listing 4-2 so that it looks like this:

```
highlight(words) {
  int numberOfKazoos;
  print(numberOfKazoos);
  print(numberOfKazoos = 94);
  return "*** " + words + " ***";
}
```

Android Studio issues a warning that the numberOfKazoos variable isn't used, but that's okay. This is only an experiment. Here's what you see in Android Studio's Run tool window when you run this code:

```
flutter: null
flutter: 94
```

The line int numberOfKazoos; is a variable declaration without an initialization. That's fair game in the Dart programming language.

When Dart executes print(numberOfKazoos); you see flutter: null in the Run tool window. Roughly speaking, null means "nothing." At this point in the program, the variable numberOfKazoos has been declared but hasn't yet been given a value, so numberOfKazoos is still null.

Finally, when Dart executes print(numberOfKazoos = 94); you see flutter: 94 in the Run tool window. Aha! The code numberOfKazoos = 94 is both a statement and an expression! Here's why:

>> As a statement, numberOfKazoos = 94 **makes the value of** numberOf Kazoos **be** 94.

>> As an expression, the value of numberOfKazoos = 94 **is** 94.

Of these two facts, the second is more difficult for people to digest. (I've known some experienced programmers who think about this the wrong way.) To execute `print(numberOfKazoos = 94);` Dart covertly substitutes 94 for the expression `numberOfKazoos = 94`, as shown in Figure 4-7.

```
                94
print (numberOfKazoos = 94);
```

```
numberOfKazoos = 100;
                     100
print (numberOfKazoos);
                     100
print (numberOfKazoos++);
                     101
print (numberOfKazoos);
```

In other words, the value `numberOfKazoos = 94` is 94. So, in addition to doing something, the code `numberOfKazoos = 94` also has a value. That's why `numberOfKazoos = 94` is both a statement and an expression.

Simple assignment statements aren't the only things that double as expressions. Try this code out for size:

```
numberOfKazoos = 100;
print(numberOfKazoos);
print(numberOfKazoos++);
print(numberOfKazoos);
```

The code's output is

```
flutter: 100
flutter: 100
flutter: 101
```

If the middle line of output surprises you, you're not alone. As a statement, `numberOfKazoos++` adds 1 to the value of `numberOfKazoos`, changing the value from 100 to 101. But, as an expression, the value of `numberOfKazoos++` is 100, not 101. (Refer to Figure 4-7.)

Here's a comforting thought. By the time Dart executes the last `print (numberOfKazoos)` statement, the value of `numberOfKazoos` has already changed to 101. Whew!

As a statement, ++numberOfKazoos (with the plus signs in front) does the same thing that numberOfKazoos++ does: It adds 1 to the value of numberOfKazoos. But, as an expression, the value of ++numberOfKazoos isn't the same as the value of numberOfKazoos++. Try it. You'll see.

Dart has some other statements whose values are expressions. For example, the following code prints flutter: 15 twice:

```
int howManyGiraffes = 10;
print(howManyGiraffes += 5);
print(howManyGiraffes);
```

And the following code prints flutter: 5000 twice:

```
int rabbitCount = 500;
print(rabbitCount *= 10);
print(rabbitCount);
```

For more info about topics like += and *=, visit this page:

```
https://dart.dev/guides/language/language-tour#operators
```

Dart's var keyword

On occasion, you might want to create a variable whose type can change. To do so, declare the variable using Dart's var keyword and leave out an initialization in the declaration. For example, the following code won't work:

```
int x = 7;
print(x);
x = "Someone's trying to turn me into a String"; // You can't do this
print(x);
```

But the following code works just fine:

```
var x;
x = 7;
print(x);
x = "I've been turned into a String"; // Dart is happy to oblige
print(x);
```

Another reason for using var is to avoid long, complicated type names. For an example, see this chapter's "Build-in types" section.

WE PAUSE FOR A FEW COMMENTS

You may have noticed some stuff beginning with two slashes (//) in some of the chapter's code examples. Two slashes signal the beginning of a comment.

A *comment* is part of a program's text. But unlike declarations, constructor calls, and other such elements, a comment's purpose is to help people understand your code. A comment is part of a good program's documentation.

The Dart programming language has three kinds of comments:

- **End-of-line comments**

  An *end-of-line comment* starts with two slashes and goes to the end of a line of type. So, in the following code snippet, the text `// Dart is happy to oblige` is an end-of-line comment:

  ```
  x = "I've been turned into a String"; // Dart is happy to oblige
  ```

  All the text in an end-of-line comment is for human eyes only. No information from the two slashes to the end of the line is translated by Dart's compiler.

- **Block comments**

  A *block comment* begins with /* and ends with */.

  A block comment can span across several lines. For example, the following code is a block comment:

  ```
  /* Temporarily commenting out this code.
     That is, omitting these statements to see what happens:
     x = "Someone's trying to turn me into a String";
     print(x); */
  ```

  Once again, no information between /* and */ gets translated by the compiler.

- **Doc comments**

  An *end-of-line doc comment* begins with three slashes (///). A *block doc comment* begins with /** and ends with */.

  A doc comment is meant to be read by people who never even look at the Dart code. But that doesn't make sense. How can you see a doc comment if you never look at the code?

  Well, a certain program called `dartdoc` (what else?) can find any doc comments in a program and turn these comments into a nice-looking web page. (For an example of such a page, visit `https://api.flutter.dev/flutter/widgets/Widget-class.html`.)

Which is better — end-of-line doc comments or block doc comments? Professional Dart programmers favor end-of-line doc comments over block doc comments. They mock block doc comments and knock block doc comments. They put no stock in block doc comments. They don't grok block doc comments. In their opinion, an end-of-line doc comment rocks, but the whole idea of a block doc comment is a crock.

One more thought about comments in general: In Chapter 3, I describe a way to display closing labels in Android Studio's editor.

```
home: Material(
   child: Text("Hello world!"),
), // Material
```

Does that final // Material look like a comment to you? Well, it's not really a comment. (Sorry about that.) Closing labels belong to a broader category of items called *code decoration*. When Android Studio creates code decoration, it doesn't add the decoration to the program's text. It only displays that decoration in the editor. If you examine a program's text using Notepad or TextEdit, you don't see the code decoration.

Built-in types

In a Dart program, every value has a *type*. Dart has ten built-in types. (See Table 4-2.)

TABLE 4-2 ### Dart's Built-In Types

Type Name	What Literals Look Like	Useful Info About the Type
Number types		
int	42	Numbers with no digits to the right of the decimal point — typically, from –9007199254740992 to 9007199254740991.
double	42.0 42.1	Numbers with digits to the right of the decimal point (possibly, all zero digits).
num	42 42.0 42.1	A number of some kind. Every int value, and every double value, is an example of a num value.

(continued)

TABLE 4-2 *(continued)*

Type Name	What Literals Look Like	Useful Info About the Type
Collection types		

List	`[2, 4, -9, 25, 18]`
	`["Hello", "Goodbye", 86]`
	`[]`
	`<int>[]`
		A bunch of values. The initial value is the 0th, the next value is the 1st, the next value is the 2nd, and so on. (With [ ], the bunch has no values in it.)

Set	`{2, 4, -9, 25, 18}`
	`{"Hello", "Goodbye", 86}`
	`{}`
	`<int>{}`
		A bunch of values with no duplicates in no particular order. (With { }, the bunch has no values in it.)

Map	`{ 'one' : 1, 'two' : 2 ,`
	`'three' : 3, 'many': 99}`
	`<String, int>{}`
		A bunch of pairs, each pair consisting of a *key* (such as `'one'`, `'two'`, `'three'`, or `'many'`) and a *value* (such as 1, 2, 3, or 99). (With { }, the bunch has no pairs in it.)

Other types		

String	`'Dart is boring'`
	`""`
	`"""The previous`
	`string is empty."""`
		A sequence of characters.

bool	`true, false`	A logical value. A variable of this type has one of only two possible values: `true` and `false`.
Runes	`Runes('I ' '\u2665' '` `you')`	A string of Unicode characters. For example, `'\u2665'` is a heart character (♥).
Symbol	`(Not applicable)`	Turns an identifier in a Dart program into a value in a Dart program. (Don't worry about it!)

You can combine types to create new types. One way to do this is to put types inside of collection types. For example, in the following declaration, the variable amounts is a List containing only int values.

```
List<int> amounts = [7, 3, 8, 2];
```

Of course, you can go crazy layering types within types within other types:

```
Map<String, Map<String, List<int>>> values = {
  "Size": {
    "Small": [1, 2, 3],
  },
};
```

In cases like that, your best bet is to use the var keyword. Dart can usually figure things out by looking at the rest of the code.

```
var values = {
  "Size": {
    "Small": [1, 2, 3],
  },
};
```

Types that aren't built-in

In addition to the types in Table 4-2, every class is a type. For example, in Listing 4-1, App0401 is the name of a type. It's a type that's defined in Listing 4-1. You can add a line to Listing 4-1 that makes a variable refer to an instance of the App0401 class. Here's one such line:

```
App0401 myApp = App0401();
```

Like many other variable declarations, this line has a type name (App0401), followed by a new variable name (myApp), followed by an initialization. The initialization makes myApp refer to a newly constructed App0401 instance.

The Dart language comes with a library full of standard, reusable code. The formal name for such a library is an *application programming interface* (API). Dart's API has declarations of many classes. For example, instances of Dart's DateTime class are moments in time, and instances of the Duration class are time intervals.

Similarly, the Flutter toolkit comes with a feature-rich API. In Listing 4-1, Widget, StatelessWidget, BuildContext, MaterialApp, Material, Center, and Text are the names of classes in the Flutter API.

Using import declarations

Woe is me! I can't read the book *Flutter For Dummies* unless I go to my local library and check out a copy. The same is true of Dart's and Flutter's library classes (well, almost). You can't use Flutter's `MaterialApp` or `Material` classes unless you start your program with

```
import 'package:flutter/material.dart';
```

If you delete this line, you can't even use any of Flutter's `Widget` classes (`StatelessWidget`, `Widget`, `Center`, and `Text`, to name a few). That's because, when you import `'package:flutter/material.dart'`, you automatically import `'package:flutter/widgets.dart'` also.

A relatively small number of Dart's API classes, like the aforementioned `DateTime` class, belong to a package named `dart.core`. You can start your program with the line

```
import 'dart:core';
```

but it won't do you any good. Classes from the `dart.core` package are always imported, whether you ask for it or not.

REMEMBER

No one (and I do mean *no one*) memorizes the names of all the classes in the Dart or Flutter libraries. When you need to know about a class, look it up by visiting `https://api.flutter.dev`.

Variations on a Theme from Die Flutter Mouse

This section shows some alternative ways of creating function declarations. Listing 4-3 has the first example.

LISTING 4-3: **Messing with Function Declarations**

```
import 'package:flutter/material.dart';

main() {
  runApp(App0403());
}

class App0403 extends StatelessWidget {
  Widget build(BuildContext context) {
    return MaterialApp(
      home: Material(
```

```
      child: Center(child: Text(highlight("Look at me"))),
    ),
  );
  }
}

highlight(words) => "*** $words ***";
```

BLING YOUR STRING

Listing 4-2 contains the following code:

```
"*** " + words + " ***"
```

The juxtaposition of plus signs and quotation marks can make code difficult to read. To make your life easier, Dart has string interpolation. With *string interpolation*, a dollar sign ($) means, "Temporarily ignore the surrounding quotation marks and find the value of the following variable." That's why, in Listing 4-3, the expression "*** $words ***" stands for "*** Look at me ***" — the same string you get in Listing 4-2.

Not impressed with string interpolation? Look over the following function and see what you think of it:

```
// The function call
getInstructions1(8, "+", ";", "'")

// The function's declaration
getInstructions1(howMany, char1, char2, char3) {
  return "Password: " +
      howMany.toString() +
      " characters; Don't use " +
      char1 +
      " " +
      char2 +
      " or " +
      char3;
}
```

Quite a mess, isn't it? The value that the getInstructions1 function returns is

```
Password: 8 characters; Don't use + ; or '
```

(continued)

(continued)

Whenever I try to write code of this kind, I forget to include some blank spaces, quotation marks, or other items. Here's how you get the same return value using string interpolation:

```
// The function call
Text(getInstructions2(8, "+", ";", "'")

// The function's declaration
getInstructions2(howMany, char1, char2, char3) {
  return "Password: $howMany characters; Don't use $char1 $char2 or $char3";
}
```

This new function, getInstructions2, is easier to create and easier to understand than getInstructions1.

When you use string interpolation, you can go a step further. Here's what you can do when you add curly braces to the mix:

```
// The function call
getInstructions3(8, "+", ";", "'")

// The function's declaration
getInstructions3(howMany, char1, char2, char3) {
  return "Password: ${howMany + 1} characters; Don't use $char1 $char2 or
    $char3";
}
```

This new getInstructions3 function returns

```
Password: 9 characters; Don't use + ; or '
```

String interpolation can handle all kinds of expressions — arithmetic expressions, logical expressions, and others.

CROSS
REFERENCE

To read all about the dollar sign ($) on the last line of Listing 4-3, see the nearby "Bling your string" sidebar.

A run of the code in Listing 4-3 is the same as that of Listing 4-2. (Refer to Figure 4-1.) In a sense, Listing 4-3 contains the same program as Listing 4-2. The notation for things is slightly different, but the things themselves are the same.

In Listing 4-3, the highlight function declaration

```
highlight(words) => "*** $words ***";
```

is shorthand for the more long-winded `highlight` declaration in Listing 4-2. When the body of a function declaration contains only one statement, you can use this quick-and-easy *fat arrow* (=>) notation.

REMEMBER

In a fat arrow function declaration, you never use the `return` keyword.

Back in Listing 4-2, I use the fat arrow notation to declare the `main` function. Just to show that I can do it, I "un-fat-arrow" this declaration in Listing 4-3.

Every Dart program has a function named `main`. When you start running a program, Dart looks for the program's `main` function declaration and starts executing whatever statements are in the declaration's body. In a Flutter app, a statement like

```
runApp(App0403());
```

tells Dart to construct an instance of `App0403` and then run that instance. The `runApp` function is part of Flutter's API.

Type names in function declarations

Listing 4-4 adds some type names to the code from Listing 4-2.

LISTING 4-4: **Better Safe than Sorry**

```
import 'package:flutter/material.dart';

void main() => runApp(App0404());

class App0404 extends StatelessWidget {
  Widget build(BuildContext context) {
    return MaterialApp(
      home: Material(
        child: Center(child: Text(highlight("Look at me")))),
      ),
    );
  }
}

String highlight(String words) {
  return "*** $words ***";
}
```

In Listing 4-4, `String` and `void` add some welcome redundancy to the code. The occurrence of `String` in (`String words`) tells Dart that, in any call to the `highlight` function, the `words` parameter must have type `String`. Armed with this extra `String` information, Dart will cough up and spit out a bad function call such as

```
highlight(19)
```

This is bad because 19 is a number, not a `String`. You may argue and say, "I'll never make the mistake of putting a number in a call to the `highlight` function." And my response is, "Yes you will, and so will I, and so will every other programmer on earth." When you're writing code, mistakes are inevitable. The trick is to catch them sooner rather than later.

Near the end of Listing 4-4, `String highlight` tells Dart that the value returned by the `highlight` function must be a `String`. If you accidentally write the following code, Dart will complain like nobody's business:

```
String highlight(String words) {
  return 99;                    //Bad code!
}
```

Sorry, chief. The value 99 isn't a `String`.

Continuing our journey through Listing 4-4, `void main` doesn't quite mean, "The `main` function must return a value of type `void`." Why not? It's okay to put a type name in front of a fat arrow declaration. So, what's different about `void main`?

Simply stated, `void` isn't a type. In a way, `void` means "no type." The word `void` reminds Dart that this `main` function isn't supposed to return anything useful. Try declaring `void main` and putting a `return` statement in the declaration's body:

```
void main() {
  runApp(App0404());
  return 0;          // Bad
}
```

If you do this, Android Studio's editor adds red marks to your code. Dart is saying, "Sorry, Bud. You can't do that."

Naming your parameters

Chapter 3 distinguishes between constructors' positional parameters and named parameters. All that fuss about the kinds of parameters applies to functions as well. For example, the highlight function in Listing 4-4 has one parameter — a positional parameter.

```
highlight("Look at me")              // A function call

String highlight(String words) {     // The function declaration
  return "*** $words ***";
}
```

If you want, you can turn words into a named parameter. Simply surround the parameter with curly braces:

```
highlight(words: "Look at me")        // A function call

String highlight({String words}) {    // The function declaration
  return "*** " + words + " ***";
}
```

You can even have a function with both positional and named parameters. In the parameter list, all the positional parameters must come before any of the named parameters. For example, the following code displays +++Look at me!+++.

```
highlight(                            // A function call
  "Look at me",
  punctuation: "!",
  symbols: "+++",
)

String highlight(                     // The function declaration
  String words, {
  String punctuation,
  String symbols,
}) {
  return symbols + words + punctuation + symbols;
}
```

What about the build function?

Listing 4-4 contains some familiar-looking code:

```
class App0404 extends StatelessWidget {
  Widget build(BuildContext context) {
    return MaterialApp(
```

Here are some facts:

>> **In this code,** `build` **is the name of a function, and**

```
Widget build(BuildContext context)
```

is the function declaration's header.

The `build` function does exactly what its name suggests. It builds something. To be precise, it builds the widget whose content is the entire Flutter app.

>> **The** `build` **function returns a value of type** `Widget`**.**

Quoting from Chapter 3, "Being an instance of one class might make you automatically be an instance of a bigger class." In fact, every instance of the `MaterialApp` class is automatically an instance of the `StatefulWidget` class, which, in turn, is automatically an instance of the `Widget` class. So there you have it — every `MaterialApp` is a `Widget`. That's why it's okay for the `build` function's `return` statement to return a `MaterialApp` object.

>> **The function's one-and-only parameter has the type** `BuildContext`**.**

When Dart builds a widget, Dart creates a `BuildContext` object and passes that to the widget's `build` function. A `BuildContext` object contains information about the widget and the widget's relationship to other widgets in the program. For more info, see Chapter 6.

In Listing 4-4, the `build` function's declaration is inside the `class App0404` definition, but the `highlight` function declaration isn't inside *any* class definition. In a sense, this `build` function "belongs to" instances of the `App0404` class.

A function that belongs to a class, or to the class's instances, has a special name. It's called a *method*. More on this in Chapter 5.

More Fun to Come!

What happens if a user taps the screen and wants a response from the app in Listing 4-4? Absolutely nothing.

Let's fix that. Turn the page to see what's in Chapter 5.

♪ *"Goodbye from us to you."* ♪
— BUFFALO BOB ON *"THE HOWDY DOODY SHOW,"* 1947–1960

Chapter **5**

Making Things Happen

The day is October 20, 1952. In Kenya, the British colonial governor declares a state of emergency. In Philadelphia, actress Melanie Mayron (granddaughter of Frances Goodman) is born. In the US, an installment of "I Love Lucy" becomes the first TV episode ever to be broadcast more than once.

What? "I Love Lucy"? Yes, "I Love Lucy." Until that day, television reruns (also known as "repeats") didn't exist. Everything on TV was brand-new.

Since then, repeat airings of TV programs have become the norm. So much of television's content is a rehash of old video that broadcasters no longer advertise a "new episode." Instead, they announce the airing of an "*all-new* episode." The word *new* is no longer good enough. Common household products aren't new; they're "new and improved."

Of course, hyping things as "new," "the best," or "the latest" can backfire. In fact, hyping of any kind can backfire. Consider the case of Stanley's Swell Shaving Cream. Back in 1954, Stanley's was the market leader. A year later, when sales were slowing down, advertisers rebranded it Stanley's Neat New Shaving Cream. The year after that, it became Stanley's Superior Shaving Cream. Sales of the product were okay for the next few years. But in the early 1960s, sales slumped and Stanley's advertisers were in a bind. What could possibly be better than "Superior Shaving Cream"? Better than Best Shaving Cream? After several long meetings, a genius in the marketing department came up with Stanley's Sensational Shocking Pink Shaving Cream — a brightly colored mixture of soap, glycerin, emollients, red dye number 2, and probably some slow-drying glue.

That was the end of the line. The idea of shaving with a pink-colored cream wasn't popular with consumers, and Stanley's company went bankrupt. Consumers talked about Stanley's Slimy Soap, Stanley's Ruby Rubbish, and, worst of all, Stanley's Disgusting Dung.

You may ask, "What in the world does Stanley's Shaving Cream have to do with developing Flutter apps?" My point is, there's a danger in overhyping a product, and overhyping an app development concept is no better. In Chapters 3 and 4, I use glowing terms to describe Flutter's programming strategies, with its constructors, functions, and other good stuff. But here in Chapter 5, I cast aspersions on those introductory examples because none of them allows the user to change anything on the screen. An app that always displays the same old text is boring, and users will rate the app with zero stars. An interesting app interacts with the user. The app's screen changes when the user enters text, taps a button, moves a slider, or does something else to get a useful response from the app. Making things happen is essential for any kind of mobile app development. So, in this chapter, you begin learning how to make things happen.

Let's All Press a Floating Action Button

When you create a new Flutter project, Android Studio makes a `main.dart` file for you. The `main.dart` file contains a cute little starter app. Listing 5-1 has a scaled-down version of that starter app.

LISTING 5-1: **Press a Button; Change the Screen**

```
import 'package:flutter/material.dart';

void main() => runApp(App0501());

class App0501 extends StatelessWidget {
  Widget build(BuildContext context) {
    return MaterialApp(
      home: MyHomePage(),
    );
  }
}

class MyHomePage extends StatefulWidget {
  _MyHomePageState createState() => _MyHomePageState();
}

class _MyHomePageState extends State {
```

```
String _pressedOrNot = "You haven't pressed the button.";

void _changeText() {
  setState(_getNewText);
}

void _getNewText() {
  _pressedOrNot = "You've pressed the button.";
}

Widget build(BuildContext context) {
  return Scaffold(
      body: Center(
        child: Text(
          _pressedOrNot,
        ),
      ),
      floatingActionButton: FloatingActionButton(
        onPressed: _changeText,
      ));
  }
}
```

WARNING

The code in Listing 5-1 captures the essence of the starter app in the October 2019 version of Android Studio. By the time you read this book, the creators of Flutter may have completely changed the starter app. If the stuff in Listing 5-1 bears little resemblance to the starter app you get when you create a new project, don't worry. Just do what you've been doing. That is, delete all of Android Studio's main.dart code, and replace it with the code in Listing 5-1.

When you launch the app in Listing 5-1, you see the text "You haven't pressed the button" and, in the screen's lower right corner, a blue circle. (See Figure 5-1.)

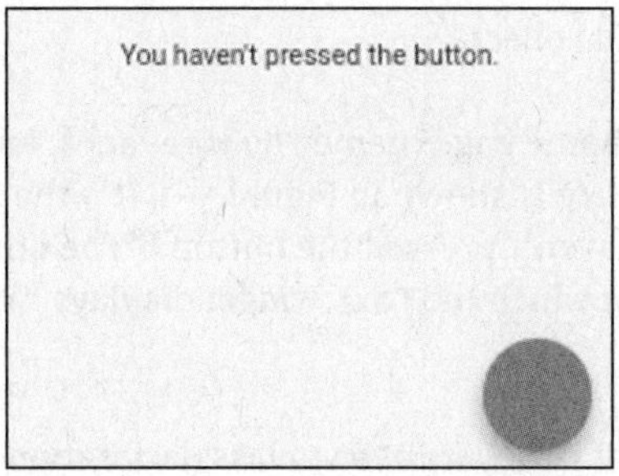

You haven't pressed the button.

FIGURE 5-1:
Before pressing
the button.

That blue circle is called a *floating action button*. It's one of the widgets that you can add to a Scaffold. When you click this app's floating action button, the words on the screen change to "You've pressed the button." (See Figure 5-2.)

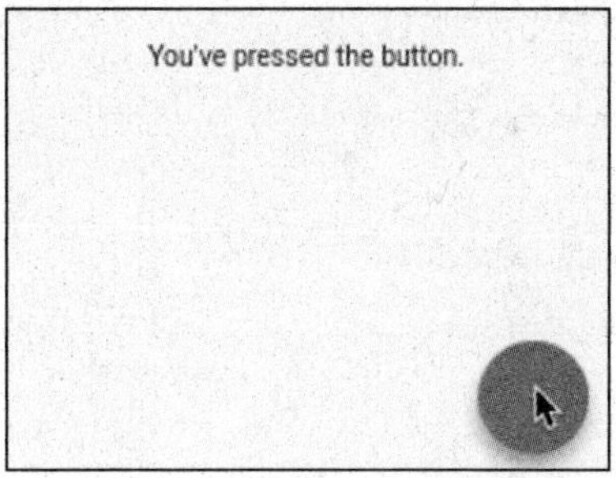

You've pressed the button.

FIGURE 5-2:
After pressing
the button.

At last! A Flutter app is making something happen!

To understand what's going on, you have to know about two kinds of widgets. To learn their names, read the next section's title.

Stateless widgets and stateful widgets

Some systems have properties that can change over time. Take, for example, your common, everyday traffic light. If it's functioning properly, it's either red, yellow, or green. Imagine that you're hurrying to get to work and you stop for a red light. Under your breath, you may grumble, "I'm annoyed that this traffic light's state is red. I wish that the state of that system would change to green." A system's *state* is a property of the system that may change over time.

TIP

This tip has nothing to do with Flutter. If you meet someone from another country, ask them the color of the middle bulb on a traffic light. During a brief conversation with five people, I got yellow, amber, gold, and orange. See how many different color names you can collect.

The app in Listing 5-1 has a home page (named MyHomePage), and that home page is in one of two states. One state is shown in Figure 5-1. It's the state in which the Text widget displays "You haven't pressed the button." The other state is shown in Figure 5-2. It's the state in which the Text widget displays "You've pressed the button."

In Listing 5-1, the first line of the MyHomePage class declaration is

```
class MyHomePage extends StatefulWidget
```

You want the look of the MyHomePage widget to be able to change itself nimbly, so you declare MyHomePage objects to be *stateful widgets*. Each MyHomePage instance has a state — something about it that may change over time.

In contrast, the App0501 class in Listing 5-1 is a *stateless widget*. The app itself (App0501) relies on its home page to keep track of whatever text is being displayed. So, the app has no need to remember whether it's in one state or another. Nothing about an App0501 instance changes during the run of this code.

Think again about a traffic light. The part with the bulbs rests on a pole that's fastened permanently to the ground. The entire assembly — pole, bulbs and all — doesn't change. But the currents running through the bulbs change every 30 seconds or so. There you have it. The entire assembly is unchanging and stateless, but a part of that assembly — the part that's responsible for showing colors — is changing and stateful. (See Figure 5-3.)

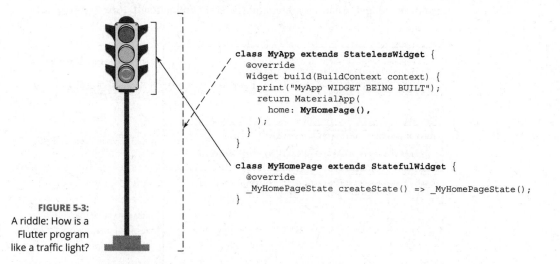

```
class MyApp extends StatelessWidget {
  @override
  Widget build(BuildContext context) {
    print("MyApp WIDGET BEING BUILT");
    return MaterialApp(
      home: MyHomePage(),
    );
  }
}

class MyHomePage extends StatefulWidget {
  @override
  _MyHomePageState createState() => _MyHomePageState();
}
```

FIGURE 5-3:
A riddle: How is a Flutter program like a traffic light?

Widgets have methods

In Listing 5-1, the declaration of the App0501 class contains a function named build. A function that's defined inside of a class declaration is called a *method*. The App0501 class has a build method. That's good because there's some fine print in the code for StatelessWidget. According to that fine print, every class that extends StatelessWidget must contain the declaration of a build method.

A stateless widget's build method tells Flutter how to build the widget. Among other things, the method describes the widget's look and behavior. Whenever you launch the program in Listing 5-1, Flutter calls the App0501 class's build method.

That `build` method constructs a `MaterialApp` instance, which, in turn, constructs a `MyHomePage` instance. And so on. From that point onward, the `MaterialApp` instance doesn't change. Yes, things inside the `MaterialApp` instance change, but the instance itself doesn't change.

How often does your town build a new traffic light assembly? Where I live, I may see one going up every two years or so. The metal part of a traffic light isn't designed to change regularly. The town planners call the traffic light assembly's `build` method only when they construct a new light. The same is true of stateless widgets in Flutter. A stateless widget isn't designed to be changed. When a stateless widget requires changing, Flutter replaces the widget.

What about stateful widgets? Do they have `build` methods? Well, they do and they don't. Every stateful widget has to have a `createState` method. The `createState` method makes an instance of Flutter's `State` class, and every `State` class has its own `build` method. In other words, a stateful widget doesn't build itself. Instead, a stateful widget creates a state, and the state builds itself. (See Figure 5-4.)

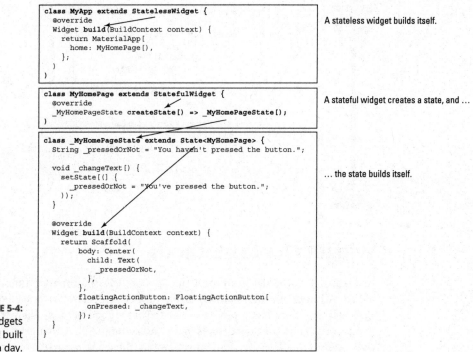

FIGURE 5-4:
Stateful widgets weren't built in a day.

"I'M TALKING TO YOU, STATELESS WIDGET — YOU MUST HAVE A BUILD METHOD!"

Every class that extends StatelessWidget must have a build method. Flutter's API enforces that rule.

But don't take my word for it. Temporarily comment out the build method declaration in Listing 5-1. That is, change the declaration of App0501 so that it looks like this:

```
class App0501 extends StatelessWidget {
//  Widget build(BuildContext context) {
//    return MaterialApp(
//      home: MyHomePage(),
//    );
//  }
}
```

When you do, you'll see some red marks in Android Studio's editor. The red marks indicate that the program contains an error; namely, that App0501 doesn't have its own build method.

TIP

To quickly comment out several lines of code, drag the mouse so that the highlight touches each of those lines. Then, if you're using Windows, press Ctrl-/. If you're using a Mac, press Cmd-/.

How does Dart enforce its build method requirement? As a novice developer, you don't have to know the answer You can skip the rest of this sidebar and go merrily on your way. But if you're curious, and you don't mind taking a little detour in your learning, try this:

In Android Studio's editor, right-click on the word StatelessWidget. On the resulting context menu, select Go To ⇨ Declaration. *Et voilá!* A new tab containing the StatelessWidget class declaration opens up in the editor. If you ignore most of the code in the StatelessWidget class declaration, you see something like this:

```
abstract class StatelessWidget extends Widget {
  // A bunch of code that you don't have to worry about, followed by ...

  Widget build(BuildContext context);
}
```

(continued)

(continued)

The first word, abstract, warns Dart that this class declaration contains methods (that is, functions) with no bodies. And, indeed, the line

```
Widget build(BuildContext context);
```

is a method header with no body. In place of a body, there's only a semicolon.

You might not be surprised to learn that StatelessWidget is an example of an *abstract class* and that the class's build method is an *abstract method*. With that in mind, I offer you these two facts:

- **You can't make a constructor call for an abstract class.**

  You can construct a Text widget by writing Text("Hello") because the Text class isn't abstract. But you can't construct a StatelessWidget by writing StatelessWidget(). That makes sense because, in the declaration of StatelessWidget, the build method isn't fully defined.

- **If you extend an abstract class, you have to provide a full declaration for each of the class's abstract methods.**

  The StatelessWidget class declaration contains the following line:

  ```
  Widget build(BuildContext context);
  ```

  Because of this, the App0501 class in Listing 5-1 must contain a full build method declaration. What's more, the declaration must specify a parameter of type BuildContext. Sure enough, the build method belonging to App0501 does the job:

  ```
  Widget build(BuildContext context) {
    return MaterialApp(
      home: MyHomePage(),
    );
  }
  ```

With a fully defined build method, the App0501 class isn't abstract. That's good because, near the top of Listing 5-1, there's a line containing an App0501() constructor call.

A typical traffic light's state changes every 30 seconds or every few minutes, and thus, the state of the light gets rebuilt. In the same way, the build method that belongs (indirectly) to a stateful widget gets called over and over again during the run of a program. That's what stateful widgets are for. They're nimble things whose appearance can easily change. In contrast, a stateless widget is like the pole of a traffic light. It's a rigid structure meant for one-time use.

Pay no attention to the framework behind the curtain

A program that displays buttons and other nice-looking things has a *graphical user interface*. Such an interface is commonly called a *GUI* (pronounced "goo-ey," as in "This peanut butter is really gooey"). In many GUI programs, things happen behind the scenes. While your app's code runs, lots of other code runs in the background. When you run a Flutter app, code that was written by the creators of Flutter runs constantly to support your own app's code. This background support code belongs to the *Flutter framework*.

Listing 5-1 has declarations for functions named main, build, createState, _getNewText, and _changeText, but the code in Listing 5-1 doesn't call any of these functions. Instead, Flutter's framework code calls these functions when a device runs the app.

Here's a blow-by-blow description:

>> **The Dart language calls the** main **function when the code in Listing 5-1 starts running.**

   The main function constructs an instance of App0501 and calls runApp to get things going. Then . . .

>> **The Flutter framework calls the** App0501 **instance's** build **function.**

   The build function constructs an instance of MyHomePage. Then . . .

>> **The Flutter framework calls the** MyHomePage **instance's** createState **function.**

   The createState function constructs an instance of _myHomePageState. Then . . .

>> **The Flutter framework calls the** _myHomePageState **instance's** build **function.**

   The build function constructs a Scaffold containing a Center with a Text widget and a FloatingActionButton widget.

To understand the Text widget's constructor, look at a few lines of code:

```
String _pressedOrNot = "You haven't pressed the button.";

// Later in the listing ...

      child: Text(
        _pressedOrNot,
      ),
```

Initially, the value of the _pressedOrNot variable is "You haven't pressed the button." So, when the app starts running, the Text widget obediently displays "You haven't pressed the button."

But the floating action button's code is a different story.

```
void _changeText() {
  setState(_getNewText);
}

void _getNewText() {
  _pressedOrNot = "You've pressed the button.";
}

// Later in the listing ...

    floatingActionButton: FloatingActionButton(
      onPressed: _changeText,
    )
```

The constructor for the FloatingActionButton has an onPressed parameter, and the value of that parameter is _changeText. What's that all about?

The onPressed parameter tells Flutter "If and when the user presses the button, have the device call the _changeText function." In fact, a lot of stuff happens when the user presses the floating action button. In the next few sections, you see some of the details.

The big event

In GUI programming, an *event* is something that happens — something that may require a response of some kind. The press of a button is an example of an event. Other examples of events include an incoming phone call, the movement of a device to a new GPS location, or the fact that one app needs information from another app.

An *event handler* is a function that's called when an event occurs. In Listing 5-1, the _changeText function is a handler for the button's onPressed event. In and of itself, the code onPressed: _changeText doesn't call the _changeText function. Instead, that code *registers the function _changeText as the official handler for floating action button presses.*

A call to the _changeText function would look like this: _changeText(). The call would end with open and close parentheses. The code onPressed: _changeText, with no parentheses, doesn't call the _changeText function. That code tells the device to remember that the name of the button's onPressed event handler is _changeText. The device uses this information when, and only when, the user presses the button.

Call me back

A phone rings four times. No one answers, but I hear a recorded announcement.

> "This is Steve Hayes — executive editor at John Wiley and Sons. I'm sorry that I'm not here to take your call. Please leave a message, and I'll get back to you as soon as I can." *<beep>*

> "Hello, Steve. This is Barry. The *Flutter For Dummies* manuscript is coming along nicely, but it's going to be several months late. Please call me so we can discuss a new timetable. Don't call me at my regular phone number. Instead, call me at my hotel in Taha'a, French Polynesia. The number is +689 49 55 55 55. Bye!"

My phone number in Taha'a is a callback number. In the same way, the functions _changeText and _getNewText in Listing 5-1 are *callbacks*. The line

```
onPressed: _changeText
```

tells the framework, "Call me back by calling my _changeText function." And the line

```
setState(_getNewText)
```

tells the framework "Call me back by calling my _getNewText function."

Callbacks are useful

You may have written programs that have no callbacks. When your program starts running, the system executes the first line of code, and keeps executing instructions until it reaches the last line of code. Everything runs as planned from start to finish. (Well, in the best of circumstances, everything runs as planned.)

A callback adds an element of uncertainty to a program. When will an event take place? When will a function be called? Where's the code that calls the function? Programs with callbacks are more difficult to understand than programs with no callbacks.

Why do you need callbacks? Can you get away without having them? To help answer this question, think about your common, everyday alarm clock. Before going to sleep, you tell the alarm clock to send sound to your ears (a callback) when the 9 A.M. event happens:

```
on9am: _rattleMyEarDrums,
```

If you didn't rely on a callback, you'd have to keep track of the time all night on your own. Like Bart and Lisa Simpson in the back seat of a car, you'd repeatedly be asking, "Is it 9 A.M. yet? Is it 9 A.M. yet? Is it 9 A.M. yet?" You certainly wouldn't get a good night's sleep. By the same token, if a Flutter program had to check every hundred milliseconds for a recent press of the button, there wouldn't be much time for the program to get anything else done. That's why you need callbacks in Flutter programs.

TECHNICAL STUFF

Programming with callbacks is called *event driven programming*. If a program doesn't use callbacks and, instead, repeatedly checks for button presses and other such things, that program is *polling*. In some situations, polling is unavoidable. But when event driven programming is possible, it's far superior to polling.

The outline of the code

One good way to look at code is to squint so that most of it's blurry and unreadable. The part that you can still read is the important part. Figure 5-5 contains my mostly blurry version of some code in Listing 5-1.

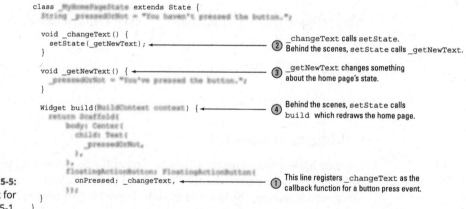

FIGURE 5-5:
What to look for in Listing 5-1.

According to Figure 5-5, this is the state management strategy in Listing 5-1:

1. Register _changeText as a callback function and wait for the user to press the floating action button.

   When, at last, the user presses the floating action button, . . .

2. Have _changeText call setState, and pass _getNewText as the one-and-only parameter in the setState function call.

The setState function calls _getNewText. When it does, . . .

3. The _getNewText function does whatever it has to do with some text.

The setState function also gets the Flutter framework to call build. When it does, . . .

4. The stuff on the user's screen is rebuilt.

The rebuilt screen displays the new text.

There's nothing special about the state management strategy in Listing 5-1. You can copy-and-paste this strategy into many other programs. Figure 5-6 shows you the general idea.

```
class _MyHomePageState extends State {
  blah, blah, blah, blabbity blah, blah, blah;

  void _handlerFunction() {
    setState(_getNewInfo);          ◄──────  ② _handlerFunction calls setState.
  }                                            Behind the scenes, setState calls _getNewInfo.

  void _getNewInfo() {             ◄──────  ③ _getNewInfo changes something
    blah, blah, blah, don't read this;          about the home page's state.
  }

  Widget build(BuildContext context) {  ◄──  ④ Behind the scenes, setState calls
    send email if(                             build, which redraws the home page.
        you've noticed(
            that I've(
                changed this text,
            );
        );
    Yada, yada, yada, sis boom bah(
        onEvent: _handlerFunction,  ◄────  ① This line registers _handlerFunction as
    );                                          the callback function for a certain kind of event.
  }
}
```

FIGURE 5-6:
What to look for in many Flutter programs.

According to Figure 5-6, these steps form a state management strategy:

1. Register a function as a callback function for an event and wait for that event to take place.

In Figure 5-6, the name of the callback function is _handlerFunction. Like all such functions, the _handlerFunction takes no parameters and returns void.

When, at last, the event takes place, . . .

2. Have the callback function call setState and pass another function as the one-and-only parameter in the setState function call.

In Figure 5-6, the name of this other function is _getNewInfo. Like all such functions, the _getNewInfo function takes no parameters and returns void.

The setState function calls _getNewInfo (or whatever name you've used, other than _getNewInfo). When it does, . . .

3. The _getNewInfo function changes something about the state of a widget.

The setState function also gets the Flutter framework to call build. When it does, . . .

4. The stuff on the user's screen is rebuilt.

The rebuilt screen displays the widget in its new state.

And so it goes.

C'mon, what really happens?

When you run a program that has a graphical user interface, lots of stuff happens behind the scenes. If you want, you can look at the framework's code, but that code can be quite complex. Besides, with any decent framework, you shouldn't have to read the framework's own code. You should be able to call the framework's functions and constructors by knowing only the stuff in the framework's documentation.

I know for sure that, when Listing 5-1 runs, the setState call results in a call to _getNewText. I know this because, when I comment out the setState call, the text doesn't change. But, I confess, I'm never completely comfortable with any GUI framework's magic. I want some sense of the framework's inner mechanisms, even if it's only a rough outline. (I'm the same way with everything. I'm not sure that the light goes out when I close the refrigerator door.)

WHAT TO DO WHEN YOU CALL setState

Try this experiment: Modify the _changeText function in Listing 5-1 this way:

```
void _changeText() {
  _getNewText();
  setState(_doNothing);
}

void _doNothing() {}
```

Move the reference to _getNewText outside of the setState function. After this move, the change of text happens before the call to setState, so setState doesn't have to call _getNewText. Of course, you still have to feed setState a function to call, so you feed it the _doNothing function. That _doNothing function keeps setState busy while it prepares to call the build method.

Does the modified code work? In this chapter's example, it does. But, in general, a change of this kind is a bad idea. Putting _getNewText inside the setState call ensures that the assignment to _pressedOrNot and the call to build happen together. In a more complicated program, the call to build might be delayed, and the results can be *strange*.

Here's another thing to consider: In Listing 5-1, the _getNewText function contains one simple assignment statement. But imagine an app that does a long, time-consuming calculation before displaying that calculation's result. The update of the screen comes in these three parts:

1. Do the calculation.

2. Change the text to be displayed so that it contains the calculation's result.

3. Have the framework call build to refresh the display.

In that case, Flutter experts recommend the following division of labor:

- Do the long, time-consuming calculation before the call to setState.
- Do the change of text in a parameter when you call setState.

In other words, keep the code that does heavy lifting outside the setState call, but put the code that changes the state's values inside the setState call. That's good advice.

To that end, I present Figure 5-7. The figure summarizes the description of event handling in the previous few sections. It illustrates some of the action in Listing 5-1, including a capsule summary of the code in the setState function. Make no mistake: Figure 5-7 is an oversimplified view of what happens when Flutter handles an event, but you might find the figure useful. I learned some things just by drawing the figure.

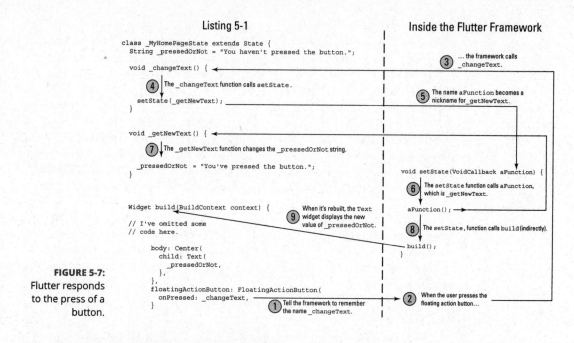

FIGURE 5-7: Flutter responds to the press of a button.

The following text appears within the figure:

Listing 5-1 · Inside the Flutter Framework

```
class _MyHomePageState extends State {
  String _pressedOrNot = "You haven't pressed the button.";

  void _changeText() {

    setState(_getNewText);
  }

  void _getNewText() {

    _pressedOrNot = "You've pressed the button.";
  }

  Widget build(BuildContext context) {
    // I've omitted some
    // code here.

      body: Center(
        child: Text(
          _pressedOrNot,
        ),
      ),
      floatingActionButton: FloatingActionButton(
        onPressed: _changeText,
  }
```

```
void setState(VoidCallback aFunction) {

  aFunction();
}

build();
}
```

③ ... the framework calls _changeText.

④ The _changeText function calls setState.

⑤ The name aFunction becomes a nickname for _getNewText.

⑦ The _getNewText function changes the _pressedOrNot string.

⑥ The setState function calls aFunction, which is _getNewText.

⑨ When it's rebuilt, the Text widget displays the new value of _pressedOrNot.

⑧ The setState, function calls build (indirectly).

① Tell the framework to remember the name _changeText.

② When the user presses the floating action button...

Enhancing Your App

The code in Listing 5-1 is a simplified version of Android Studio's starter app. That's nice, but maybe you want to know more about the starter app. To that end, Listing 5-2 includes a few more features — features that enhance the look and behavior of the simple Flutter demo program.

LISTING 5-2: **Inching Toward Android Studio's Starter App**

```
import 'package:flutter/material.dart';

void main() => runApp(App0502());

class App0502 extends StatelessWidget {
  @override
  Widget build(BuildContext context) {
    return MaterialApp(
      title: 'Flutter Demo',
      theme: ThemeData(
        primarySwatch: Colors.blue,
      ),
      home: MyHomePage(),
    );
  }
}
```

```
class MyHomePage extends StatefulWidget {
  @override
  _MyHomePageState createState() => _MyHomePageState();
}

class _MyHomePageState extends State {
  int _counter = 0;

  void _incrementCounter() {
    setState(() {
      _counter++;
    });
  }

  @override
  Widget build(BuildContext context) {
    return Scaffold(
      appBar: AppBar(
        title: Text("Listing 5-2"),
      ),
      body: Center(
        child: Column(
          mainAxisAlignment: MainAxisAlignment.center,
          children: <Widget>[
            Text(
              'You have pushed the button this many times:',
            ),
            Text(
              '$_counter',
              style: Theme.of(context).textTheme.display1,
            ),
          ],
        ),
      ),
      floatingActionButton: FloatingActionButton(
        onPressed: _incrementCounter,
        tooltip: 'Increment',
        child: Icon(Icons.add),
      ),
    );
  }
}
```

Figures 5-8 and 5-9 show a run of the code in Listing 5-2. Figure 5-8 is what you see when the app starts running, and Figure 5-9 is what you see after one click of the floating action button. On subsequent clicks, you see the numbers 2, 3, 4, and so on.

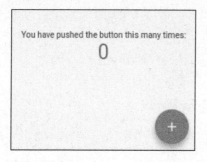

FIGURE 5-8:
Before the first button press.

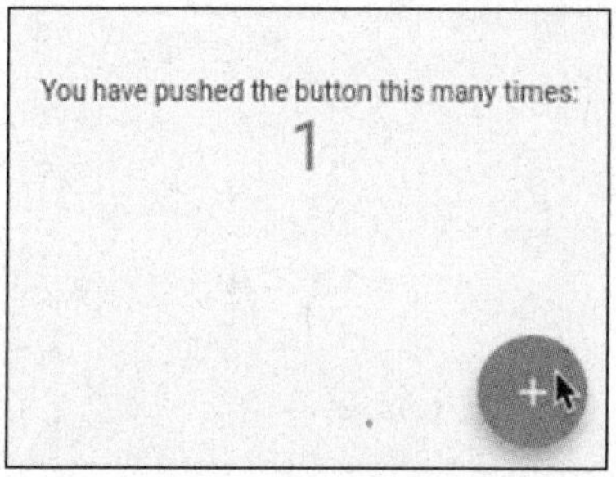

FIGURE 5-9:
After the first button press.

Whenever the user clicks the floating action button, the number on the screen increases by 1. To make this happen, Listing 5-2 has three references to the variable named _counter. Figure 5-10 illustrates the role of the _counter variable in the running of the app.

The app's Text widget displays the value of the _counter variable. So, when the app starts running, the Text widget displays 0. When the user first presses the floating action button and the Flutter framework calls setState, the _counter variable becomes 1. So, the number 1 appears in the center of the app's screen. When the user presses the action button again, _counter becomes 2, and so on.

More parameters, please

Listing 5-2 introduces some tried-and-true constructor parameters. For example, the MaterialApp constructor has title and theme parameters.

>> The title (in this example, Flutter Demo) appears only on Android phones, and only when the user conjures up the Recent Apps list.

>> The value of theme is a ThemeData instance (thus, the use of the ThemeData constructor in Listing 5-2).

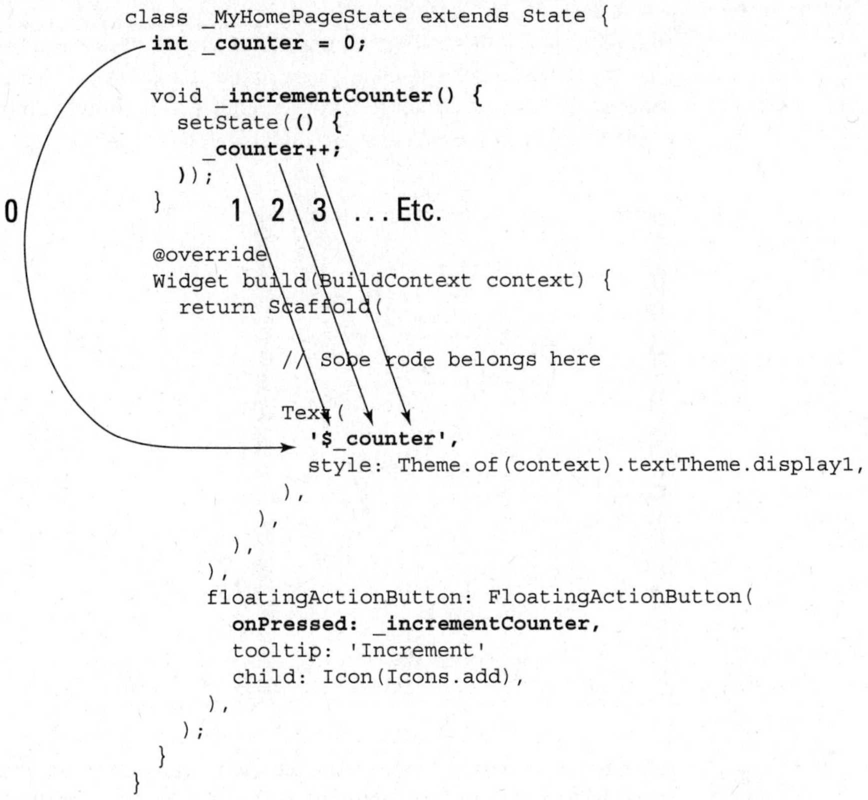

```
class _MyHomePageState extends State {
  int _counter = 0;

  void _incrementCounter() {
    setState(() {
      _counter++;
    ));
  }

  @override
  Widget build(BuildContext context) {
    return Scaffold(

        // Some code belongs here

        Text(
          '$_counter',
          style: Theme.of(context).textTheme.display1,
        ),
      ),
    ),
  ),
  floatingActionButton: FloatingActionButton(
    onPressed: _incrementCounter,
    tooltip: 'Increment'
    child: Icon(Icons.add),
  ),
);
  }
}
```

0   1 2 3 . . . Etc.

FIGURE 5-10:
Updating the
Text widget.

In the world of app design, themes are vitally important. A *theme* is a bunch of choices that apply to all parts of an app. For example, "Use the Roboto font for all elements that aren't related to accessibility" is a choice, and that choice can be part of a theme.

The choice made in Listing 5-2 is "Use the blue color swatch throughout the app." A *swatch* is a bunch of similar colors — variations on a single color that can be used throughout the app. The Colors.blue swatch contains ten shades of blue, ranging from very light to very dark. (For a look at some pretty swatches, see https://api.flutter.dev/flutter/material/Colors-class.html.)

As an experiment, run the code in Listing 5-2, and then change Colors.blue to Colors.deepOrange or Colors.blueGrey. When you save the change, all elements in the app suddenly look different. That's cool! You don't have to specify each widget's color. The theme maintains a consistent look among all widgets on the screen. For a big app with more than one page, the theme maintains a consistent look from one page to another. This helps the user understand the flow of elements in the app.

In Listing 5-2, a Text widget's `style` parameter uses a roundabout way to get a TextStyle instance. The code `Theme.of(context).textTheme.display1` represents a TextStyle with large text size. Figure 5-11 shows you the options that are available when you use `Theme.of(context).textTheme`.

FIGURE 5-11:
Flutter's
TextTheme
styles.

WARNING

A particular style may be too large for the screens on some phones. For example, to create Figure 5-11, I ran an emulator with a Pixel 3 XL virtual device. But with a plain old Pixel 3 in portrait mode, the word *display4* is too large for the width of the screen. The digit *4* appears on a line of its own.

As it is with the MaterialApp theme, the notion of a text theme is mighty handy. When you rely on Flutter's `Theme.of(context).textTheme` values, you provide a uniform look for all the text elements in your app. You can also take comfort in the fact that you're using standard values — nice-looking values chosen by professional app designers.

**ON THE
WEB**

Names like `display1` in the Flutter API don't correspond exactly to the names in Google's Material Design specifications, and I suspect that the options available in Flutter's API will change soon. For more on the Material Design specs, visit this page:

```
https://material.io/design/typography/#
```

Finally, the floating action button in Listing 5-2 has `tooltip` and `child` parameters.

>> **The** tooltip **string shows up when a user long-presses the button.**

When you touch the screen and keep your finger in the same place for a second or two, you're *long-pressing* that part of the screen. The app in Listing 5-2 displays the word Increment whenever the user long-presses the floating action button.

>> **For the button's** child, **you construct an** Icon **instance.**

The Icon instance displays a tiny image from Flutter's Icons class; namely, the Icons.add image. Sure enough, that image is a plus sign. (Refer to Figures 5-8 and 5-9.)

For a list of images in Flutter's Icons class, visit

```
https://api.flutter.dev/flutter/material/Icons-class.html
```

You can read more about parameters in Listing 5-2 and discover other useful parameters by visiting Flutter's documentation pages. For a brief introduction to those pages, refer to Chapter 3.

The override annotation

The line @override, which appears several times in Listing 5-2, is called an *annotation*. In Dart, an annotation begins with the at-sign (@).

A statement, such as _pressedOrNot = "You've pressed the button.", tells Dart what to do during the run of a program. But an annotation is different. An annotation tells Dart something *about* part of a Dart program. An @override annotation reminds Dart that the class you're extending has a matching declaration.

For example, consider the following code in Listing 5-2:

```
class App0502 extends StatelessWidget {
  @override
  Widget build(BuildContext context) {
```

The line @override says "The StatelessWidget class, which this App0502 class extends, has its own build(BuildContext context) method declaration." And indeed, according to this chapter's earlier sidebar "I'm talking to you, stateless widget — you must have a build method!" the StatelessWidget class in the Flutter API code has a build(BuildContext context) method with no body. It all works out nicely.

Listing 5-2 has @override annotations, but Listing 5-1 doesn't. Look at that! You can get away without having @override annotations! So, why bother having them?

The answer is "safety." The more information you give Dart about your code, the less likely it is that Dart will let you do something wrong. If you make a mistake and declare your build method incorrectly, Dart might warn you. "Hey! You said that you intend to override the build method that's declared in the StatelessWidget class, but your new build method doesn't do that correctly. Fix it, my friend!"

CROSS
REFERENCE

You can make Dart warn you about methods that don't match with their @override annotations. For details, visit https://dart.dev/guides/language/analysis-options.

What does <Widget> mean?

In Listing 5-2, the column's list of children starts with some extra stuff:

```
children: <Widget>[
  Text(
    'You have pushed the button this many times:',
  ),
  Text(
    '$_counter',
    style: Theme.of(context).textTheme.display1,
  ),
]
```

The <Widget> word, with its surrounding angle brackets, is called a *generic*, and a list that starts with a generic is called a *parameterized list*. In Listing 5-2, the <Widget> generic tells Dart that each of the list's values is, in one way or another, a Widget. According to Chapter 3, every instance of the Text class is an instance of the Widget class, so the <Widget> generic isn't lying.

In many situations, the use of generics is a safety issue. Consider the following two lines of code:

```
var words1 = ["Hello", "Goodbye", 1108];          // No error message
var words2 = <String>["Hello", "Goodbye", 1108];  // Error message!
```

You may plan to fill your list with String values, but when you declare words1 and words2, you accidentally include the int value 1108. The words1 list isn't parameterized, so Dart doesn't catch the error. But the words2 list is parameterized with the `<String>` generic, so Dart catches the mistake and refuses to run the code. An error message says `The element type 'int' can't be assigned to the list type 'String'`. To this, you should respond, "Good catch, Dart. Thank you very much."

Anonymous functions

In the Dart programming language, some functions don't have names. Take a look at the following code:

```
void _incrementCounter() {
  setState(_addOne);
}

void _addOne() {
  _counter++;
}
```

Imagine that your app contains no other references to _addOne. In that case, you've made up the name _addOne and used the name only once in your app. Why bother giving something a name if you'll be using the name only once? "Let's give this ear of corn the name 'sinkadillie'. And now, let's eat sinkadillie."

To create a function with no name, you remove the name. If the function's header has a return type, you remove that too. So, for example,

```
void _addOne() {
  _counter++;
}
```

becomes

```
          () {
  _counter++;
}
```

When you make this be the parameter for the `setState` function call, it looks like this:

```
void _incrementCounter() {
  setState(() {
    _counter++;
  });
}
```

CONFRONTING THE GREAT VOID

Take a nostalgic look at some code from the beginning of this chapter. It's in Listing 5-1.

```
void _changeText() {
  setState(_getNewText);
}
```

And later, in Listing 5-1:

```
floatingActionButton: FloatingActionButton(
    onPressed: _changeText,
))
```

The button press triggers a call to _changeText, and the _changeText function calls setState(_getNewText). Why not eliminate the middleman and have onPressed point directly to setState(_getNewText)? The resulting code would look something like this:

```
floatingActionButton: FloatingActionButton(
  onPressed: setState(_getNewText),        // This doesn't
  work.
))
```

When you write this code, an error message says, "The expression here has a type of 'void' and, therefore, can't be used." Flutter wants the onPressed parameter to be a function, but the expression setState(_getNewText) isn't a function. It's a call to setState, and a call to setState returns void. (See this sidebar's first figure.)

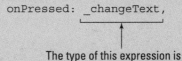

The type of this expression is
VoidCallback. That's good!

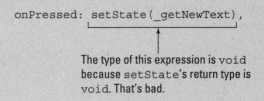

The type of this expression is void
because setState's return type is
void. That's bad.

A VoidCallback function is a function that takes no arguments and has the return type void. A common reason for creating a VoidCallback function is . . . well . . . to call a function back. Flutter wants the onPressed parameter to be a VoidCallback function, and the _changeText function fulfills the criteria for being a VoidCallback function. So, in Listing 5-1, the code onPressed: _changeText is fine and dandy.

But setState(_getNewText) isn't a VoidCallback. No, setState(_getNewText) is a plain old void. So the code onPressed: setState(_getNewText) falls flat on its face.

How can you fix the problem? You can revert to the original Listing 5-1 code, or you can save the day by using yet another anonymous function. All you do is add () => before the reference to setState, like so:

```
floatingActionButton: FloatingActionButton(
  onPressed: () => setState(_getNewText),
)
```

This sidebar's second figure describes the miraculous change that takes place when you add a few characters to your code. What was formerly a call to setState becomes a VoidCallback, and everyone is happy. Most importantly, Dart is happy. Your program runs correctly.

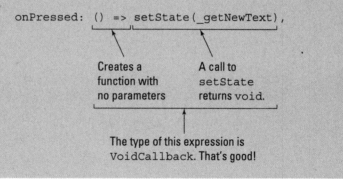

That's what you have in Listing 5-2.

A function with no name is called an *anonymous function*. When an anonymous function contains more than one statement, those statements must be enclosed in curly braces. But if the function contains only one statement, you can use fat arrow notation. For example, in Listing 5-2, the following code would work just fine:

```
void _incrementCounter() {
  setState(() => _counter++);
}
```

What belongs where

In Listing 5-2, the _counter variable's declaration is inside the _MyHomePage State class but outside of that class's _incrementCounter and build methods. A variable of this kind is called an *instance variable* or a *field*. (It depends on whom you ask.)

Why did I declare the _counter variable in that particular place? Why not put the declaration somewhere else in the code? I could write a whole chapter to answer the question in detail, but you don't want to read all that, and I certainly don't want to write it. Instead, I suggest some experiments for you to try:

1. **Starting with the code in Listing 5-2, add a reference to _counter inside the** MyHomePage **class. (See Figure 5-12.)**

```
void main() => runApp(App0502());

class App0502 extends StatelessWidget {
  // Blah, blah, blah ...
}

class MyHomePage extends StatefulWidget {
  @override
  _MyHomePageState createState() => _MyHomePageState();
  _counter = 86;  // This line is incorrect.
}

class _MyHomePageState extends State {
  int _counter = 0;

  void _incrementCounter() {
    setState(() {
      _counter++;
    });
  }

  @override
  Widget build(BuildContext context) {
    // Yada, yada ...
  }
}
```

FIGURE 5-12:
References to the boldface _counter variable are valid only inside the grey box.

Android Studio marks this new reference with a jagged red underline. The underline shames you into admitting that this additional reference was a bad idea. You've declared the _counter variable in the _MyHomePageState class, but you're trying to reference the variable in a different class; namely, the MyHomePage class.

Whenever you declare a variable inside of a class, that variable is *local* to the class. You can't refer to that variable outside the class. In particular, you can't refer to that variable inside a different class.

Don't you hate it when authors contradict themselves? There *is* a way to refer to a variable outside of its class's code. I cover it in detail in Chapter 7.

CROSS REFERENCE

2. **Remove the reference to** _counter **that you added in Step 1. Then move the declaration of** _counter **to the end of the** _MyHomePageState **class. (See Figure 5-13.)**

```
void main() => runApp(App0502());

class App0502 extends StatelessWidget {
  // Blah, blah, blah ...
}

class MyHomePage extends StatefulWidget {
  // Yada, yada ...
}

class _MyHomePageState extends State {
  void _incrementCounter() {
    setState(() {
      _counter++;
    });
  }

  @override
  Widget build(BuildContext context) {
    // Whatever ...
  }

  int _counter = 0;
}
```

FIGURE 5-13: References to the boldface _counter variable are valid inside the grey box.

Near the start of the _MyHomePageState class, you do _counter++. But you don't declare the _counter variable until the end of the _MyHomePageState class. Nevertheless, the program runs correctly. The moral of this story is, you don't have to declare a variable before you refer to that variable. Nice!

3. **Move the declaration of** _counter **so that it's inside the body of the** _incrementCounter **function. (See Figure 5-14.)**

When you do, you see an error marker on the occurrence of _counter in the build function. You've declared the _counter variable inside the _incrementCounter function, but you're trying to reference that variable in a different function; namely, the build function.

Whenever you declare a variable inside a function, that variable is local to the function. You can't refer to that variable outside the function. In particular, you can't refer to that variable inside a different function.

```
void main() => runApp(App0502());

class App0502 extends StatelessWidget {
  // Blah, blah, blah ...
}

class MyHomePage extends StatefulWidget {
  // Yada, yada ...
}

class _MyHomePageState extends State {

  void _incrementCounter() {
    int _counter = 0;
    setState(() {
      _counter++;
    });
  }

  @override
  Widget build(BuildContext context) {
    // Whatever ...
    Test{
      '$_counter',
    }
  }
}
```

4. **Keep the declaration of** _counter **inside the** _incrementCounter **function, and add another** _counter **declaration inside the** build **function. Initialize the** build **function's** _counter **variable to** 99. **(See Figure 5-15.)**

When you do this, the error message from Step 3 goes away. So the code is correct. Right?

No! The code isn't correct. When you run the code, the number in the center of the device is 99, and its value never changes. Pressing the floating action button has no effect. What's going on?

```
void main() => runApp(App0502());

class App0502 extends StatelessWidget {
  // Blah, blah, blah ...
}

class MyHomePage extends StatefulWidget {
  // Yada, yada ...
}

class _MyHomePageState extends State {

  void _incrementCounter() {
    int _counter = 0;
    setState(() {
      _counter++;
    });
  }

  @override
  Widget build(BuildContext context) {
    int _counter = 99;
    // Whatever ...
  }
}
```

FIGURE 5-15:
You can refer to one _counter variable only in the upper grey region; you can refer to the other _counter variable only in the lower grey region.

0

99

With this revised code, you have two different _counter variables — one that's local to the _incrementCounter function and another that's local to the build function. The statement _counter++ adds 1 to one of these _counter variables, but it doesn't add 1 to the other _counter variable. It's like having two people named Barry Burd — one living in New Jersey and the other in California. If you add a dollar to one of their bank accounts, the other person doesn't automatically get an additional dollar.

5. **Have only one** _counter **declaration. Put it just before the start of the** _MyHomePageState **class. (See Figure 5-16.)**

   After making this change, the editor doesn't display any error markers. Maybe you click the Run icon, anticipating bad news. Either the app doesn't run, or it runs and behaves badly. But, lo and behold, the app runs correctly!

   A declaration that's not inside a class or a function is called a *top-level* declaration, and a top-level name can be referenced anywhere in your program. (Well, almost anywhere. There are some limits. In particular, see the later section "Names that start with an underscore.")

6. **Have two** _counter **variable declarations — one at the top level, and another inside the** _MyHomePageState **class. Initialize the top-level** _counter **to** 2873 **and the latter** _counter **to** 0. **(See Figure 5-17.)**

   Before testing this version of the code, end the run of any other version. Start this version of the code afresh.

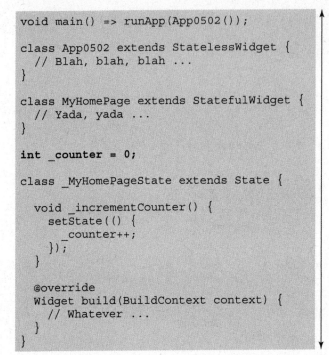

```
void main() => runApp(App0502());

class App0502 extends StatelessWidget {
  // Blah, blah, blah ...
}

class MyHomePage extends StatefulWidget {
  // Yada, yada ...
}

int _counter = 0;

class _MyHomePageState extends State {

  void _incrementCounter() {
    setState(() {
      _counter++;
    });
  }

  @override
  Widget build(BuildContext context) {
    // Whatever ...
  }
}
```

FIGURE 5-16:
Use a top-level
name anywhere
in your .dart file.

When this modified app starts running, the number in the center of the screen is 0, not 2873. The top-level declaration of _counter has no effect because it's shadowed by the declaration in the _MyHomePageState class.

The _counter declaration in the _MyHomePageState class applies to the code inside the _MyHomePageState class. The top-level _counter declaration applies everywhere else in this file's code.

TECHNICAL STUFF

This section is all about classes, methods, and variables. The section describes an instance variable as a variable whose declaration is inside of a class, but not inside any of the class's methods. That's *almost* a correct description of an instance variable. To be precise, an instance variable's declaration is one that doesn't contain the word static @@ a word that you encounter in Chapters 7 and 8. Until you read Chapters 7 and 8, don't worry about it.

Names that start with an underscore

Someday soon, when you're a big-shot Flutter developer, you'll create a large, complicated app that involves several different .dart files. A file's import statements will make code from one file available for use in another file. But how does this work? Are there any restrictions? Figure 5-18 says it all.

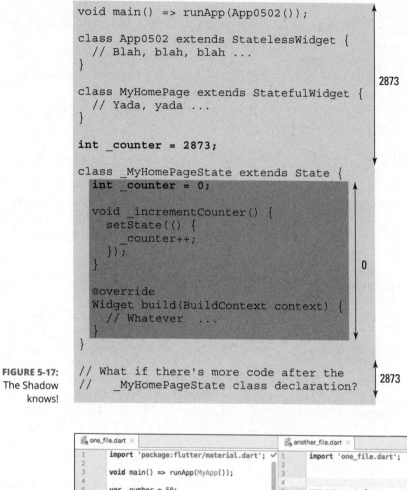

```
void main() => runApp(App0502());

class App0502 extends StatelessWidget {
  // Blah, blah, blah ...
}

class MyHomePage extends StatefulWidget {
  // Yada, yada ...
}

int _counter = 2873;

class _MyHomePageState extends State {
  int _counter = 0;

  void _incrementCounter() {
    setState(() {
      _counter++;
    });
  }

  @override
  Widget build(BuildContext context) {
    // Whatever  ...
  }
}

// What if there's more code after the
//    _MyHomePageState class declaration?
```

2873

0

2873

FIGURE 5-17:
The Shadow
knows!

```
one_file.dart ×                                    another_file.dart ×
1   import 'package:flutter/material.dart';   ✓  1   import 'one_file.dart';
2                                                2
3   void main() => runApp(MyApp());              3
4                                                4
5   var _number = 50;                            5   var num = _number;
6   var amount = 10;                             6   var amnt = amount;
7                                                7
8   class MyApp extends StatelessWidget {
9     @override
10      Widget build(BuildContext context) {
11        return MaterialApp(
```

FIGURE 5-18:
"I got plenty
numbers left."
(Google it.)

A variable or function whose name begins with an underscore (_) is local to the file in which it's declared and can't be referenced in other .dart files. All other names can be imported and shared among all the files in an application. In Figure 5-18, the _number variable can be used only in one_file.dart. But, because of an import statement, the amount variable is available in both one_file.dart and another_file.dart.

TECHNICAL STUFF

If you're used to writing code in languages like Java, forget about access modifiers such as public and private. The Dart language doesn't have those things.

TOP-LEVEL NAMES AREN'T ALWAYS BEST

In Step 5 of this section's instructions, you declare _counter at the top level, and the program runs without a hitch. If it's okay to declare _counter at the top level, why don't you do that in Listing 5-2? Well, you should expect more from a program than that it simply runs correctly. In addition to running correctly, a good program is sturdy. The program doesn't break when someone changes a bit of code.

In Listing 5-2, the only use of the _counter variable is inside the _MyHomePageState class. A programmer who's working on the _MyHomePageState class's code should be able to mess with the _counter variable. But other programmers, those who work on other parts of the app, have no need to reference the _counter variable. By keeping access to _counter inside the _MyHomePageState class, you're protecting the variable from accidental misuse by programmers who don't need to reference it. (Object-oriented programmers call this *encapsulation*.)

The program in Listing 5-2 isn't a large, industrial-strength app. So, in that program, anyone who writes code outside the _MyHomePageState class is likely to know all about the code inside the _MyHomePageState class. But for real-life applications in which teams of programmers work on different parts of the code, protecting one part of the code from the other parts is important. No, it's not important. It's absolutely essential.

Remember: In any program that you write, limit access to variable names and other names as much as you can. Don't declare them at the top level if you don't have to. It's safer that way.

Whew!

This is a heavy-duty chapter. If you've spent the evening reading every word of it, you're probably a bit tired. But that's okay. Take a breather. Make yourself a cup of tea. Sit in your easy chair, and relax with a performance of *The Well-Tempered Clavier* (Praeludium 1, BWV 846).

Chapter 6 continues the theme of widgets responding to user actions. In that chapter, you slide sliders, switch switches, drop dropdown lists, and do other fun things. Go for it (but don't forget to unwind a bit first)!

Chapter **6**

Laying Things Out

A ccording to folklore, the size of a fish tank determines the sizes of the goldfish in the tank. A goldfish in a small tank can be only one or two inches long, but the same goldfish in a larger tank grows to be ten inches long. It's as if a fish's cells sense the boundaries of the fish's living space, and the cells stop growing when they feel that doing so would be impractical.

Several online resources say that the tank size phenomenon is a myth, but that doesn't stop me from comparing it with Flutter layouts. (Nothing stops me from making comparisons with Flutter layouts.)

In a Flutter layout, widgets are nested inside of other widgets. The outer widget sends a constraint to the inner widget:

"You can be as wide as you want, as long as your width is between 0 and 400 density-independent pixels."

Later on, the inner widget sends its exact height to the outer widget:

"I'm 200 density-independent pixels wide."

The outer widget uses that information to position the inner widget:

"Because you're 200 density-independent pixels wide, I'll position your left edge 100 pixels from my left edge."

Of course, this is a simplified version of the true scenario. But it's a useful starting point for understanding the way Flutter layouts work. Most importantly, this outer/inner communication works its way all along an app's widget chain.

Imagine having four widgets. Starting from the outermost widget (such as the Material widget), call these widgets "great-grandmother", "grandmother", "mother", and "Elsie." Here's how Flutter decides how to draw these widgets:

1. Great-grandmother tells grandmother how big she (grandmother) can be.

2. Grandmother tells mother how big she (mother) can be.

3. Mother tells Elsie how big she (Elsie) can be.

4. Elsie decides how big she is and tells mother.

5. Mother determines Elsie's position, decides how big she (mother) is, and then tells grandmother.

6. Grandmother determines mother's position, decides how big she (grand-mother) is, and then tells great-grandmother.

7. Great-grandmother determines mother's position and then decides how big she (great-grandmother is).

Yes, the details are fuzzy. But it helps to keep this pattern in mind as you read about Flutter layouts.

The Big Picture

Listings 6-1 and 6-2 introduce a handful of Flutter layout concepts, and Figure 6-1 shows what you see when you run these listings together.

LISTING 6-1: **Reuse This Code**

```
// App06Main.dart

import 'package:flutter/material.dart';

import 'App0602.dart'; // Change this line to App0605, App0606, and so on.

void main() => runApp(App06Main());
```

```
class App06Main extends StatelessWidget {
  @override
  Widget build(BuildContext context) {
    return MaterialApp(
      home: _MyHomePage(),
    );
  }
}

class _MyHomePage extends StatelessWidget {
  @override
  Widget build(BuildContext context) {
    return Material(
      color: Colors.grey[400],
      child: Padding(
        padding: const EdgeInsets.symmetric(
          horizontal: 20.0,
        ),
        child: buildColumn(context),
      ),
    );
  }
}

Widget buildTitleText() {
  return Text(
    "My Pet Shop",
    textScaleFactor: 3.0,
    textAlign: TextAlign.center,
  );
}

Widget buildRoundedBox(
  String label, {
  double height = 88.0,
}) {
  return Container(
    height: height,
    width: 88.0,
    alignment: Alignment(0.0, 0.0),
    decoration: BoxDecoration(
      color: Colors.white,
      border: Border.all(color: Colors.black),
      borderRadius: BorderRadius.all(
        Radius.circular(10.0),
      ),
    ),
```

```
    child: Text(
      label,
      textAlign: TextAlign.center,
    ),
  );
}
```

LISTING 6-2: **A Very Simple Layout**

```
// App0602.dart

import 'package:flutter/material.dart';

import 'App06Main.dart';

Widget buildColumn(BuildContext context) {
  return Column(
    mainAxisAlignment: MainAxisAlignment.center,
    crossAxisAlignment: CrossAxisAlignment.stretch,
    children: <Widget>[
      buildTitleText(),
      SizedBox(height: 20.0),
      buildRoundedBox(
        "Sale Today",
        height: 150.0,
      ),
    ],
  );
}
```

FIGURE 6-1:
A sale at
My Pet Shop.

CROSS
REFERENCE

The code in Listing 6-1 refers to code in Listing 6-2, and vice versa. As long as these two files are in the same Android Studio project, running the app in Listing 6-1 automatically uses code from Listing 6-2. This works because of the import declarations near the top of each of the listings. For info about import declarations, refer to Chapter 4.

Listings 6-1 and 6-2 illustrate some coding concepts along with a bunch of useful Flutter features. I cover these in the next several sections.

Creating bite-size pieces of code

In Listings 6-1 and 6-2, I create some of the widgets by making method calls.

```
child: buildColumn(context),

// ... And elsewhere, ...

Column(
  // ... Blah, blah, ...
  children: <Widget>[
    buildTitleText(),
    SizedBox(height: 20.0),
    buildRoundedBox(
    // ... Etc.
```

Each method call takes the place of a longer piece of code — one that describes a particular widget in detail. I create these methods because doing so makes the code easier to read and digest. With a glance at Listing 6-2, you can tell that the Column consists of title text, a sized box, and a rounded box. You don't know any of the details until you look at the buildTitleText and buildRoundedBox method declarations in Listing 6-1, but that's okay. With the code divided into methods this way, you don't lose sight of the app's overall outline.

In the design of good software, planning is essential. But sometimes your plans change. Imagine this scenario: You start writing some code that you believe will be fairly simple. After several minutes (or, sometimes, several hours), you realize that the code has become large and unwieldy. So you decide to divide the code into methods. To do this, you can take advantage of one of Android Studio's handy refactoring features. Here's how it works:

1. **Start with a constructor call that you want to replace with your own method call.**

   For example, you want to replace the Text constructor call in the following code snippet:

   ```
   children: <Widget>[
     Text(
       "My Pet Shop",
   ```

```
        textScaleFactor: 3.0,
        textAlign: TextAlign.center,
    ),
    SizedBox(height: 20.0),
```

2. **Place the mouse cursor on the constructor call's name.**

   For the snippet in Step 1, click on the word Text.

3. **On Android Studio's main menu, select Refactor ⇨ Extract ⇨ Method.**

   As a result, Android Studio displays the Extract Method dialog box.

4. **In the Extract Method dialog box, type a name for your new method.**

   For a constructor named Text, Android Studio suggests the method name buildText. But, to create Listings 6-1 and 6-2, I made up the name buildTitleText.

5. **In the Extract Method dialog box, press Refactor.**

   As if by magic, Android Studio adds a new method declaration to your code and replaces the original widget constructor with a call to the method.

   The new method's return type is whatever kind of widget your code is trying to construct. For example, starting with the code in Step 1, the method's first two lines might look like this:

```
Text buildTitleText() {
    return Text(
```

6. **Do yourself a favor and change the type in the method's header to** Widget.

```
Widget buildTitleText() {
    return Text(
```

   Every instance of the Text class is an instance of the Widget class, so this change doesn't do any harm. In addition, the change adds a tiny bit of flexibility that may eventually save you some mental energy. Maybe later, you decide to surround the method's Text widget with a Center widget.

```
// Baby, you're no good . . .
Text buildTitleText() {
    return Center(
        child: Text(
```

After you make this change, your code is messed up because the header's return type is inaccurate. Yes, every instance of the Text class is an instance of the Widget class. But, no, an instance of the Center class isn't an instance of the Text class. Your method returns an instance of Center, but the method's header expects the method to return an instance of Text. Don't you wish you had changed the first word in the header to Widget? Do it sooner rather than later. That way, you won't be distracted when you're concentrating on making changes in the method's body.

Creating a parameter list

In Listing 6-1, the header of the buildRoundedBox declaration looks like this:

```
Widget buildRoundedBox(
  String label, {
  double height = 88.0,
})
```

The method has two parameters: label and height.

>> **The label parameter is a positional parameter.**

It's a positional parameter because it's not surrounded by curly braces. In a header, all the positional parameters must come before any of the named parameters.

>> **The height parameter is a named parameter.**

It's a named parameter because it's surrounded by curly braces.

In a call to this method, you can omit the height parameter. When you do, the parameter's default value is 88.0.

With these facts in mind, the following calls to buildRoundedBox are both valid:

```
buildRoundedBox(          // Flutter style guidelines recommend having a
  "Flutter",              //    trailing comma at the end of every list.
  height: 1000.0,         //    It's the comma after the height parameter.
)

buildRoundedBox("Flutter") // In the method header, the height parameter
                           //    has the default value 88.0.
```

Here are some calls that aren't valid:

```
buildRoundedBox(            // In a function call, all positional parameters
  height: 1000.0,           //   must come before any named parameters.
  "Flutter",
)

buildRoundedBox(
  label: "Flutter",         // The label parameter is a positional parameter,
  height: 1000.0,           //   not a named parameter.
)

buildRoundedBox(
  "Flutter",                // The height parameter is a named parameter,
  1000.0,                   //   not a positional parameter.
)

buildRoundedBox()           // You can't omit the label parameter, because
                            //   the label parameter has no default value.
```

CROSS
REFERENCE

For info about positional parameters and named parameters, refer to Chapter 3. For the basics on declaring functions, refer to Chapter 4.

CROSS
REFERENCE

In Listing 6-2, the declaration of buildColumn has a BuildContext parameter. You may ask, "What good is this BuildContext parameter? The body of the buildColumn method makes no reference to this parameter's value." For an answer, see the last section of this chapter.

Living color

Chapter 5 introduces Flutter's Colors class with basic things like Colors.grey and Colors.black. In fact, the Colors class provides 12 different shades of grey, 7 shades of black, 28 shades of blue, and a similar variety for other colors. For example, the shades of grey are named Colors.grey[50] (the lightest), Colors.grey[100], Colors.grey[200], Colors.grey[300], and so on, up to Colors.grey[900] (the darkest). You can't put arbitrary numbers inside the brackets, so things like Colors.grey[101] and Colors.grey[350] simply don't exist. But one shade — Colors.grey[500] — is special. You can abbreviate Colors.grey[500] by writing Colors.grey without having a number in brackets.

If you want extra-fine control over the look of your app, you can use Flutter's Color.fromRGBO constructor. (That's Color singular, as opposed to Colors plural.) The letters RGBO stand for Red, Green, Blue, and Opacity. In the constructor, the values of Red, Green, and Blue range from 0 to 255, and the value of Opacity ranges from 0.0 to 1.0. For example, `Color.fromRGBO(255, 0, 0, 1.0)` stands for completely opaque Red. Table 6-1 has some other examples:

TABLE 6-1 **Sample Parameters for the Color.fromRGBO Constructor**

Parameter List	What the Parameter List Means
(0, 255, 0, 1.0)	Green
(0, 0, 255, 1.0)	Blue
(255, 0, 255, 1.0)	Purple (equal amounts of Red and Blue)
(0, 0, 0, 1.0)	Black
(255, 255, 255, 1.0)	White
(190, 190, 190, 1.0)	Grey (approximately 75% whiteness)
(255, 0, 0, 0.5)	50% transparent Red
(255, 0, 0, 0.0)	Nothing (complete transparency, no matter what the Red, Green, and Blue values are)

ON THE WEB

To find out about other options for describing colors, visit Flutter's `Color` class documentation page:

`https://api.flutter.dev/flutter/dart-ui/Color-class.html`

Adding padding

Flutter's `Padding` widget puts some empty space between its outermost edge and its child. In Listing 6-1, the code

```
Padding(
  padding: const EdgeInsets.symmetric(
    horizontal: 20.0,
  ),
  child: buildColumn(context),
```

surrounds the `buildColumn` call with 20.0 units of empty space on the left and the right. (Refer to Figure 6-1.) With no padding, the column would touch the left and right edges of the user's screen, and so would the white Sale Today box inside the column. That wouldn't look nice.

In Flutter, a line such as `horizontal: 20.0` stands for 20.0 density-independent pixels. A *density-independent pixel* (dp) has no fixed size. Instead, the size of a density-independent pixel depends on the user's hardware. In particular, every inch of the user's screen is roughly 96 dp long. That makes every centimeter approximately 38 pixels long. According to Flutter's official documentation, the rule about having 96 dp per inch "may be inaccurate, sometimes by a significant margin." Run this section's app on your own phone, and you'll see what they mean.

In Flutter, you describe padding of any kind by constructing an `EdgeInsets` object. The `EdgeInsets.symmetric` constructor in Listing 6-1 has one parameter — a `horizontal` parameter. In addition to the `horizontal` parameter, an `EdgeInsets.symmetric` constructor can have a `vertical` parameter, like so:

```
Padding(
  padding: const EdgeInsets.symmetric(
    horizontal: 20.0,
    vertical: 10.0,
  )
)
```

A `vertical` parameter adds empty space on the top and bottom of the child widget.

Table 6-2 lists some alternatives to the `EdgeInsets.symmetric` constructor.

TABLE 6-2 EdgeInsets Constructor Calls

Constructor Call	How Much Blank Space Surrounds the Child Widget
`EdgeInsets.all(20.0)`	`20.0 dp on all four sides`

`EdgeInsets.only(`
`left: 15.0,`
`top: 10.0,`
`)`
	`15.0 dp on the left`
	`10.0 dp on top`

`EdgeInsets.only(`
`top: 10.0,`
`right: 15.0,`
`bottom: 15.0,`
`)`
	`10.0 dp on top`
	`15.0 dp on the right`
	`15.0 dp on the bottom`

`EdgeInsets.fromLTRB(`
`5.0,`
`10.0,`
`3.0,`
`2.0,`
`)`
	`5.0 dp on the left`
	`10.0 dp on top`
	`3.0 dp on the right`
	`2.0 dp on the bottom`

When I started working on the code in Listing 6-1, the listing had no `Padding` widget. The call to `buildColumn` was a direct descendant of the `Material` widget:

```
return Material(
  color: Colors.grey[400],
  child: buildColumn(context),
);
```

I used the Alt+Enter trick from Chapter 3 to surround the `buildColumn` call with the new `Padding` widget. When I did this, Android Studio also added its own `const` `EdgeInsets` code. I tinkered with Android Studio's code a bit, but I didn't remove the code's `const` keyword. For the inside story on Dart's `const` keyword, see Chapter 7.

The `Padding` widget adds blank space inside of itself. To add space outside of a widget, see the section "Your friend, the Container widget," later in this chapter.

Your humble servant, the Column widget

Think about it: Without Flutter's `Column` widget, you wouldn't be able to position one widget above another. Everything on a user's screen would be squished into one place. The screen would be unreadable, and no one would use Flutter. You wouldn't be reading this book. I wouldn't earn any royalties. What an awful world it would be!

The `Column` widget in Listing 6-2 has two properties related to alignment:

```
Column(
  mainAxisAlignment: MainAxisAlignment.center,
  crossAxisAlignment: CrossAxisAlignment.stretch,
  // ... And so on.
```

The `mainAxisAlignment` property comes up in Chapter 3. It describes the way children are positioned from the top to the bottom of the column. With `MainAxisAlignment.center`, children gather about halfway down from the top of the screen. (Refer to Figure 6-1.) In contrast, the `crossAxisAlignment` describes how children are situated from side to side within the column. (See Figure 6-2.)

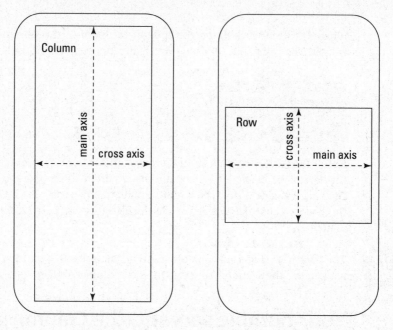

A column's crossAxisAlignment can make a big difference in the way the column's children appear on the screen. For example, if you comment out the crossAxisAlignment line in Listing 6-2, you see the screen shown in Figure 6-3.

In Listing 6-2, the CrossAxisAlignment.stretch value tells the column that its children should fill the entire cross axis. This means that, regardless of the children's explicit width values, children shrink or widen so that they run across the entire column. If you don't believe me, try the following experiment:

1. **Run the code in Listing 6-1.**

   Use the iPhone simulator, the Android emulator, or a real physical phone. Start with the device in portrait mode, as in Figure 6-1.

2. **Turn the device sideways so that the device is in landscape mode.**

    If you're running a virtual device, press Command-right arrow (on a Mac) or Ctrl+right arrow (on Windows). If you're running a physical device, turn the darn thing sideways.

3. **Observe the change in the size of the Sale Today box.**

    No matter how wide the screen is, the Sale Today box stretches almost all the way across. The `width: 88.0` setting in Listing 6-1 has no effect.

You can read more about axis alignments in the sections that follow.

TIP

When you turn a device sideways, the device might not switch between portrait and landscape modes. This is true for both physical devices (real phones and tablets) and virtual devices (emulators and simulators). If your device's orientation refuses to change, try this:

>> On an Android device, in Settings ⇨ Display, turn on Auto Rotate Screen.

>> On an iPhone or iPad, swipe up from the bottom of the screen, and press the button that displays a lock and a circular arrow.

With an emulator or a simulator, you can try turning the computer monitor sideways, but that probably won't work.

The SizedBox widget

If I planned to live on a desert island and I could bring only seven widgets with me, those seven widgets would be `Column`, `Row`, `SizedBox`, `Container`, `Expanded`, `Spacer`, and `Padding`. (If I could bring only two kinds of food with me, the two kinds of food would be cheeseburgers and chocolate.)

A `SizedBox` is a rectangle that developers use for taking up space. A `SizedBox` has a `width`, a `height`, and possibly a `child`. Very often, only the `width` or the `height` matters.

Listing 6-2 has a `SizedBox` of height 20.0 sitting between the title text and the rounded box. Without the `SizedBox`, there would be no space between the title text and the rounded box.

TIP

A `Spacer` is like a `SizedBox`, except that a `Spacer` uses `flex` instead of explicit `height` and `width` parameters. For a look at Flutter's `flex` property, see the section "Flexing some muscles," later in this chapter.

Your friend, the Container widget

In Listing 6-2, the box displaying the words *Sale Today* uses a `Container` widget. A `Container` is a widget that contains something. (That's not surprising.) While the widget is containing something, it has properties like `height`, `width`, `alignment`, `decoration`, `padding`, and `margin`.

The height and width parameters

You might be curious about a particular line in Listing 6-1:

```
return Container(
  height: height,
```

What could `height: height` possibly mean? The height is what it is? The height is the height is the height?

To find out what's going on, place the cursor on the second occurrence of the word `height` — the one after the colon. When you do, Android Studio highlights that occurrence along with one other. (See Figure 6-4.)

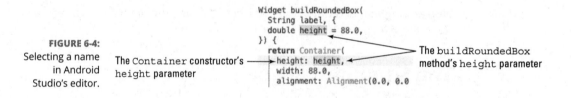

FIGURE 6-4: Selecting a name in Android Studio's editor.

Noticeably absent is any highlight on the `height` that's immediately before the colon. Listing 6-1 has two variables named `height`. One is a parameter of build-RoundedBox; the other is a parameter of the `Container` constructor. The line

```
height: height,
```

makes the `Container` parameter have the same value as the `buildRoundedBox` parameter. (The `buildRoundedBox` parameter gets its value from the call in Listing 6-2.)

WARNING

In a `Container` constructor call, the `height` and `width` parameters are suggestions — not absolute sizes. For details, refer to the section "Your humble servant, the Column widget," earlier in this chapter. And, while you're at it, check out the section "Using the Expanded Widget," later in this chapter.

The alignment parameter

To align a child within a `Container` widget, you don't use `mainAxisAlignment` or `crossAxisAlignment`. Instead, you use the plain old `alignment` parameter. In Listing 6-1, the line

```
alignment: Alignment(0.0, 0.0)
```

tells Flutter to put the child of the container in the center of the container. Figure 6-5 illustrates the secrets behind the `Alignment` class.

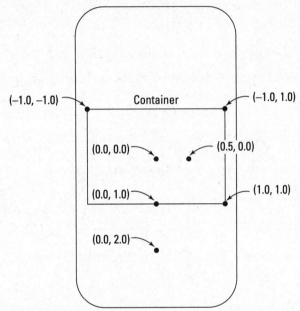

FIGURE 6-5:
Using a container's alignment parameter.

The decoration parameter

As the name suggests, `decoration` is something that livens up an otherwise dull-looking widget. In Listing 6-1, the `BoxDecoration` constructor has three parameters of its own:

>> `color`: The widget's fill color.

This property fills the Sale Today box in Figure 6-1 with white.

Both the `Container` and `BoxDecoration` constructors have `color` parameters. When you put a `BoxDecoration` inside of a `Container`, have a `color` parameter for the `BoxDecoration`, not the `Container`. If you have both, your program may crash.

WARNING

» `border`: The outline surrounding the widget.

Listing 6-1 uses the `Border.all` constructor, which describes a border on all four sides of the Sale Today box.

To create a border whose sides aren't all the same, use Flutter's `Border` constructor (without the `.all` part). Here's an example:

```
Border(
    top: BorderSide(width: 5.0, color: Colors.black),
    bottom: BorderSide(width: 5.0, color: Colors.black),
    left: BorderSide(width: 3.0, color: Colors.blue),
    right: BorderSide(width: 3.0, color: Colors.blue),
    )
```

» `borderRadius`: The amount of curvature of the widget's border.

Figure 6-6 shows what happens when you use different values for the `borderRadius` parameter.

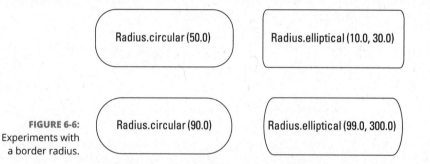

FIGURE 6-6:
Experiments with a border radius.

The padding and margin parameters

The `Container` constructor call in Listing 6-1 has no `padding` or `margin` parameters, but `padding` and `margin` can be useful in other settings. To find out how `padding` and `margin` work, look first at Listing 6-3.

LISTING 6-3: **Without Padding or Margin**

```
// App0603.dart

import 'package:flutter/material.dart';

void main() => runApp(App0602());
```

```
class App0602 extends StatelessWidget {
  @override
  Widget build(BuildContext context) {
    return MaterialApp(
      home: Material(
        color: Colors.grey[50],
        child: Container(
          color: Colors.grey[500],
          child: Container(
            color: Colors.grey[700],
          ),
        ),
      ),
    );
  }
}
```

Listing 6-3 has a container within another container that's within a Material widget. The inner container is grey[700], which is fairly dark grey. The outer container is a lighter grey, and the Material widget background is grey[50], which is almost white.

I told my editor that I wanted to use up page space with a figure devoted to a run of Listing 6-3, but he said no. I wonder why! Who could object to a figure that's nothing but a dark grey rectangle?

When you run the app in Listing 6-3, the inner container completely covers the outer container, which, in turn, completely covers the Material widget. Each of these widgets expands to fill its parent, so each of the three widgets takes up the entire screen. The only widget you can see is the innermost, dark grey container. What a waste!

To remedy this situation, Listing 6-4 uses both padding and margin. Figure 6-7 shows you the result.

LISTING 6-4: **With Padding and Margin**

```
// App0604.dart

import 'package:flutter/material.dart';

void main() => runApp(App0603());

class App0603 extends StatelessWidget {
```

```
  @override
  Widget build(BuildContext context) {
    return MaterialApp(
      home: SafeArea(
        child: Material(
          color: Colors.grey[50],
          child: Container(
            color: Colors.grey[500],
            padding: EdgeInsets.all(80.0),
            margin: EdgeInsets.all(40.0),
            child: Container(
              color: Colors.grey[700],
            ),
          ),
        ),
      ),
    );
  }
}
```

The middle container's

Outermost edge

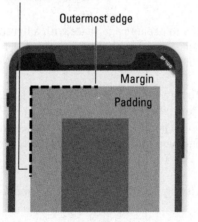

FIGURE 6-7:
Padding versus
margin.

Listing 6-4 is all about the middle container — the one whose color is a medium shade of grey. I've marked up Figure 6-7 to make the result crystal-clear. The general rules are as follows:

>> *Padding* **is the space between a widget's outermost edges and the widget's child.**

   In Figure 6-7, the medium grey stuff is padding.

In Figure 6-7, the white (or nearly white) stuff is the margin.

From what I observe, Flutter developers use padding a lot but use margin sparingly.

REMEMBER

You can add padding to almost any widget without putting that widget inside a `Container`. To do so, simply put the widget inside of a `Padding` widget. For an example, look for the `Padding` widget in Listing 6-1.

When you think about a mobile device, you probably imagine a rectangular screen. Does this mean that an entire rectangle is available for use by your app? It doesn't. The top of the rectangle may have a notch. The corners of the rectangle may be rounded instead of square. The operating system (iOS or Android) may consume parts of the screen with an Action Bar or other junk.

To avoid items in this obstacle course, Flutter has a `SafeArea` widget. The `SafeArea` is the part of the screen that's available for the free, unencumbered use by your app. In Listing 6-4, a `SafeArea` helps me show the padding and margin in all their glory. Without that `SafeArea`, the top part of the margin might be covered by stuff that's not part of my app.

Nesting Rows and Columns

You hardly ever see an app with only one column of widgets. Most of the time, you see widgets alongside other widgets, widgets arranged in grids, widgets at angles to other widgets, and so on. The most straightforward way to arrange Flutter widgets is to put columns inside of rows and rows inside of columns. Listing 6-5 has an example, and Figure 6-8 shows you the results.

LISTING 6-5: **A Row Within a Column**

```
// App0605.dart

import 'package:flutter/material.dart';

import 'App06Main.dart';

Widget buildColumn(BuildContext context) {
  return Column(
```

```
      mainAxisAlignment: MainAxisAlignment.center,
      crossAxisAlignment: CrossAxisAlignment.stretch,
      children: <Widget>[
        buildTitleText(),
        SizedBox(height: 20.0),
        _buildRowOfThree(),
      ],
    );
  }

  Widget _buildRowOfThree() {
    return Row(
      mainAxisAlignment: MainAxisAlignment.spaceBetween,
      children: <Widget>[
        buildRoundedBox("Cat"),
        buildRoundedBox("Dog"),
        buildRoundedBox("Ape"),
      ],
    );
  }
```

FIGURE 6-8:
Animals for sale.

In Listing 6-1, the Column widget's crossAxisAlignment property forces the Sale Today box to be as wide as it could possibly be. That happens because the Sale Today box is one of the Column widget's children. But in Listing 6-5, the Cat, Dog, and Ape boxes aren't children of the Column widget. Instead, they're *grandchildren* of the Column widget. So, for Listing 6-5, the major factor positioning the Cat, Dog, and Ape boxes is the Row widget's mainAxisAlignment property.

To see this in action, change the lines

```
return Row(
  mainAxisAlignment: MainAxisAlignment.spaceBetween,
```

in Listing 6-5 to the following lines:

```
return Row(
  mainAxisAlignment: MainAxisAlignment.center,
```

When you do, you see the arrangement shown in Figure 6-9.

FIGURE 6-9:
Animals in cramped quarters.

CROSS REFERENCE

To find out about values you can give to a mainAxisAlignment property, refer to Chapter 3.

More Levels of Nesting

Every sack had seven cats,

Every cat had seven kits . . .

FROM A TRADITIONAL ENGLISH LANGUAGE NURSERY RHYME

Yes, you can create a row within a column within a row within a column within a row. You can go on like that for a very long time. This section has two modest examples. The first example (Listing 6-6) has a row of captioned boxes.

LISTING 6-6: **(Does This Listing Have Three Captions?)**

```
// App0606.dart

import 'package:flutter/material.dart';

import 'App06Main.dart';

Widget buildColumn(BuildContext context) {
  return Column(
    mainAxisAlignment: MainAxisAlignment.center,
    crossAxisAlignment: CrossAxisAlignment.stretch,
    children: <Widget>[
      buildTitleText(),
      SizedBox(height: 20.0),
      _buildCaptionedRow(),
    ],
  );
}
```

```
Widget _buildCaptionedRow() {
  return Row(
    mainAxisAlignment: MainAxisAlignment.spaceBetween,
    children: <Widget>[
      _buildCaptionedItem(
        "Cat",
        caption: "Meow",
      ),
      _buildCaptionedItem(
        "Dog",
        caption: "Woof",
      ),
      _buildCaptionedItem(
        "Ape",
        caption: "Chatter",
      ),
    ],
  );
}

Column _buildCaptionedItem(String label, {String caption}) {
  return Column(
    children: <Widget>[
      buildRoundedBox(label),
      SizedBox(
        height: 5.0,
      ),
      Text(
        caption,
        textScaleFactor: 1.25,
      ),
    ],
  );
}
```

Figure 6-10 shows a run of the code from Listing 6-6.

FIGURE 6-10: Noisy animals for sale.

The next example, Listing 6-7, does something a bit different. In Listing 6-7, two boxes share the space where one box might be.

LISTING 6-7: **More Widget Nesting**

```dart
// App0607.dart

import 'package:flutter/material.dart';

import 'App06Main.dart';

Widget buildColumn(BuildContext context) {
  return Column(
    mainAxisAlignment: MainAxisAlignment.center,
    crossAxisAlignment: CrossAxisAlignment.stretch,
    children: <Widget>[
      buildTitleText(),
      SizedBox(height: 20.0),
      _buildColumnWithinRow(),
    ],
  );
}

Widget _buildColumnWithinRow() {
  return Row(
    mainAxisAlignment: MainAxisAlignment.spaceBetween,
    children: <Widget>[
      buildRoundedBox("Cat"),
      SizedBox(width: 20.0),
      buildRoundedBox("Dog"),
      SizedBox(width: 20.0),
      Column(
        children: <Widget>[
          buildRoundedBox(
            "Big ox",
            height: 36.0,
          ),
          SizedBox(height: 16.0),
          buildRoundedBox(
            "Small ox",
            height: 36.0,
          ),
        ],
      ),
    ],
  );
}
```

Figure 6-11 shows a run of the code from Listing 6-7.

Using the Expanded Widget

Start with the code in Listing 6-5, and add two more boxes to the row:

```
Widget _buildRowOfThree() {
  return Row(
    mainAxisAlignment: MainAxisAlignment.spaceBetween,
    children: <Widget>[
      buildRoundedBox("Cat"),
      buildRoundedBox("Dog"),
      buildRoundedBox("Ape"),
      buildRoundedBox("Ox"),
      buildRoundedBox("Gnu"),
    ],
  );
}
```

Yes, the method name is still _buildRowOfThree. If the name bothers you, you can either change the name or Google the *Hitchhiker's Guide to the Galaxy* trilogy.

When you run this modified code on a not-too-large phone in portrait mode, you see the ugly display in Figure 6-12. (If your phone is too large to see the ugliness, add more buildRoundedBox calls.)

The segment on the right side of Figure 6-12 (the stuff that looks like barricade tape) indicates *overflow*. To put it crudely, you've created a blivit. The row is trying to be wider than the phone's screen. Look near the top of Android Studio's Run tool window and you see the following message:

```
A RenderFlex overflowed by 67 pixels on the right.
```

What else is new?

When you line up too many boxes side-by-side, the screen becomes overcrowded. That's not surprising. But some layout situations aren't so obvious. You can stumble into an overflow problem when you least expect it.

What can you do when your app overflows? Here's an off-the-wall suggestion: Tell each of the boxes to expand. (You read that correctly: Tell them to expand!) Listing 6-8 has the code, and Figure 6-13 shows you the results.

LISTING 6-8: **Expanding Your Widgets**

```dart
// App0608.dart

import 'package:flutter/material.dart';

import 'App06Main.dart';

Widget buildColumn(BuildContext context) {
  return Column(
    mainAxisAlignment: MainAxisAlignment.center,
    crossAxisAlignment: CrossAxisAlignment.stretch,
    children: <Widget>[
      buildTitleText(),
      SizedBox(height: 20.0),
      _buildRowOfFive(),
    ],
  );
}

Widget _buildRowOfFive() {
  return Row(
    mainAxisAlignment: MainAxisAlignment.spaceBetween,
    children: <Widget>[
      _buildExpandedBox("Cat"),
      _buildExpandedBox("Dog"),
      _buildExpandedBox("Ape"),
      _buildExpandedBox("Ox"),
      _buildExpandedBox("Gnu"),
```

```
    ],
  );
}

Widget _buildExpandedBox(
  String label, {
  double height = 88.0,
}) {
  return Expanded(
    child: buildRoundedBox(
      label,
      height: height,
    ),
  );
}
```

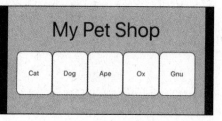

FIGURE 6-13:
A nice row of five.

I quote from the official Flutter documentation (`https://api.flutter.dev/flutter/widgets/Expanded-class.html`):

> A widget that expands a child of a Row, Column, or Flex so that the child fills the available space.

> Using an Expanded widget makes a child of a Row, Column, or Flex expand to fill the available space along the main axis (horizontally for a Row or vertically for a Column). If multiple children are expanded, the available space is divided among them according to the flex factor.

In spite of its name, the Expanded widget doesn't necessarily make its child bigger. Instead, the Expanded widget makes its child fill the available space along with any other widgets that are competing for that space. If that available space differs from the code's explicit height or width value, so be it. Listing 6-8 inherits the line

```
width: 88.0,
```

to describe the width of each rounded box. But, in Figure 6-13, none of the boxes is 88.0 dp wide. When I run the app on an iPhone 11 Pro Max, each box is only 74.8 dp wide.

Expanded versus unexpanded

The code in the previous section surrounds each of a row's boxes with the Expanded widget. In this section, Listing 6-9 shows you what happens when you use Expanded more sparingly.

LISTING 6-9: **Expanding One of Three Widgets**

```
// App0609.dart

import 'package:flutter/material.dart';

import 'App06Main.dart';

Widget buildColumn(BuildContext context) {
  return Column(
    mainAxisAlignment: MainAxisAlignment.center,
    crossAxisAlignment: CrossAxisAlignment.stretch,
    children: <Widget>[
      buildTitleText(),
      SizedBox(height: 20.0),
      _buildRowOfThree(),
    ],
  );
}

Widget _buildRowOfThree() {
  return Row(
    mainAxisAlignment: MainAxisAlignment.spaceBetween,
    children: <Widget>[
      buildRoundedBox(
        "Giraffe",
        height: 150.0,
      ),
      SizedBox(width: 10.0),
      buildRoundedBox(
        "Wombat",
        height: 36.0,
      ),
      SizedBox(width: 10.0),
      _buildExpandedBox(
        "Store Manager",
```

```
          height: 36.0,
        ),
      ],
    );
  }

Widget _buildExpandedBox(
  String label, {
  double height = 88.0,
}) {
  return Expanded(
    child: buildRoundedBox(
      label,
      height: height,
    ),
  );
}
```

The code in Listing 6-9 surrounds only one box — the Store Manager box — with an Expanded widget. Here's what happens:

>> The code gets width: 88.0 from the buildRoundedBox method in Listing 6-1, so the Giraffe and Wombat boxes are 88.0 dp wide each.

>> Two SizedBox widgets are 10.0 dp wide each.

So far, the total is 196.0 dp.

>> Because the Store Manager box sits inside an Expanded widget, the remaining screen width goes to the Store Manager box. (See Figure 6-14.)

My Pet Shop

Giraffe   Wombat   Store Manager

FIGURE 6-14:
The store
manager
takes up space.

Use of the Expanded widget affects a widget's size along its parent's main axis, but not along its parent's cross axis. So, in Figure 6-14, the Store Manager box grows from side to side (along the row's main axis) but doesn't grow from top to bottom (along the row's cross axis). In fact, only the numbers 150.0, 36.0, and

36.0 in the `_buildRowOfThree` method (see Listing 6-9) have any influence on the heights of the boxes.

With a bit of tweaking, the code in Listing 6-9 can provide more evidence that an Expanded widget isn't necessarily a large widget. Try these two experiments:

1. **Rerun the code from Listings 6-1 and 6-9. But, in the** `buildRoundedBox` **method declaration, change** `width: 88.0` **to** `width: 130.0`.

   On my iPhone 11 Pro Max simulator, the widths of the Giraffe and Wombat boxes are 130.0 dp each. But the width of the Expanded Store Manager box is only 94.0 dp. The Giraffe and Wombat boxes are quite large. So, when the Store Manager box fills the remaining available space, that space is only 94.0 dp wide. (See Figure 6-15.)

FIGURE 6-15:
Expanding to fit
into a small
space.

2. **In the** `buildRoundedBox` **method declaration, change** `width` **from its value in Step 1 (** `width: 130.0` **) to** `width: 180.0`.

   With the Giraffe and Wombat boxes and the `SizedBox` widgets taking up 380.0 dp, there's no room left on my iPhone 11 Pro Max simulator for the Store Manager box. Alas! I see the black-and-yellow stripe, indicating RenderBox overflow. (See Figure 6-16.) The Expanded widget isn't a miracle worker. It doesn't help solve every problem.

FIGURE 6-16:
More barricade
tape.

Expanded widget saves the day

Listings 6-10 and 6-11 illustrate a nasty situation that may arise when you mix rows and columns at various levels.

LISTING 6-10: **A Listing That's Doomed to Failure**

```
// App0610.dart -- BAD CODE

import 'package:flutter/material.dart';

import 'App06Main.dart';
import 'constraints_logger.dart';

Widget buildColumn(BuildContext context) {
  return Row(
    children: [
      _buildRowOfThree(),
    ],
  );
}

Widget _buildRowOfThree() {
  return ConstraintsLogger(
    comment: 'In _buildRowOfThree',
    child: Row(
      children: <Widget>[
        _buildExpandedBox("Cat"),
        _buildExpandedBox("Dog"),
        _buildExpandedBox("Ape"),
      ],
    ),
  );
}

Widget _buildExpandedBox(
  String label, {
  double height = 88.0,
}) {
  return Expanded(
    child: buildRoundedBox(
      label,
      height: height,
    ),
  );
}
```

LISTING 6-11: **An Aid For Debugging**

```
// constraints_logger.dart

import 'package:flutter/material.dart';

class ConstraintsLogger extends StatelessWidget {
  final String comment;
  final Widget child;

  ConstraintsLogger({
    this.comment = "",
    @required this.child,
  }) : assert(comment != null);

  Widget build(BuildContext context) {
    return LayoutBuilder(
      builder: (BuildContext context, BoxConstraints constraints) {
        print('$comment: $constraints to ${child.runtimeType}');
        return child;
      },
    );
  }
}
```

When you run the code in Listings 6-10 and 6-11, three things happen:

>> **Nothing appears on your device's screen except maybe a dull, grey background.**

>> **In Android Studio's Run tool window, you see the following error message:**

```
RenderFlex children have non-zero flex but incoming width
constraints are unbounded.
```

Flutter developers start groaning when they see this message.

Later on, in the Run tool window . . .

```
If a parent is to shrink-wrap its child, the child
cannot simultaneously expand to fit its parent.
```

>> **Also, in the Run tool window, you see a message like this one:**

```
I/flutter ( 5317): In _buildRowOfThree:
BoxConstraints(0.0<=w<=Infinity, 0.0<=h<=683.4) to Row
```

This I/flutter message tells you that the layout's inner row is being handed a width constraint that has something to do with Infinity. This informative 0.0<=w<=Infinity message comes to you courtesy of the code in Listing 6-11.

What do all these messages mean? In a Flutter app, your widgets form a tree. Figure 6-17 shows a tree of widgets as it's depicted in Android Studio's Flutter Inspector.

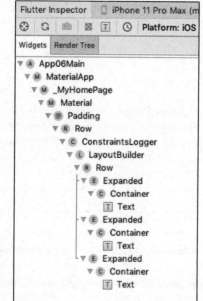

To display your widgets, Flutter travels in two directions:

>> **Along the tree from top to bottom**

During this travel, each widget tells its children what sizes they can be. In Flutter terminology, each parent widget *passes constraints* to its children.

For example, a Run tool window message says that, in Listing 6-11, the outer row passes the width constraint of 0.0<=w<=Infinity to the inner row. Because of the word Infinity, this constraint is called an *unbounded constraint*.

If you're looking for an example of a *bounded constraint*, look at the same Run tool window message. The outer row passes the height constraint of

`0.0<=h<=683.4` to the inner row. That constraint is bounded by the value 683.4 dp.

Eventually, Flutter reaches the bottom of your app's widget tree. At that point . . .

>> **Along the tree again — this time, from bottom to top**

During this travel, each child widget tells its parent exactly what size it wants to be. The parent collects this information from each of its children and uses the information to assign positions to the children.

Sometimes this works well, but in Listing 6-11, it fails miserably.

In Listing 6-11, because each animal box is inside an Expanded widget, the inner row doesn't know how large it should be. The inner row needs to be given a width in order to divide up the space among the animal boxes. But the outer row has given an unbounded constraint to the inner row. Instead of telling the inner row its width, the outer row is asking the inner row for its width. Nobody wants to take responsibility, so Flutter doesn't know what to do. (See Figure 6-18.)

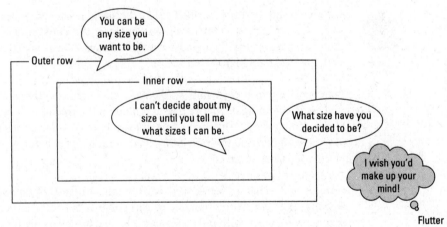

FIGURE 6-18:
My first graphic
novel.

How can you fix this unpleasant problem? Oddly enough, another Expanded widget comes to the rescue.

```
Widget _buildRowOfThree() {
  return Expanded(
    child: ConstraintsLogger(
      comment: 'In _buildRowOfThree',
      child: Row(
        children: <Widget>[
```

```
            _buildExpandedBox("Cat"),
            _buildExpandedBox("Dog"),
            _buildExpandedBox("Ape"),
          ],
        ),
      ),
    );
  }
```

This new Expanded widget passes bounded constraints down the widget tree, as you can see from this new message in the Run tool window:

```
I/flutter ( 5317): In _buildRowOfThree:
BoxConstraints(w=371.4, 0.0<=h<=683.4) to Row
```

The new Expanded widget tells the inner row that its width must be exactly 371.4 dp, so the confusion that's illustrated in Figure 6-18 goes away. Flutter knows how to display the app's widgets, and you see three nicely arranged animal boxes on your device's screen. Problem solved!

TECHNICAL STUFF

The constraint w=371.4 is called a *tight constraint* because it gives the row an exact size with no leeway whatsoever. In contrast, the constraint 0.0<=h<=683.4 is called a *loose constraint*. The loose constraint says, "Be as short as 0.0 dp high and as tall as 683.4 dp high. See if I care."

This business with constraints and sizes may seem overly complicated. But the process of scanning down the tree and then up the tree is an important part of the Flutter framework. The two-scan approach makes for efficient rebuilding of stateful widgets. And the rebuilding of stateful widgets is fundamental to the way Flutter apps are designed.

Some layout schemes work well with small numbers of components but start slowing down when the number of components becomes large. Flutter's layout scheme works well with only a few widgets and scales nicely for complicated layouts with large numbers of widgets.

REMEMBER

The ConstraintsLogger widget is for debugging purposes only. Before publishing an app, remove all uses of the ConstraintsLogger from your code.

Flexing some muscles

Using Flutter's Expanded widget, you can specify the relative sizes of the children inside a column or a row. Listing 6-12 has an example.

LISTING 6-12: **How to Specify Relative Sizes**

```
// App0612.dart

import 'package:flutter/material.dart';

import 'App06Main.dart';

Widget buildColumn(BuildContext context) {
  return Column(
    mainAxisAlignment: MainAxisAlignment.center,
    crossAxisAlignment: CrossAxisAlignment.stretch,
    children: <Widget>[
      buildTitleText(),
      SizedBox(height: 20.0),
      _buildRowOfThree(),
    ],
  );
}

Widget _buildRowOfThree() {
  return Row(
    mainAxisAlignment: MainAxisAlignment.spaceBetween,
    children: <Widget>[
      _buildExpandedBox(
        "Moose",
      ),
      _buildExpandedBox(
        "Squirrel",
        flex: 1,
      ),
      _buildExpandedBox(
        "Dinosaur",
        flex: 3,
      ),
    ],
  );
}

Widget _buildExpandedBox(
  String label, {
  double height = 88.0,
  int flex,
}) {
  return Expanded(
    flex: flex,
    child: buildRoundedBox(
```

```
      label,
      height: height,
    ),
  );
}
```

What will happen to our heroes, the Moose and the Squirrel, in Listing 6-12? To find out, see Figure 6-19.

FIGURE 6-19:
The squirrel is
small; the
dinosaur is big.

Notice the frequent use of the word `flex` in Listing 6-12. An `Expanded` widget can have a `flex` value, also known as a flex factor. A *flex factor* decides how much space the widget consumes relative to the other widgets in the row or column.

Listing 6-12 has three boxes:

>> Moose, with no flex value (the value `null`)

>> Squirrel, with flex value 1

>> Dinosaur, with flex value 3

Here's the lowdown on the resulting size of each box:

Because the Moose box has a `null` flex value, the Moose box has whatever width comes explicitly from the `_buildExpandedBox` method. The Moose box's width is 88.0. (Refer to Figure 6-19.)

Both the Squirrel and Dinosaur boxes have non-null, non-zero flex values. So those two boxes share the space that remains after the Moose box is in place. With flex values of Squirrel: 1, Dinosaur: 3, the Dinosaur box is three times the width of the Squirrel box. On my Pixel 2 emulator, the Squirrel box is 70.9 dp wide, and the Dinosaur box is 212.5 dp wide. That's the way flex values work.

TECHNICAL STUFF

In addition to the Expanded widget's flex property, Flutter has classes named Flex and Flexible. It's easy to confuse the three of them. Every Flex instance is either a Row instance or a Column instance. And every Expanded instance is an instance of the Flexible class. A Flexible instance can have a flex value, but a Flexible instance doesn't force its child to fill the available space. How about that!

How Big Is My Device?

The title of this section is a question, and the answer is "You don't know." I can run a Flutter app on a small iPhone 6, or in a web page on a 50-inch screen. You want your app to look good no matter what size my device happens to be. How can you do that? Listing 6-13 has an answer.

LISTING 6-13: Checking Device Orientation

```
// App0613.dart

import 'package:flutter/material.dart';

import 'App06Main.dart';

Widget buildColumn(context) {
  if (MediaQuery.of(context).orientation == Orientation.landscape) {
    return _buildOneLargeRow();
  } else {
    return _buildTwoSmallRows();
  }
}

Widget _buildOneLargeRow() {
  return Column(
    mainAxisAlignment: MainAxisAlignment.center,
    children: <Widget>[
      Row(
        mainAxisAlignment: MainAxisAlignment.spaceEvenly,
        children: <Widget>[
          buildRoundedBox("Aardvark"),
          buildRoundedBox("Baboon"),
          buildRoundedBox("Unicorn"),
          buildRoundedBox("Eel"),
          buildRoundedBox("Emu"),
          buildRoundedBox("Platypus"),
        ],
```

```
      ),
    ],
  );
}

Widget _buildTwoSmallRows() {
  return Column(
    mainAxisAlignment: MainAxisAlignment.center,
    children: [
      Row(
        mainAxisAlignment: MainAxisAlignment.spaceEvenly,
        children: [
          buildRoundedBox("Aardvark"),
          buildRoundedBox("Baboon"),
          buildRoundedBox("Unicorn"),
        ],
      ),
      SizedBox(
        height: 30.0,
      ),
      Row(
        mainAxisAlignment: MainAxisAlignment.spaceEvenly,
        children: [
          buildRoundedBox("Eel"),
          buildRoundedBox("Emu"),
          buildRoundedBox("Platypus"),
        ],
      ),
    ],
  );
}
```

Figures 6-20 and 6-21 show what happens when you run the code in Listing 6-13. When the device is in portrait mode, you see two rows, with three boxes on each row. But when the device is in landscape mode, you see only one row, with six boxes.

The difference comes about because of the if statement in Listing 6-13.

```
if (MediaQuery.of(context).orientation == Orientation.landscape) {
  return _buildOneLargeRow();
} else {
  return _buildTwoSmallRows();
}
```

FIGURE 6-20:
Listing 6-13 in
portrait mode.

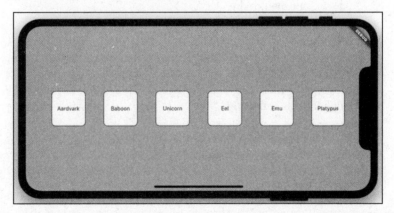

FIGURE 6-21:
Listing 6-13 in
landscape mode.

Yes, the Dart programming language has an `if` statement. It works the same way that `if` statements work in other programming languages.

```
if (a certain condition is true) {
  Do this stuff;
```

```
} otherwise {
  Do this other stuff;
}
```

In the name MediaQuery, the word Media refers to the screen that runs your app. When you call MediaQuery.of(context), you get back a treasure trove of information about that screen, such as

>> orientation: Whether the device is in portrait mode or landscape mode

>> size.height and size.width: The number of dp units from top to bottom and across the device's screen

>> size.longestSide and size.shortestSide: The larger and smaller screen size values, regardless of which is the height and which is the width

>> size.aspectRatio: The screen's width divided by its height

>> devicePixelRatio: The number of physical pixels for each dp unit

>> padding, viewInsets, and viewPadding: The parts of the display that aren't available to the Flutter app developer, such as the parts covered up by the phone's notch or (at times) the soft keyboard

>> alwaysUse24HourFormat: The device's time display setting

>> platformBrightness: The device's current brightness setting

>> ... and many more

For example, a Pixel C tablet with 2560-by-1800 dp is big enough to display a row of six animal boxes in either portrait or landscape mode. To prepare for your app to run on such a device, you may not want to rely on the device's orientation property. In that case, you can replace the condition in Listing 6-13 with something like the following:

```
if (MediaQuery.of(context).size.width >= 500.0) {
  return _buildOneLargeRow();
} else {
  return _buildTwoSmallRows();
}
```

Notice the word context in the code MediaQuery.of(context). In order to query media, Flutter has to know the context in which the app is running. That's why, starting with this chapter's very first listing, the _MyHomePage class's build method has a BuildContext context parameter. Listing 6-1 has this method call:

```
buildColumn(context)
```

And other listings have method declarations with this header:

```
Widget buildColumn(BuildContext context)
```

Listings 6-2 to 6-12 make no use of that context parameter. But what if, in Listing 6-1, I omit the method's context parameter, like so:

```
buildColumn()
```

Then everything is hunky-dory until Listing 6-13, which has no access to the context and is unable to call MediaQuery.of(context). What a pity!

When I created Listing 6-1, I added the context parameter because I anticipated the need for the context value in this chapter's last listing — Listing 6-13. Yes, I'm a very smart dude.

Well, that's not really true. When I started writing this chapter, I didn't anticipate the need for the context value. I didn't see the context issue coming until I started writing this last section. At that point, I went back and modified every single listing so that the context would be available to Listing 6-13. Oh, well! Everybody has to make course corrections. It's part of life, and it's certainly part of professional app development.

On to the next chapter. . . .

3 Details, Details

Chapter **7**

Interacting with the User

L ove is in the air! The sun is shining. The birds are singing. My heart is all a-Flutter. (Pun intended.)

Doris D. Developer wants to find a mate, and she has two important criteria. First, she wants someone who's 18 or older. Second, she's looking for someone who loves developing Flutter apps. What better way for Doris to achieve her goal than for her to write her own dating app?

This chapter covers Doris's outstanding work. To create the app, Doris uses several kinds of widgets: a text field, a slider, a dropdown button, and some others. A widget of this kind — one that the user sees and interacts with — is called a *control element*, or simply a *control*.

Doris's app also has some layout widgets, such as Center, Row, and Column, but these layout widgets aren't called *controls*. The user doesn't really see them, and certainly doesn't interact with them. This chapter's emphasis is on the controls, not on the layout widgets or the app's other assorted parts.

Doris's final dating app isn't full-featured by commercial standards, but the code for the app is a few hundred lines long. That's why Doris develops the app in small pieces — first one control, and then another, and another, and so on. Each piece is a small, free-standing practice app.

The first practice app deals with a simple question: Is the prospective mate at least 18 years old?

A Simple Switch

A Switch is a control that's in one of two possible states: on or off, yes or no, true or false, happy or sad, over 18 or not. Listing 7-1 has the code for the practice Switch app.

LISTING 7-1: **How Old Are You?**

```dart
import 'package:flutter/material.dart';

void main() => runApp(App0701());

class App0701 extends StatelessWidget {
  @override
  Widget build(BuildContext context) {
    return MaterialApp(
      home: MyHomePage(),
    );
  }
}

class MyHomePage extends StatefulWidget {
  @override
  _MyHomePageState createState() => _MyHomePageState();
}

const _youAre = 'You are';
const _compatible = 'compatible with\nDoris D. Developer.';

class _MyHomePageState extends State<MyHomePage> {
  bool _ageSwitchValue = false;
  String _messageToUser = "$_youAre NOT $_compatible";

  /// State

  @override
  Widget build(BuildContext context) {
    return Scaffold(
      appBar: AppBar(
        title: Text("Are you compatible with Doris?"),
      ),
      body: Padding(
        padding: const EdgeInsets.all(8.0),
        child: Column(
          children: <Widget>[
            _buildAgeSwitch(),
```

```
        _buildResultArea(),
      ],
    ),
  ),
);
}


/// Build

Widget _buildAgeSwitch() {
  return Row(
    children: <Widget>[
      Text("Are you 18 or older?"),
      Switch(
        value: _ageSwitchValue,
        onChanged: _updateAgeSwitch,
      ),
    ],
  );
}


Widget _buildResultArea() {
  return Text(_messageToUser, textAlign: TextAlign.center);
}


/// Actions

void _updateAgeSwitch(bool newValue) {
  setState(() {
    _ageSwitchValue = newValue;
    _messageToUser =
        _youAre + (_ageSwitchValue ? " " : " NOT ") + _compatible;
  });
}
}
```

Figures 7-1 and 7-2 show the app in its two possible states.

This chapter's listings are practice apps. They're bite-size samples of Doris's big, beautiful dating app. But even "bite-size" programs can be long and complicated. To keep this chapter's listings short, I reuse code from one listing to another. I bend a few rules and ignore some good programming practices to make the listings compatible with one another. But, don't worry. Each listing works correctly, and each listing illustrates useful Flutter development concepts. You can find the entire dating app in Appendix A and in the stuff that you download from this book's website (www.allmycode.com/Flutter).

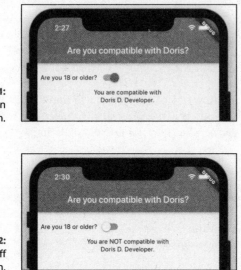

The code in Listing 7-1 isn't much different from the code in Chapter 5. In Chapter 5, the floating action button has an onPressed parameter. In Listing 7-1, the Switch widget has something similar. Listing 7-1 has an onChanged parameter. The onChanged parameter's value is a function; namely, the _updateAgeSwitch function. When the user flips the switch, that flip triggers the switch's onChanged event, causing the Flutter framework to call the _updateAgeSwitch function.

Unlike the event handling functions in Chapter 5, the _updateAgeSwitch function in Listing 7-1 isn't a VoidCallback. A VoidCallback function takes no parameters, but the _updateAgeSwitch function has a parameter. The parameter's name is newValue:

```
void _updateAgeSwitch(bool newValue)
```

When the Flutter framework calls _updateAgeSwitch, the framework passes the Switch widget's new position (off or on) to the newValue parameter. Because the type of newValue is bool, newValue is either false or true. It's false when the switch is off and true when the switch is on.

If _updateAgeSwitch isn't a VoidCallback, what is it? (That was a rhetorical question, so I answer it for you. . . .) The _updateAgeSwitch function is of type ValueChanged<bool>. A ValueChanged function takes one parameter and returns void. The function's parameter can be of any type, but a ValueChanged<bool> function's parameter must be of type bool. In the same way, a ValueChanged<double> function's parameter must be of type double. And so on.

Make no mistake about it: Even though the term ValueChanged<bool> doesn't have the word Callback in it, the _updateAgeSwitch function is a callback. When the user flips the Switch widget, the Flutter framework calls your code back. Yes, the _updateAgeSwitch function is a callback. It's just not a VoidCallback.

With many controls, nothing much happens if you don't change the control's value and call setState. For a few laughs, I tried commenting out the setState call in the body of the _updateAgeSwitch function in Listing 7-1:

```
void _updateAgeSwitch(bool newValue) {
  // setState(() {
  _ageSwitchValue = newValue;
  _messageToUser = _youAre + (_ageSwitchValue ? " " : " NOT ") + _compatible;
  // });
}
```

Then I uncommented the setState call and commented out the assignment statements:

```
void _updateAgeSwitch(bool newValue) {
  setState(() {
//      _ageSwitchValue = newValue;
//      _messageToUser =
//          _youAre + (_ageSwitchValue ? " " : " NOT ") + _compatible;
  });
}
```

In both cases, I restarted the program and then tapped on the switch. Not only did the _messageToUser refuse to change, but the switch didn't even budge. That settles it! The look of the switch is completely dependent on the _ageSwitchValue variable and the call to setState. If you don't assign anything to _ageSwitch Value or you don't call setState, the switch is completely unresponsive.

Dart's const keyword

Here's my cardinal rule: Once I've made a decision, I never change my mind. The only exception to this rule is when I change my mind about the cardinal rule.

In app development, the issue of change is very important. The term *variable* comes from the word *vary*, which means "change." But some things shouldn't change. In Listing 7-1, I refer to the strings 'You are' and 'compatible with\nDoris D. Developer' more than once, so I create handy names _youAre and _compatiblc for these strings. That way, I don't have to type things like 'compatible with\nDoris D. Developer' more than once. I don't risk typing the phrase correctly one time and incorrectly another time.

But what if the value of _youAre is allowed to change throughout the run of the program? A developer who's working with my code might mistakenly write

```
_youAre = 'sweet';
```

I don't want that to happen. I want _youAre to stand for 'You are' throughout the run of the program. Android Studio should flag the assignment _youAre = 'sweet' as an error. That's why, in Listing 7-1, I declare _youAre with the word const. Dart's const keyword is short for *constant*. As a constant, the value of _youAre cannot change. The same holds true for the declaration of _compatible in Listing 7-1. The use of Dart's const keyword is a safety measure, and it's a darn good one!

TECHNICAL
STUFF

In case you're wondering, \n in 'compatible with\nDoris D. Developer' tells Dart to go to a new line of text. That way, Doris D. Developer appears on a line of its own. (See Figures 7-1 and 7-2.) The character combination \n is called an *escape sequence*.

TIP

Referring to the code in Listing 7-1, an experienced developer might say, "the _youAre constant" or "the _youAre variable." The former is more accurate, but the latter is acceptable.

TECHNICAL
STUFF

Dart has two keywords to indicate that certain things shouldn't change: const and final. The const keyword says, "Don't change this value at any time during a run of the app." The final keyword says, "Don't change this value unless you encounter this declaration again." The difference between const and final has many subtle consequences, so I don't open that can of worms in this chapter. Instead, simply remember that programs with const may run a bit faster than programs with final. You can put any old const declaration at the top level of your code or inside a function declaration. But, for a const at the start of a class, the story is different. The following code is illegal:

```
// Don't do this:
class _MyHomePageState extends State<MyHomePage> {
  const _youAre = 'You are';
```

But this code is just fine:

Prod: Note the bold code.-BB

```
// Do this instead:
class _MyHomePageState extends State<MyHomePage> {
  static const _youAre = 'You are';
```

**CROSS
REFERENCE**

For the real scoop on Dart's `static` keyword, see the "Callout 4" section, later in this chapter.

Compatible or NOT?

For some users, the Dating app should say, "You are compatible with Doris D. Developer." For other users, the app should add *NOT* to its message. That's why Listing 7-1 contains the following code:

```
_messageToUser =
    _youAre + (_ageSwitchValue ? " " : " NOT ") + _compatible;
```

The expression `_ageSwitchValue ? " " : " NOT "` is a *conditional expression*, and the combination of `?` and `:` in that expression is Dart's *conditional operator*. Figure 7-3 shows you how Dart evaluates a conditional expression.

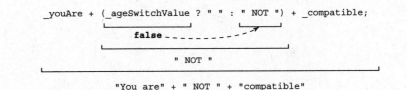

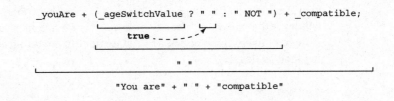

FIGURE 7-3:
Evaluating a
conditional
expression.

A conditional expression looks like this:

```
condition ? expression1 : expression2
```

When the `condition` is true, the value of the whole expression is whatever you find in the `expression1` part. But, when the `condition` is false, the value of the whole expression is whatever you find in the `expression2` part.

In addition to its conditional expressions, Dart has `if` statements. A conditional expression is like an `if` statement but, unlike an `if` statement, a conditional expression has a value. That value can be assigned to a variable.

To illustrate the point, I give you an `if` statement whose effect is the same as the conditional expression in Listing 7-1:

```
if (_ageSwitchValue) {
  _messageToUser = _youAre + " " + _compatible;
} else {
  _messageToUser = _youAre + " NOT " + _compatible;
}
```

Translated into plain English, this `if` statement says:

```
If the bool variable _ageSwitchValue has the value true,
  _messageToUser = _youAre + " " + _compatible;
otherwise
  _messageToUser = _youAre + " NOT " + _compatible;
```

In some situations, choosing between an `if` statement and a conditional expression is a matter of taste. But in Listing 7-1, the conditional expression is a clear winner. After all, an `if` statement doesn't have a value. You can't assign an `if` statement to anything or add an `if` statement to anything. So, code of the following kind is illegal:

```
// THIS CODE IS INVALID.
_messageToUser =
  _youAre +

  if (_ageSwitchValue) {
    " ";
  } else {
    " NOT ";
  } +

_compatible;
```

TECHNICAL STUFF

Another name for Dart's conditional operator is the *ternary operator*. The word *ternary* means "three," and the operator has three parts: one before the question mark, a second between the question mark and the colon, and a third after the colon.

Wait For It!

Today's users are impatient. They want instant feedback. How do I know this? A bunch of actors convinced me. Here's the story:

A long time ago, in a theater far, far from Broadway, I saw a musical comedy in the company of nine other people. Three of them were my friends, two of them were watching from third-row seats, and the other four were the play's performers. I remember this event for two reasons. First, it was the beginning of my lifelong philosophy about making performers feel good. The play's jokes weren't funny, but I laughed out loud at every one of them. The singing was out of tune, but I clapped vigorously after each song. Eventually, we were all having a good time, and the actors didn't regret playing to a six-person audience.

The other memorable part of this event was the play's signature song. It was kind of silly, but it stuck in my mind for years and years. To this day, my wife and I chuckle whenever we howl out the song's first few measures. The title of this tune was "Immediate Gratification." It was a mockery of modern culture, in which every need is urgent and every desire must be fulfilled.

In following this line of thought, I present a humble widget known as the Raised Button. A button isn't much. You press it, and something happens. You press it again, and something may or may not happen. Buttons used to be the go-to control for web developers and app developers. But these days, buttons are passé. When a user flips a switch, the app responds immediately. There's no waiting around to find a button to press. The old light-grey rectangle with the word *Submit* on it has taken a back seat.

In celebration of the good old days, this section's example shuns the quick response of the app in Listing 7-1. When the user flicks a switch, the switch simply moves. The app doesn't say, "You're compatible" or "You're not compatible" until the user presses a button. Come sit on the porch and relax while this app runs! The code is in Listing 7-2.

LISTING 7-2: **Responding to a Button Press**

```
// Copy the code up to and including the _buildAgeSwitch
// method from Listing 7-1 here.

  Widget _buildResultArea() {
    return Row(
      children: <Widget>[
        RaisedButton(
          child: Text("Submit"),
          onPressed: _updateResults,
        ),
        SizedBox(
          width: 15.0,
        ),
        Text(_messageToUser, textAlign: TextAlign.center),
```

(continued)

LISTING 7-2: *(continued)*

```
      ],
    );
  }

  /// Actions

  void _updateAgeSwitch(bool newValue) {
    setState(() {
      _ageSwitchValue = newValue;
    });
  }

  void _updateResults() {
    setState(() {
      _messageToUser = 'You are' +
          (_ageSwitchValue ? " " : " NOT ") +
          'compatible with \nDoris D. Developer.';
    });
  }
}
```

Figure 7-4 shows a snapshot from a run of the code in Listing 7-2.

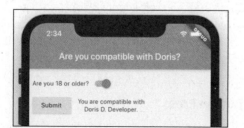

FIGURE 7-4:
Good news!

When it's combined with some code from Listing 7-1, the app in Listing 7-2 has both onPressed and onChanged event handlers. In particular:

>> **The function** _updateAgeSwitch **handles** onChanged **events for the switch.**

When the user taps the switch, the appearance of the switch changes from off to on or from on to off.

>> **The function** _updateResults **handles** onPressed **events for the button.**

When the user presses the button, the app's message catches up with the switch's status. If the switch is on, the message becomes, "You are compatible." If the switch is off, the message becomes "You are NOT compatible."

Between the moment when the user flicks the switch and the time when the user presses the button, the message on the screen might be inconsistent with the switch's state. In an online form with several questions, that's not a problem. The user doesn't expect to see a result until after the concluding button press. But in this chapter's practice apps, each with only one question for the user, the lack of coordination between the user's answer and the message that's displayed is problematic. These practice apps don't win any user experience awards.

Fortunately, Doris doesn't publish her practice apps. Instead, she publishes an app that combines all the controls from her practice apps and more.

ON THE WEB

You can download and run Doris's full-fledged dating app. It's the file named `App_endix.dart` in the download from this book's website. If you need immediate gratification and downloading code isn't fast for you, just flip this book's pages until you reach Appendix A.

So, what's next? I know! How about a slider?

How Much Do You Love Flutter?

Doris the Developer wants to meet someone who loves to create Flutter apps. Her homemade dating app includes a slider with values from 1 to 10. Scores of 8 and above are acceptable. Anyone with a response of 7 or below can take a hike.

Listing 7-3 has the highlights of Doris's practice slider app.

CROSS REFERENCE

To see the rest of Doris's slider practice app, look for the App0703 project in the download from this book's website. (Quick! Visit www.allmycode.com/Flutter right away!)

LISTING 7-3: **For the Love of Flutter**

```
// This is not a complete program. (No way!)

class _MyHomePageState extends State<MyHomePage> {
  double _loveFlutterSliderValue = 1.0;

  Widget _buildLoveFlutterSlider() {
    return // ...
        Text("On a scale of 1 to 10, "
            "how much do you love developing Flutter apps?"),
```

(continued)

LISTING 7-3:   *(continued)*

```
        Slider(
          min: 1.0,
          max: 10.0,
          divisions: 9,
          value: _loveFlutterSliderValue,
          onChanged: _updateLoveFlutterSlider,
          label: '${_loveFlutterSliderValue.toInt()}',
        ),

    }

    void _updateLoveFlutterSlider(double newValue) {
      setState(() {
        _loveFlutterSliderValue = newValue;
      });
    }

    void _updateResults() {
      setState(() {
        _messageToUser = _youAre +
            (_loveFlutterSliderValue >= 8 ? " " : " NOT ") +
            _compatible;
      });
    }
}
```

Figure 7-5 shows a run of the slider app with the slider set all the way to 10. (How else do you expect me to set the "love Flutter" slider?)

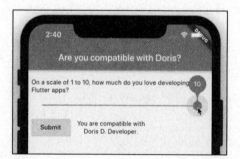

FIGURE 7-5:
Love at first byte.

The `Slider` constructor call in Listing 7-3 has these six parameters:

>> `min`: The slider's smallest value.

The little gizmo that moves from left to right along a slider is called a *thumb*. The position of the thumb determines the slider's *value*. So `min` is the value of the slider when the slider's thumb is at the leftmost point. The `min` parameter has type `double`.

>> `max`: The slider's largest value.

This is the value of the slider (again, a `double`) when the thumb is at the rightmost point.

A slider's values may increase going from left to right or from right to left. Before displaying a slider, Flutter checks a `textDirection` property. If the value is `TextDirection.ltr`, the slider's minimum value is on the left. But if the `textDirection` property's value is `TextDirection.rtl`, the slider's minimum value is on the right. Apps written for speakers of Arabic, Farsi, Hebrew, Pashto, and Urdu use `TextDirection.rtl`. Other apps use `TextDirection.ltr`. In case you're wondering, Flutter doesn't support boustrophedon writing — an ancient style in which alternate lines flow from left to right and then from right to left.

>> `divisions`: The number of spaces between points where the thumb can be placed. (See Figure 7-6.)

Values (points where the thumb can stop): →   1   2   3   4   5   6   7   8   9   10

Divisions: →   1   2   3   4   5   6   7   8   9

The slider in Listing 7-3 can be placed at values 1.0, 2.0, 3.0, and so on, up to 10.0.

If you omit the `divisions` parameter, or if you set that parameter to `null`, the thumb can be placed anywhere along the slider. For example, with the following constructor, the slider's value can be 0.0, 0.20571428571428554, 0.917142857142857, 1.0, or almost any other number between 0 and 1.

```
Slider(
  min: 0.0,
  max: 1.0,
  value: _loveFlutterSliderValue,
  onChanged: _updateLoveFlutterSlider,
)
```

>> value: A number in the range from min to max.

This parameter determines the thumb's position.

>> onChanged: The event handling function for changes to the slider.

When the user moves the slider's thumb, the Flutter framework calls this function.

>> label: The widget that's displayed on the slider's value indicator.

As the user moves the thumb, an additional shape appears. That shape is the slider's *value indicator*. In Figure 7-5, the bubble with the number 10 on it is the slider's value indicator.

Despite its name, the value indicator doesn't necessarily display a Text widget showing the slider's value. In fact, the value indicator can display anything you want it to display. (Well, almost anything.)

Luckily for us, the widget on the slider in Listing 7-3 displays _loveFlutter SliderValue — the slider's very own value. But remember: If you don't want numbers like 0.20571428571428554 to appear in the value indicator, you have to convert the slider's double values into int values. That's why, in Listing 7-3, the widget on the slider's value indicator displays _loveFlutter SliderValue.toInt( ), not plain old _loveFlutterSliderValue.

TIP

If you don't specify a label parameter, or if you specify a label but make it null, the value indicator never appears.

Dealing with Text Fields

In this section, I introduce Doris's friend Irving. Unlike Doris, Irving wants a companion with lots of money. To this end, Irving asks Doris to create a variation on her dating app. Irving's custom-made app has two text fields — one for a user's name and another for the user's income. If the user's income is $100,000 or more, the app reports "compatible." Otherwise, the app reports "incompatible." Figure 7-7 has an illustrated version of the app's _MyHomePageState class. To see the rest of Irving's app, look for the App0704 project in the download from this book's website.

① Reserve the names _nameFieldController and _incomeFieldController to refer to instances of the TextEditingController class.

```
class _MyHomePageState extends State<MyHomePage> {
  TextEditingController _nameFieldController, _incomeFieldController;
  String _messageToUser;

  @override
  void initState() {
    super.initState();
    _nameFieldController = TextEditingController();
    _incomeFieldController = TextEditingController();
    _messageToUser = "";
  }
```

② When you initialize this _MyHomePageState, create two TextEditingController objects.

```
// Later in the code ...

Widget _buildNameTextField() {
  return Container(
    padding: EdgeInsets.symmetric(vertical: 4.0, horizontal: 8.0),
    child: TextField(
      controller: _nameFieldController,
      decoration: _buildDecoration("Your name:"),
    ),
  );
}
```

③ Associate _nameFieldController with the name text field and _incomeFieldController with the income text field.

```
Widget _buildIncomeTextField() {
  return Container(
    padding: EdgeInsets.symmetric(vertical: 4.0, horizontal: 8.0),
    child: TextField(
      controller: _incomeFieldController,
      decoration: _buildDecoration("Your income:"),
      keyboardType: TextInputType.number,
    ),
  );
}

// Later in the code ...

void _updateResults() {
  bool _richUser = int.parse(_incomeFieldController.text) >= 1000000;
  setState(() {
    _messageToUser = _nameFieldController.text +
      "\n" +
      _youAre +
      (_richUser ? " " : " NOT ") +
      _compatible;
  });
}
```

④ The expressions _nameFieldController.text and _incomeFieldController.text stand for the characters in the two text fields.

```
  @override
  void dispose() {
    _nameFieldController.dispose();
    _incomeFieldController.dispose();
    super.dispose();
  }
}
```

⑤ When the Flutter framework disposes of the _MyHomePageState instance, call each controller's own dispose method.

FIGURE 7-7:
(Also known as Listing 7-4.) How much do you earn?

TECHNICAL
STUFF

To keep the size of Figure 7-7 manageable, I omitted the declaration of _buildDecoration. In case you're wondering, here's that method's code:

```
InputDecoration _buildDecoration(String label) {
  return InputDecoration(
    labelText: label,
    border: OutlineInputBorder(
```

CHAPTER 7 **Interacting with the User**   221

```
        borderRadius: BorderRadius.all(Radius.circular(10.0)),
      ),
    );
  }
```

Figure 7-8 shows Pat's pathetic attempt to be deemed compatible with Irving. With an income of $61,937, Pat doesn't have a chance. (In 2018, the median income for households in the United States was $61,937. Irving's sights are set too high.)

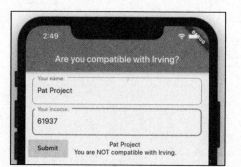

FIGURE 7-8:
Bad news for Pat.

Text fields have the same kinds of event handlers that switches and sliders have. In particular, a TextField constructor can have an onChanged event handler — a function that looks like this:

```
void _updateStuff(String newValue) {
  // When the user types a character, do something with
  // the characters inside the text field (the newValue).
}
```

But what about the press of a button? Is there a nice way to find out what's in a text field when the field's characters aren't changing? Yes, there is. It's the TextEditingController — a stand-out feature in Figure 7-7.

In fact, Figure 7-7 has two TextEditingController objects — one for the Your Name field and another for the Your Income field. The next several paragraphs add details to the numbered callouts in Figure 7-7.

Callouts 1 and 2

In a Flutter program, constructor calls rule the roost. You get a `Text` widget with a constructor call like `Text("Hello")`. You get a `Column` and two `Text` widgets with code like `Column(children: [Text('a'), Text('b')])`.

When you issue a constructor call, the call itself stands for an object. For example, the call `Text("Hello")` stands for a particular `Text` widget — an instance of the `Text` class. You can assign the call to a variable and use that variable elsewhere in your code:

```
@override
Widget build(BuildContext context) {
  Text myTextInstance = Text("I'm reusable");
  return Scaffold(
    appBar: AppBar(
      title: myTextInstance,
    ),
    body: Column(
      children: <Widget>[
        myTextInstance,
      ],
    ),
  );
}
```

In many cases, you can separate the variable declaration from the call:

```
Text myTextInstance;

// More code here, and elsewhere ...

myTextInstance = Text("I'm reusable");
```

In Figure 7-7, the declaration of the two controller variables (_nameField Controller and _incomeFieldController) is separate from the corresponding TextEditingController constructor calls. I do this in order to introduce Flutter's initState and dispose methods.

A State object is like anything else in the world — it comes into being and, eventually, it goes away. Flutter calls initState when a State instance comes into being, and calls dispose when the State instance goes away.

NULL POUR LES NULS

You can declare a variable name without assigning anything to that variable. If you do, the variable's starting value is null, which means "absolutely nothing." In many cases, that's exactly what you want to do.

But you have to be careful. An unwanted null value can be dangerous. For example, the following code crashes like a reckless car on the New Jersey Turnpike:

```
main() {
  int quantity;
  print(quantity.isEven);  // null.isEven -- You can't do this
}
```

On the other hand, if you assign something to the quantity variable, the code runs without a hitch:

```
main() {
  int quantity;
  quantity = 22;
  print(quantity.isEven);  // Outputs the word "true" (without quotes)
}
```

Here's a mistake that I sometimes make: I create a variable declaration that doesn't assign a value to its variable. Then I forget to assign a value to that variable elsewhere in the code. Oops! My code crashes. My advice is, try not to make that mistake.

It may not be obvious, but the code in Figure 7-7 refers to two different initState methods. The declaration that begins with void initState() describes a method that belongs to the _MyHomePageState class. But the _MyHomePageState class extends Flutter's own State class, and that State class has its own initState declaration. (See Figure 7-9.)

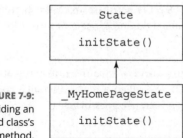

FIGURE 7-9:
Overriding an extended class's initState method.

When you have two methods named initState, how do you distinguish one from another? Well, what if you meet a woman named Mary, whose child is also named Mary? Chances are, the child doesn't call her mother "Mary." Instead, the child calls her mother "Mom" or something like that. For her mother's birthday, she buys a souvenir mug displaying the words *Super Mom*, and her mother smiles politely on receiving another useless gift.

The same kind of thing happens when two classes — a parent and its child — have methods named initState. The child class (_MyHomePageState) has to call the initState method belonging to its parent class (Flutter's State class). To do so, the child class calls super.initState(). Unlike the Mary situation, the use of the keyword super isn't meant to be flattering. It's simply a reference to the initState method that's defined in the parent class. (I can't resist: The keyword super may not be flattering, but it's certainly Fluttering.)

To stretch the mother/daughter metaphor a bit further, imagine that Super Mom Mary is a real estate agent. In that case, the child can't buy a house without first consulting her mother. The child's decideWhichHouse method must include a call to the mother's decideWhichHouse method, like so:

```
// The child's method declaration:
@override
void decideWhichHouse() {
  super.decideWhichHouse();
  // Etc.
}
```

That may be the situation when your code overrides Flutter's initState method. In some versions of Flutter, if you don't call super.initState(), your code won't run.

Callout 3

Each TextField constructor can have its own controller parameter. A text field's controller mediates the flow of information between the text field and other parts of the app. (For details, jump to the later section "Callout 4.")

Elsewhere in the TextField constructor call, the TextInputType.number parameter in the income text field's constructor tells a device to display a soft keyboard with only digits on the keys. Alternatives include TextInputType.phone, TextInputType.emailAdress, TextInputType.datetime, and others. For an authoritative list of TextInputType choices, visit https://api.flutter.dev/flutter/services/TextInputType-class.html.

This tip applies while you develop and test your app. The Android emulator and iPhone simulator have options to suppress the appearance of the soft keyboard, allowing input with only your development computer's keyboard. If that option is turned on, you don't see the effect of the TextInputType.number parameter. If you type a letter on your computer keyboard, that letter appears in your app's text field.

If you plan to run your app on a real, physical phone, you should test the app with the virtual device's soft keyboard enabled. When you do, you might see some troublesome effects that you weren't expecting. For example, when you move from a text field to another kind of control, the soft keyboard doesn't go away. To make the soft keyboard go away automatically, enclose the scaffold in a gesture detector. Here's how you do it:

```
Widget build(BuildContext context) {
  return GestureDetector(
    onTap: () {
      final currentFocus = FocusScope.of(context);
      if (!currentFocus.hasPrimaryFocus) {
        currentFocus.unfocus();
      }
    },
    child: Scaffold(
    // ... Etc.
```

For more chitchat about the GestureDetector, see Chapter 9.

Callout 4

In Figure 7-7, the expression _nameFieldController.text stands for the characters that appear in the Name text field, and _incomeFieldController.text stands for the characters in the Income text field. If the code included the statement

```
_nameFieldController.text = "May I. Havanother";
```

execution of that statement would change whatever was already in the Name text field to *May I. Havanother.*

In Figure 7-7, the expression _nameFieldController.text adds the user's name to the outgoing message. The expression _incomeFieldController.text stands for whatever characters the user has entered in the app's Income field, but those characters come with a slight catch. The stuff in a text field is always a String value, never a numeric value. In Figure 7-8, Pat enters 61937 in the Income text field, so the value of _incomeFieldController.text is "61937" (the String), not 61937 (the number).

Luckily, Dart's int class has a parse method. If the value of _incomeField Controller.text is "61937" (the String), the value of int.parse(_income FieldController.text) is 61937 (the int number value). In Figure 7-7, the code

```
int.parse(_incomeFieldController.text) >= 1000000
```

compares a number like 61937 to Irving's high-demand number of 1000000. The result of the comparison is either true or false, so the value of _richUser becomes either true or false.

WHAT DOES A DARN DOT DO?

In object-oriented programming, an object can have certain things called *properties*. Using dot notation, you can refer to each of those properties.

Here are a few examples:

- **Every** String **instance has** length **and** isEmpty **properties.**

  The value of "Dart".length is 4, and the value of "".isEmpty is true.

- **Every** int **value has** isEven, isNegative, **and** bitLength **properties.**

  The value of 44.isEven is true, and the value of 99.isNegative is false. The value of 99.bitLength is 7 because the binary representation of 99 is 1100011, which has 7 bits.

- **Every** TextEditingController **instance has a** text **property.**

  In Figure 7-7, the value of _nameFieldController.text is whatever string of characters appears in the Name text field.

You can apply dot notation to expressions of all kinds. For example, the value of (29 + 10).isEven is false. With phrase = "I like Dart", the value of phrase.length is 11.

(continued)

(continued)

Properties are examples of things called *members*. A class's members also include the class's variables and methods. Consider the following:

- **Every** String **instance has methods named** toUpperCase, endsWith, split, trim, **and many others.**

  The value of "Attention!".toUpperCase() is "ATTENTION!".

  The value of " Holy moly! ".trim() is "Holy moly!".

- **Every** int **value has methods named** abs, toRadixString, **and several others.**

  The value of (-182).abs() is 182 because 182 is the absolute value of -182. The value of 99.toRadixString(2) is 1100011 because the binary (base 2) representation of 99 is 1100011.

There's nothing mysterious about the members of a class. Here's a class named Account and a main function that calls the Account class's constructor:

```
class Account {
  // Two member variables:
  String customerName;
  int balance;

  // A member method:
  void deposit({int amount}) {
    balance += amount;
  }
}

void main() {
  // A call to the Account class's constructor:
  Account myAccount = Account();

  // References to the Account class's members:
  myAccount.customerName = "Barry Burd";
  myAccount.balance = 100;
  myAccount.deposit(amount: 20);
  print(myAccount.customerName);
  print(myAccount.balance);
}

/*
 * Output:
 * Barry Burd
 * 120
 */
```

The classes in this book's Flutter listings have members too. For example, the class in Figure 7-7 has several members, including _nameFieldController, _incomeField Controller, _messageToUser, initState, and build.

Some classes have things called *static members*. A static member belongs to an entire class, not to any of the class's instances. For example, the int class has a static method named parse. Because the parse method is static, you put the name of the class (the word int) before the dot. You *don't* put any particular int value before the dot. Here are some examples:

- **The value of** int.parse("1951") **is the number** 1951.

- **Expressions such as** 1951.parse("1951"), 1951.parse() **and** 1951.parse **are invalid.**

  None of these works because, in each case, the value before the dot isn't the class name int. Instead, the value before the dot is an object — an instance of the int class.

- **Putting any expression with an** int **value before** .parse **is invalid.**

  For example, the following code breaks your program:

  ```
  int numberOfClowns;
  int otherNumber = numberOfClowns.parse("2020");
  ```

Creating a static member is no big deal. Simply add the word static to your member declaration, like so:

```
class Automobile {
  static int numberOfWheels = 4;
}

void main() {
  Automobile jalopy = Automobile();
  // print(jalopy.numberOfWheels);  This is incorrect.
  print(Automobile.numberOfWheels);
}

/*
 * Output:
 * 4
 */
```

TIP

Figure 7-7 calls Dart's `int.parse` method — a handy method indeed! But Dart has an even better method. It's called `int.tryParse`. It's a lot like `int.parse`, but it's safer to use. When you call `int.tryParse('This is not a number')`, the app doesn't blow up in your face.

Callout 5

Much of the fuss in earlier paragraphs about the `initState` method applies equally to Flutter's `dispose` method. Before a `State` class gets the heave-ho, the Flutter framework calls the code's `dispose` method. In Figure 7-7, the `dispose` method does these three things:

>> **It calls the** `dispose` **method belonging to the** `_nameFieldController`.

The `dispose` method for `_nameFieldController` trashes that controller, freeing up any resources that the controller happens to be hogging.

>> **It calls the** `dispose` **method belonging to the** `_incomeFieldController`.

Goodbye, `_incomeFieldController`. Glad to see that your resources are being freed up.

>> **It calls the** `State` **class's** `dispose` **method.**

The `State` class's `dispose` method, built solidly into the Flutter framework, cleans up any other stuff having to do with `_MyHomePageState`. As it is with `initState`, your own code's `dispose` method must call `super.dispose()`.

Creating Radio Buttons

Every dating app has a question about the user's gender. For this question, Doris decides on a group of radio buttons. Listing 7-5 has much of Doris's radio button code.

ON THE WEB

For the rest of Doris's practice app with radio buttons, see App0705 in the files that you download from this book's website:

www.allmycode.com/Flutter

LISTING 7-5: **How Do You Identify?**

```dart
// This is not a complete program.
// Some trees have been saved.
// The trees are happy about that.

enum Gender { Female, Male, Other }

String shorten(Gender gender) => gender.toString().replaceAll("Gender.", "");

class _MyHomePageState extends State<MyHomePage> {
  String _messageToUser = "";
  Gender _genderRadioValue;

// And later ...

  Widget _buildGenderRadio() {
    return Row(
      children: <Widget>[
        Text(shorten(Gender.Female)),
        Radio(
          value: Gender.Female,
          groupValue: _genderRadioValue,
          onChanged: _updateGenderRadio,
        ),
        SizedBox(width: 25.0),
        Text(shorten(Gender.Male)),
        Radio(
          value: Gender.Male,
          groupValue: _genderRadioValue,
          onChanged: _updateGenderRadio,
        ),
        SizedBox(width: 25.0),
        Text(shorten(Gender.Other)),
        Radio(
          value: Gender.Other,
          groupValue: _genderRadioValue,
          onChanged: _updateGenderRadio,
        ),
      ],
    );
  }

  Widget _buildResultArea() {
    return Row(
```

(continued)

LISTING 7-5: *(continued)*

```
        children: <Widget>[
          RaisedButton(
            child: Text("Submit"),
            onPressed: _genderRadioValue != null ? _updateResults : null,
          ),
          SizedBox(
            width: 15.0,
          ),
          Text(
            _messageToUser,
            textAlign: TextAlign.center,
          ),
        ],
      );
    }


    /// Actions

    void _updateGenderRadio(Gender newValue) {
      setState(() {
        _genderRadioValue = newValue;
      });
    }


    void _updateResults() {
      setState(() {
        _messageToUser =
            "You selected ${shorten(_genderRadioValue)}.";
      });
    }
}
```

Figures 7-10 and 7-11 show snapshots from a run of the code in Listing 7-5.

FIGURE 7-10:
Before selecting a
radio button.

FIGURE 7-11:
After selecting a
radio button and
pressing Submit.

Creating an enum

Chapter 3 introduces Flutter's built-in `Brightness` enum with its values `Brightness.light` and `Brightness.dark`. That's nice, but why let the creators of Flutter have all the fun? You can define your own enum by doing what you see in Listing 7-5.

```
enum Gender { Female, Male, Other }
```

With this declaration, your code has three new values; namely, `Gender.Female`, `Gender.Male`, and `Gender.Other`. You can use these values in the rest of the app's code.

Building the radio group

The code in Listing 7-5 has three radio buttons. Each radio button has its own `value` but, taken together, all three buttons have only one `groupValue`. In fact, the common `groupValue` is what ties the three buttons together. When a user selects the button with value `Gender.Female`, the `groupValue` of all three becomes `Gender.Female`. It's as if part of the code suddenly looked like this:

```
// Don't try this at home. This is fake code.
Radio(
  value: Gender.Female,
  groupValue: Gender.Female,
),
Radio(
  value: Gender.Male,
  groupValue: Gender.Female,
),
Radio(
  value: Gender.Other,
  groupValue: Gender.Female,
),
```

Each radio button has its own onChanged parameter. In Listing 7-5, the function that handles onChanged events (the _updateGenderRadio function) does exactly what you would expect — it changes the radio buttons' groupValue to whatever value the user has selected.

WHY BOTHER?

A reader from Minnesota asks, "What good is the enum declaration in Listing 7-5? Why can't I assign the String values "Female", "Male", and "Other" directly to the three radio buttons?"

Good question, reader! Thanks for asking. The answer is, "You're correct. You can assign String values to the radio buttons." You don't really need an enum to create a group of radio buttons. The following code with no enum is valid:

```
String _genderRadioValue;

// And later ...

Radio(
  value: "Female",
  groupValue: _genderRadioValue,
  onChanged: _updateGenderRadio,
),
Radio(
  value: "Male",
  groupValue: _genderRadioValue,
  onChanged: _updateGenderRadio,
),
Radio(
  value: "Other",
  groupValue: _genderRadioValue,
  onChanged: _updateGenderRadio,
),

// And later ...

void _updateGenderRadio(String newValue) {
  setState(() {
    _genderRadioValue = newValue;
  });
}

void _updateResults() {
  setState(() {
```

```
                    _messageToUser = "You selected $_genderRadioValue.";
            });
        }
```

So, in Listing 7-5, why do I bother creating the Gender enum? And the answer is, genders aren't strings. Being male doesn't mean that a person carries around the four letters *m*, then *a*, then *l*, and then *e*. Instead, maleness is one of two or more possibilities, another possibility being femaleness. The best way to represent genders in the code is to enumerate the alternatives, not to use a few strings and hope that no one misspells them.

Consider this code that uses the String type:

```
String _genderRadioValue = "Femail";
```

The code is incorrect but, as far as the Dart language is concerned, the code is peachy keen.

Now, consider this code that uses an enum type:

```
enum Gender { Female, Male, Other }
Gender _genderRadioValue = Gender.Femail;
```

The code is incorrect, and Dart refuses to accept it. With the declaration of the Gender enum, the programmer guarantees that the only possible values of _genderRadio Value are Gender.Female, Gender.Male, and Gender.Other. That's good programming practice. Safety first!

Displaying the user's choice

The shorten method in Listing 7-5 is a workaround for a slightly annoying Dart language feature. In Dart, every enum value has a toString method which, in theory, gives you a useful way to display the value. The problem is that, when you apply the toString method, the result is always a verbose name. For example, Gender.Female.toString() is "Gender.Female", and that's not quite what you want to display. In Figure 7-10, the user sees the sentence *You selected Female* instead of the overly technical sentence *You selected Gender.Female* sentence.

Applying the replaceAll("Gender.", "") method call turns "Gender." into the empty string, so "Gender.Female" becomes plain old "Female". Problem solved! — or maybe not.

Look at the declaration of _genderRadioValue in Listing 7-5:

```
Gender _genderRadioValue;
```

This declaration doesn't assign anything to _genderRadioValue, so _gender RadioValue starts off being null. That's good because having null for _gender RadioValue means that none of the radio group's buttons is checked. That's exactly what you want when the app starts running.

But what if the user presses Submit without selecting one of the radio buttons? Then _genderRadioValue is still null, so the shorten method's gender parameter is null. Inside the shorten method, you have the following nasty situation:

```
String shorten(Gender null) => null.toString().replaceAll("Gender.", "");
```

Oops! When you apply toString() to null, you get "null" (the string consisting of four characters). If you don't do anything about that, the message on the user's screen becomes *You selected null.* That's not user-friendly!

"null" is a four-letter word.

In Listing 7-5, the Submit button's onPressed handler responds appropriately whenever _genderRadioValue is null. Here's the code:

```
RaisedButton(
    child: Text("Submit"),
    onPressed: _genderRadioValue != null ? _updateResults : null,
),
```

If _genderRadioValue isn't null, the handler is a nice, conventional _update Results method — a method that creates a _messageToUser and displays that message inside a Text widget. Nothing special there.

But when _genderRadioValue is null, the Submit button's onPressed handler is also null. And the good news is, a RaisedButton with a null handler is completely disabled. The user can see the button, but the button's surface is greyed out, and pressing the button has no effect. That's great! If no gender is selected and the user tries to press the Submit button, nothing happens and no message appears.

¿WHAT DO ?. AND ?? DO?

In Listing 7-5, the Submit button is lifeless until the user selects a gender. Are there other ways to approach the no-selection-yet problem? This sidebar explores two of the alternatives. First, here's a boring alternative:

```
RaisedButton(
  child: Text("Submit"),
  onPressed: _updateResults,
),

// And later in the code ...

void _updateResults() {
  setState(() {
    if (_genderRadioValue != null) {
      _messageToUser = "You selected ${shorten(_genderRadioValue)}.";
    } else {
      _messageToUser = "You selected nothing yet.";
    }
  });
}
```

In this version of the code, the Submit button is always enabled, and the method that handles a button click (the _updateResults method) treats _genderRadioValue being null as a special case. (See this sidebar's first figure.) Putting an if statement inside the _updateResults method certainly works but, like I say, it's boring.

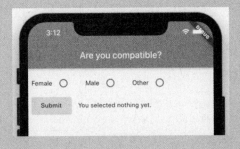

What's not boring are Dart's null-aware operators. Here's some code:

```
String shorten(Gender gender) => gender?.toString()?.
    replaceAll("Gender.", "");
_messageToUser =
    "You selected ${shorten(_genderRadioValue) ?? 'nothing yet'}.";
```

(continued)

(continued)

A *null-aware operator* is a thingamajig that does something special when you apply it to a `null` value. Take, for example, Dart's `?.` operator.

- **If** gender **is** `null`, **then** gender`.toString()` **is** `"null"`.

  That's what happens when you don't use Dart's `?.` operator. In Dart, everything has its own `toString` method. What better string representation for the `null` value than the string `"null"`?

- **If** gender **is** `null`, **then** gender`?.toString()` **is** `null`.

  That's what happens when you use Dart's `?.` operator. Whenever *someValue* is `null`, *someValue*`?.`*something_else* is `null`. That's the rule.

This sidebar's second figure illustrates the behavior of the `shorten` method with and without `?.` operators.

```
String shorten(Gender gender) => gender.toString().replaceAll("Gender.", "");
                         |____|      |_____|
                          null         null
                                    |_____|
                                          "null"
                                    |_____|
                                        "null" (You don't want that.)
```

```
String shorten(Gender gender) => gender?.toString()?.replaceAll("Gender.", "");
                         |____|      |_____|
                          null         null
                                    |_____|
                                           null
                                    |_____|
                                         null (You want that!)
```

```
String shorten(Gender gender) => gender?.toString().replaceAll("Gender.", "");
                         |____|      |_____|
                          null         null
                                    |_____|
                                           null
                                    |_____|
                                    You can't apply replaceAll to null.
```

```
String shorten(Gender gender) => gender.toString()?.replaceAll("Gender.", "");
                         |____|      |_____|
                          null         null
                                    |_____|
                                          "null"
                                    |_____|
                                      "null" (You don't want that.)
```

What can you do when the entire shorten method returns null? Another one of Dart's null-aware operators — the ?? operator — can take care of the null value. The expression

```
shorten(_genderRadioValue) ?? 'nothing yet'
```

stands for either shorten(_genderRadioValue) or 'nothing yet'. To be a bit more precise,

- The ?? expression stands for shorten(_genderRadioValue) unless shorten(_genderRadioValue) is null.

- If shorten(_genderRadioValue) is null, the ?? expression stands for 'nothing yet'.

The ?? operator has a name. It's called the *if-null* operator. When you use the if-null operator in combination with ?. operators, you get a result like the one in this sidebar's first figure.

Creating a Dropdown Button

As soon as word gets around about Doris's dating app, everyone wants a piece of the action. Doris's friend Hilda wants a dropdown button to gauge the potential mate's level of commitment. Hilda wants a committed relationship and possibly marriage. Listing 7-6 shows some of the code that Doris writes for Hilda. Figures 7-12, 7-13, and 7-14 show the code in action.*

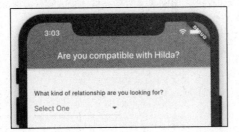

FIGURE 7-12:
The user hasn't decided yet.

---

* Thanks to David Nesterov–Rappoport, for creating the Heart and BrokenHeart images shown in Figures 7-13 and 7-14.

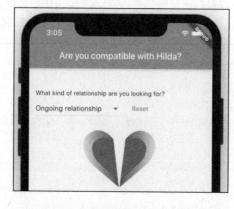

FIGURE 7-13:
A user with
cold feet.

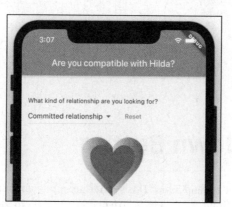

FIGURE 7-14:
A serious user.

LISTING 7-6: **What Are You Looking For?**

```
// This listing is missing some parts. See App0705 in the files that
// you download from this book's website (www.allmycode.com/Flutter).

enum Relationship {
  Friend,
  OneDate,
  Ongoing,
  Committed,
  Marriage,
}

Map<Relationship, String> show = {
  Relationship.Friend: "Friend",
  Relationship.OneDate: "One date",
  Relationship.Ongoing: "Ongoing relationship",
  Relationship.Committed: "Committed relationship",
  Relationship.Marriage: "Marriage",
};
```

```
List<DropdownMenuItem<Relationship>> _relationshipsList = [
  DropdownMenuItem(
    value: Relationship.Friend,
    child: Text(show[Relationship.Friend]),
  ),
  DropdownMenuItem(
    value: Relationship.OneDate,
    child: Text(show[Relationship.OneDate]),
  ),
  DropdownMenuItem(
    value: Relationship.Ongoing,
    child: Text(show[Relationship.Ongoing]),
  ),
  DropdownMenuItem(
    value: Relationship.Committed,
    child: Text(show[Relationship.Committed]),
  ),
  DropdownMenuItem(
    value: Relationship.Marriage,
    child: Text(show[Relationship.Marriage]),
  ),
];

class _MyHomePageState extends State<MyHomePage> {
  Relationship _relationshipDropdownValue;

// And later in the program ...

  /// Build

  Widget _buildDropdownButtonRow() {
    return Row(
      mainAxisAlignment: MainAxisAlignment.start,
      children: <Widget>[
        DropdownButton<Relationship>(
          items: _relationshipsList,
          onChanged: _updateRelationshipDropdown,
          value: _relationshipDropdownValue,
          hint: Text("Select One"),
        ),
        if (_relationshipDropdownValue != null)
          FlatButton(
            child: Text(
              "Reset",
              style: TextStyle(color: Colors.blue),
            ),
```

(continued)

LISTING 7-6:   *(continued)*

```
                onPressed: _reset,
          ),
      ],
    );
  }

  Widget _buildResultsImage() {
    if (_relationshipDropdownValue != null) {
      return Image.asset((_relationshipDropdownValue.index >= 3)
          ? "Heart.png"
          : "BrokenHeart.png");
    } else {
      return SizedBox();
    }
  }

  /// Actions

  void _reset() {
    setState(() {
      _relationshipDropdownValue = null;
    });
  }

  void _updateRelationshipDropdown(Relationship newValue) {
    setState(() {
      _relationshipDropdownValue = newValue;
    });
  }
}
```

Building the dropdown button

A DropdownButton constructor has several parameters, one of which is a list of items. Each item is an instance of the DropdownMenuItem class. Each such instance has a value and a child. (See Figure 7-15.)

>> **An item's** value **is something that identifies that particular item.**

In Listing 7-6, the items' values are Relationship.Friend, Relationship. OneDate, and so on. They're all members of the Relationship enum. You don't want things like Relationship.OneDate appearing on the surface of a menu item, so . . .

>> **An item's** child **is the thing that's displayed on that item.**

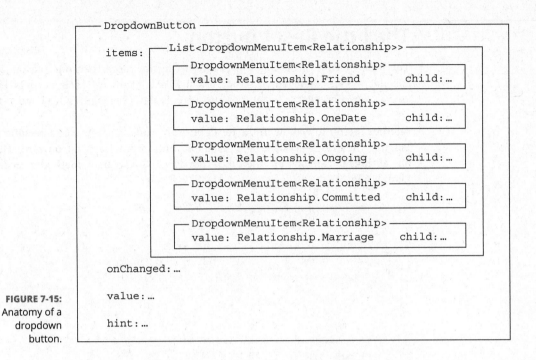

FIGURE 7-15:
Anatomy of a
dropdown
button.

In Listing 7-6, the items' children are all Text widgets, but you can display all kinds of things on the dropdown items. For example, an item's child can be a Row containing a Text widget and an Icon widget.

In addition to its list of items, a DropdownButton constructor has onChanged, value, and hint parameters.

>> **The** onChanged **parameter does what such parameters do in so many other constructors.**

The parameter refers to a function that handles the user's taps, presses, tweaks, and pokes.

>> **At any moment, the** value **parameter refers to whichever dropdown button item is selected.**

>> **The** hint **parameter tells Flutter what to display when none of the dropdown button's items has been selected.**

In this section's example, Flutter displays the words *Select One*.

A dropdown button's hint is typically displayed before the user has chosen any of the button's items. But Listing 7-6 has a Reset button. When the user presses the Reset button, the button's onPressed handler sets _relationshipDropdownValue back to null, so the dropdown button's hint reappears.

The little Reset button

The Reset button in Listing 7-6 is interesting for more than one reason. First, it's not a RaisedButton. Instead, it's a FlatButton. A FlatButton is like a RaisedButton except . . . well, a FlatButton is flat. (See Figures 7-13 and 7-14.)

Another reason to wallow in the Reset button's code is because of a peculiar Dart language feature — one that's available only from Dart 2.3 onward. Here's an abridged version of the _buildDropdownButtonRow method's code in Listing 7-6:

```
Widget _buildDropdownButtonRow() {
  return Row(

    children: <Widget>[
      DropdownButton<Relationship>(

      ),

      if (_relationshipDropdownValue != null)
        FlatButton(

        ),
    ],
  );
}
```

In this code, the Row widget's children parameter is a list, and the list consists of two items: a DropdownButton and something that looks like an if statement. But appearances can be deceiving. The thing in Listing 7-6 isn't an if statement. The thing in Listing 7-6 is a *collection if*. In Chapter 4, I unceremoniously sneak in the word *collection* to describe Dart's List, Set, and Map types. A collection if helps you define an instance of one of those types.

In Listing 7-6, the meaning of the collection if is exactly what you'd guess. If _relationshipDropdownValue isn't null, the list includes a FlatButton. Otherwise, the list doesn't include a FlatButton. That makes sense because, when _relationshipDropdownValue is null, there's no sense in offering the user an option to make it be null.

CROSS REFERENCE

In addition to its collection if, the Dart programming language has a collection for. You can read about the collection for in Chapter 8.

Making a Map

Chapter 4 introduces Dart's types, one of which is the `Map` type. A `Map` is a lot like a dictionary. To find the definition of a word, you look up the word in a dictionary. To find a user-friendly representation of the enum value `Relationship.OneDate`, you look up `Relationship.OneDate` in the `show` map.

Relationship.Friend /ri-lAY-shuhn-ship frEnd/ *n.* Friend.

Relationship.OneDate /ri-lAY-shuhn-ship wUHn dAYt/ *n.* One date.

Relationship.Ongoing /ri-lAY-shuhn-ship AWn-goh-ing/ *adj.* Ongoing relationship.

Relationship.Committed /ri-lAY-shuhn-ship kuh-mIt-uhd / *adj.* Committed relationship.

Relationship.Marriage /ri-lAY-shuhn-ship mAIR-ij / *n.* Marriage.

To be a bit more precise, a `Map` is a bunch of pairs, each pair consisting of a key and a value. In Listing 7-6, the variable `show` refers to a map whose keys are `Relationship.Friend`, `Relationship.OneDate`, and so on. The map's values are `"Friend"`, `"One date"`, `"Ongoing relationship"`, and so on. See Table 7-1.

TABLE 7-1

The show Map

Key	Value	Index
Relationship.Friend	"Friend"	0
Relationship.OneDate	"One date"	1
Relationship.Ongoing	"Ongoing relationship"	2
Relationship.Committed	"Committed relationship"	3
Relationship.Marriage	"Marriage"	4

In a Dart program, you use brackets to look up a value in a map. For example, in Listing 7-6, looking up `show[Relationship.OneDate]` gives you the string `"One date"`.

In addition to their keys and values, each map entry has an *index*. An entry's index is its position number in the declaration of the map, starting with position number 0. Doris's buddy Hilda wants a committed relationship and possibly marriage. So the code in Listing 7-6 checks this condition:

When this condition is true, the app displays a heart to indicate a good match. Otherwise, the app displays a broken heart. (Sorry, Hilda.)

Onward and Upward

Doris's work on the dating app has paid off in spades. Doris is now in a committed relationship with an equally geeky Flutter developer — one who's well over 18 and who earns just enough money to live comfortably. Doris and her mate will live happily ever after, or at least until Google changes the Dart language specification and breaks some of Doris's code.

The next chapter is about navigation. How can your app go from one page to another? When the user finishes using the new page, how can your app go back? With more than one page in your app, how can the pages share information? For the answers to these questions, simply turn to this book's next page!

Chapter **8**

Navigation, Lists, and Other Goodies

n researching this chapter, I learned some interesting things about the art of page-turning:

» The web has many sites to help musicians solve their page-turning problems. Some sites offer advice on the best ways to turn pages manually. Others offer mechanical solutions with foot pedals to control flipping devices. Scholarly papers survey the alternatives and draw conclusions based on studies.

» For nonmusicians, several sites describe build-it-yourself page-turning contraptions. None of these devices improves the homey look of a person's living room or study.

» One site describes, in ten steps, how a person can use their hands to turn the page of a book. The site has illustrations and detailed instructions for each of the ten steps. (I thought I already knew how to turn pages, but maybe I was wrong!)

» On one forum, I saw a link to a site that sells the most professional page-turning device. When I clicked the link, a run-on sentence announced, "We are sorry, the requested page could not be found." Maybe what they meant was, "The requested page-turning device could not be found."

>> Flutter's Navigator class can transition within an app from one page to another. In fact, Flutter's navigation features are so important that one book has an entire chapter devoted to the subject. The name of the book is *Flutter For Dummies*, and the chapter in that book is Chapter 8.

Extending a Dart Class

If I'm not careful, the code listings in this book can become unbearably long. A simple example to illustrate one new concept may consume several pages. You'd need magic powers to find each listing's new and interesting code. To combat this difficulty, I divide some sections' examples into two files — one file containing boilerplate code and another file containing the section's new features. When I march from one section to the next, I reuse the file containing the boilerplate code and introduce a separate file containing only the new features.

All is well and good until I try to split a particular class's code between two files. Imagine that I have two files. One file's name is ReuseMe.dart:

```
// This is ReuseMe.dart

import 'MoreCode.dart';

class ReuseMe {
  int x = 229;
}

main() => ReuseMe().displayNicely();
```

The other file's name is MoreCode.dart.

```
// This is a bad version of MoreCode.dart

import 'ReuseMe.dart';

void displayNicely() {
  print('The value of x is $x.');
}
```

What could possibly go wrong?

Here's what goes wrong: The declaration of displayNicely isn't inside the ReuseMe class. In this pair of files, displayNicely is a lonely function that sits outside of any particular class. This causes two problems:

» The line ReuseMe().displayNicely() makes no sense.

» The displayNicely function can't casually refer to the ReuseMe class's x variable.

This code is bogus. Throw it out!

But wait! A sneaky trick can rescue this example. Since Dart's 2.7 version, I can add methods to a class without putting them inside the class's code. I indicate this business using Dart's extension keyword. Here's how I do it:

```
// This is a good version of MoreCode.dart

import 'ReuseMe.dart';

extension MyExtension on ReuseMe {
  void displayNicely() {
    print('The value of x is $x.');
  }
}
```

After making this change, the displayNicely function becomes a method belonging to the ReuseMe class. Dart behaves as if I had written the following code:

```
// The extension keyword makes Dart pretend that I wrote this code:

class ReuseMe {
  int x = 229;

  void displayNicely() {
    print('The value of x is $x.');
  }
}
```

Inside the displayNicely method's body, the name x refers to the ReuseMe class's x variable. And every instance of the ReuseMe class has a displayNicely method. So the call ReuseMe().displayNicely() makes perfect sense.

Everything works. And, best of all, I can swap out the MoreCode.dart file for another version of the file whenever I want.

```
// Another good version of MoreCode.dart

import 'ReuseMe.dart';

extension MyExtension on ReuseMe {
  void displayNicely() {
    print('   * $x *   ');
    print('  ** $x **  ');
    print(' *** $x *** ');
    print('**** $x ****');
  }
}
```

I can change the `displayNicely` function without touching the file that contains the original `ReuseMe` class declaration. That's handy!

Extensions aren't available in all versions of Dart. If Android Studio complains to you about your use of extensions, look for the `environment` section of your project's `pubspec.yaml` file. That `environment` section may look something like this:

```
environment:
  sdk: ">=2.1.0 <3.0.0"
```

Change the lower Dart version number like so:

```
environment:
  sdk: ">=2.6.0 <3.0.0"
```

The name of an extension distinguishes that extension from any other extensions on the same class. For example, imagine that I've defined `MyExtension` and you've defined `YourExtension`, both on the `ReuseMe` class:

```
extension YourExtension on ReuseMe {
  void displayNicely() {
    print('!!! $x !!!');
  }
}
```

With two extensions declaring `displayNicely` methods, the expression `ReuseMe().displayNicely()` is ambiguous. To clear up the confusion, name one of the extensions explicitly:

```
YourExtension(ReuseMe()).displayNicely()
```

From One Page to Another

You've probably used an app with a master-detail interface. A *master-detail interface* has two pages. The first page displays a list of items. When the user selects an item in the list, a second page displays details about that item. This chapter's first example (in Listings 8-1 and 8-2) has a stripped-down master-detail interface. And why do I say "stripped-down"? The master page's list consists of only one item — the name of a particular movie.

LISTING 8-1: **Reuse This Code**

```
// App08Main.dart

import 'package:flutter/material.dart';

import 'App0802.dart'; // Change this line to App0803, App0804, and so on.

void main() => runApp(App08Main());

class App08Main extends StatelessWidget {
  @override
  Widget build(BuildContext context) {
    return MaterialApp(
      home: MovieTitlePage(),
    );
  }
}


class MovieTitlePage extends StatefulWidget {
  @override
  MovieTitlePageState createState() => MovieTitlePageState();
}

class MovieTitlePageState extends State<MovieTitlePage> {
  @override
  Widget build(BuildContext context) {
    return Scaffold(
      appBar: AppBar(
        title: Text(
          'Movie Title',
        ),
      ),
      body: Padding(
        padding: const EdgeInsets.all(16.0),
        child: Center(
```

(continued)

| LISTING 8-1: | *(continued)* |

```
              child: buildTitlePageCore(),
          ),
        ),
      );
    }
  }


  class DetailPage extends StatelessWidget {
    final overview = '(From themoviedb.com) One day at work, unsuccessful '
        'puppeteer Craig finds a portal into the head of actor John '
        'Malkovich. The portal soon becomes a passion for anybody who '
        'enters its mad and controlling world of overtaking another human '
        'body.';

    @override
    Widget build(BuildContext context) {
      return Scaffold(
        appBar: AppBar(
          title: Text(
            'Details',
          ),
        ),
        body: Padding(
          padding: const EdgeInsets.all(16.0),
          child: Center(
            child: buildDetailPageCore(context),
          ),
        ),
      );
    }
  }
```

| LISTING 8-2: | **Basic Navigation** |

```
// App0802.dart

import 'package:flutter/material.dart';

import 'App08Main.dart';

extension MoreMovieTitlePage on MovieTitlePageState {
  goToDetailPage() {
    Navigator.push(
      context,
      MaterialPageRoute(
```

```
      builder: (context) => DetailPage(),
    ),
  );
}

Widget buildTitlePageCore() {
  return Column(
    crossAxisAlignment: CrossAxisAlignment.center,
    children: <Widget>[
      Text(
        'Being John Malkovich',
        textScaleFactor: 1.5,
      ),
      SizedBox(height: 16.0),
      RaisedButton.icon(
        icon: Icon(Icons.arrow_forward),
        label: Text('Details'),
        onPressed: goToDetailPage,
      ),
    ],
  );
}
}

extension MoreDetailPage on DetailPage {
  Widget buildDetailPageCore(context) {
    return Column(
      crossAxisAlignment: CrossAxisAlignment.center,
      children: <Widget>[
        Text(
          overview,
        ),
      ],
    );
  }
}
```

To run this chapter's first app, your project must contain both Listing 8-1 and Listing 8-2. Each of these listings depends on code from the other listing. In fact, many of this chapter's listings depend on the code from Listing 8-1.

Listings 8-1 and 8-2 must be in separate .dart files because both listings contain import declarations.

Listing 8-2 doesn't have a main method. So, to run the app in Listings 8-1 and 8-2, you look for the App08Main.dart tab above Android Studio's editor. You right-click that tab and then select Run 'App08Main.dart' from the menu that appears.

Figures 8-1 and 8-2 show the pages generated by the code in Listings 8-1 and 8-2.

FIGURE 8-1:
A very simple
master page.

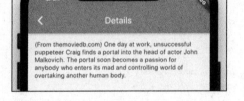

FIGURE 8-2:
A very simple
detail page.

Figure 8-1 shows the app's starting page — a page with a RaisedButton on it. When the user presses this button, Flutter calls the goToDetailPage method in Listing 8-2. The goToDetailPage method calls the Navigator class's push method. The parameters of the push method point directly to the DetailPage class. So the app jumps to its second page — the DetailClass page in Figure 8-2.

The upper left corner of Figure 8-2 has a little backward-pointing arrow. Flutter creates that arrow automatically whenever it navigates to a page that has an app bar. When the user presses that arrow, the app returns to the first page — the MovieTitlePage.

An icon on a button

For a tiny bit of cuteness, I add an icon (a little forward-pointing arrow) to the RaisedButton in Figure 8-1. To make this happen, I use the word *icon* a bunch of times in Listing 8-2. Rather than call the ordinary RaisedButton constructor, I call Flutter's RaisedButton.icon constructor. Then, for the constructor's icon parameter, I write Icon(Icons.arrow_forward), which means, "Construct an actual Icon widget whose appearance is that of Flutter's built-in Icons.arrow_forward value."

Flutter has a whole bunch of built-in icons. Most of them are familiar user interface icons, like volume_up, warning, and signal_cellular_4_bar. But others are ones you don't expect to find. For example, Flutter has a pets icon (a picture of a paw), a casino icon (the face of a die), and an airline_seat_legroom_reduced icon (a person scrunched into a small space).

Pushing and popping

Here's some useful terminology:

>> A page that calls Navigator.push is a *source* page.

   In Listings 8-1 and 8-2, the MovieTitlePage is a source page.

>> A page that the user sees as a result of a Navigator.push call is a *destination* page.

   In Listings 8-1 and 8-2, the DetailPage is a destination page.

Some transitions go from a source page to a destination page; others go from a destination page back to a source page. In this section's example,

>> The user presses the RaisedButton in Figure 8-1 to go from source to destination.

>> The user presses the app bar's Back button in Figure 8-2 to go from destination to source.

For the most part, a mobile app's transitions form a structure known as a *stack*. To create a stack, you pile each new page on top of all the existing pages. Then, when you're ready to remove a page, you remove the page that's at the top of the stack. It's like a seniority system for pages. The youngest page is the first to be removed. With this *Last-In-First-Out* (LIFO) rule, the user forms a clear mental image of his or her place among the app's pages.

Here's a bit more terminology:

>> When you add something to the top of a stack, you're *pushing* it onto the stack.

>> When you remove something from the top of a stack, you're *popping* it off the stack.

In Listing 8-2, the name `Navigator.push` suggests the pushing of a page onto a stack of pages. In fact, when I think about page transitions, I always imagine pages on top of pages. The most recent page obscures the older pages that lie below it. During a run of this chapter's first app, the `DetailPage` sits comfortably on top of the `MovieTitlePage`, completely obscuring the `MovieTitlePage` from the user's view.

In some situations, the notion of piling one page on top of another isn't appropriate. Maybe you don't want to push a destination page on top of a source page. Instead, you want to replace a source page with a destination page. To do this in Listing 8-2, you make one tiny change: You change the words `Navigator.push` to the words `Navigator.pushReplacement`. When you do, the `MovieTitlePage` looks as it does in Figure 8-1, but the `DetailPage` differs a bit from the image in Figure 8-2. In the new `DetailPage`, the app bar has no Back button.

In Flutter, screens and pages are called *routes*. That's why Listing 8-2 contains a `MaterialPageRoute` constructor call.

To make your app look like an iPhone app, use Flutter's Cupertino widgets instead of the Material Design widgets and construct a `CupertinoPageRoute` rather than a `MaterialPageRoute`. A `CupertinoPageRoute` makes page transitions look "Apple-like." For more on Flutter's Cupertino widgets, refer to Chapter 3.

Passing Data from Source to Destination

Sometimes, you want to pass information from one page to another. The next example (see Listing 8-3) shows you how a source sends information to a destination.

Before you try to run this section's app, change one of the `import` lines in Listing 8-1. Change `'App0802.dart'` to `'App0803.dart'`. Make similar changes to run Listings 8-3, 8-4, 8-5, 8-7, 8-8, and 8-10.

LISTING 8-3: **From Movie Title Page to Detail Page**

```
// App0803.dart

import 'package:flutter/material.dart';

import 'App08Main.dart';

extension MoreMovieTitlePage on MovieTitlePageState {
  static bool _isFavorite = true; // You can change this to false.
```

```
goToDetailPage() {
  Navigator.push(
    context,
    MaterialPageRoute(
      builder: (context) => DetailPage(),
      settings: RouteSettings(
        arguments: _isFavorite,
      ),
    ),
  );
}


Widget buildTitlePageCore() {
  return Column(
    crossAxisAlignment: CrossAxisAlignment.center,
    children: <Widget>[
      Text(
        'Being John Malkovich',
        textScaleFactor: 1.5,
      ),
      SizedBox(height: 16.0),
      RaisedButton.icon(
        icon: Icon(Icons.arrow_forward),
        label: Text('Details'),
        onPressed: goToDetailPage,
      ),
    ],
  );
}
}


extension MoreDetailPage on DetailPage {
  Widget buildDetailPageCore(context) {
    return Column(
      crossAxisAlignment: CrossAxisAlignment.center,
      children: <Widget>[
        Text(
          overview,
        ),
        Visibility(
          visible: ModalRoute.of(context).settings.arguments ?? false,
          child: Icon(Icons.favorite),
        ),
      ],
    );
  }
}
```

Figure 8-3 shows you the `DetailPage` generated by the code in Listings 8-1 and 8-3. A little heart indicates that *Being John Malkovich* is a favorite movie.

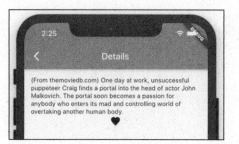

FIGURE 8-3:
The Favorite icon on the detail page.

Figure 8-4 illustrates the trip made by the `_isFavorite` variable's value in a run of this section's example.

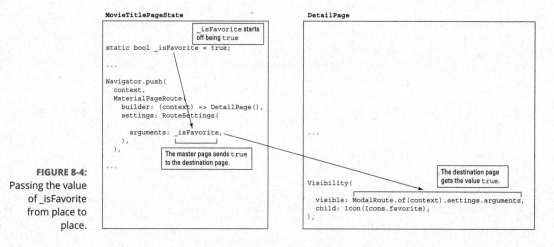

FIGURE 8-4:
Passing the value of _isFavorite from place to place.

When Flutter displays the detail page, the value of

```
ModalRoute.of(context).settings.arguments
```

is `true`. It's as if the code near the bottom of Listing 8-3 looked like this:

```
// Remember, I said "as if" the code looked like this...
Visibility(
  visible: true,
  child: Icon(Icons.favorite),
),
```

A `Visibility` widget either shows or hides its child depending on the value of its `visible` parameter. So, in this example, Flutter's built-in `favorite` icon appears on the user's screen.

In Listing 8-3, you can change the declaration of `_isFavorite` like this:

```
static bool _isFavorite = false;
```

When you do, the movie title page passes `false` to the detail page. So, the `Visibility` widget's `visible` property becomes `false`, and the little `favorite` icon doesn't appear.

WARNING

In Listing 8-3, the variable `_isFavorite` is `static`. One consequence of this is that hot restarting the app doesn't work. If you change `_isFavorite` from `true` to `false`, and then save your code, the little heart icon doesn't go away. To make that change in the value of `_isFavorite` take effect, stop the run of the app and then start it again.

RUBE GOLDBERG WOULD BE PLEASED

I admit it: I've never seen a more complicated way of making a tiny icon appear than the way it's done in Listing 8-3. But remember, passing information from one page to another is important, whether you're passing a simple `_isFavorite` value or a large chunk of medical data. Dividing an app into pages keeps the pages uncluttered. It also lends continuity to the flow of an app.

Chapter 5 tells you that Dart has top-level variables — variables that aren't declared inside of a class. If you put all of your app's code in one file, all the code in your app can refer directly to those top-level variables. So why do you need this section's `arguments` feature? Why not let your master and detail pages share the values of top-level variables?

The answer is, top-level variables can be dangerous. While Mary withdraws funds on one page, another page processes an automatic payment and nearly empties Mary's account. As a result, Mary overdraws her account and owes a hefty fee to the bank. That's not good.

Use top-level variables sparingly. Don't use top-level variables to pass information between pages. Instead, use Flutter's `arguments` feature.

In this section, I commit a major-league sin. I want to keep this chapter's examples as simple as possible, so Listings 8-1 and 8-3 provide no way for the user to change the _isFavorite value. Instead, I invite you, the reader, to reach into Listing 8-3, change _isFavorite to false, and then rerun the code. It's a horrible way to unfavorite a movie — like telling banking account customers to edit their account pages' source code — but it gets the job done.

A STATIC VARIABLE

In Listing 8-3, the declaration of _isFavorite starts with the word static. Any variable that you declare in an extension, rather than inside any of the extension's methods, must be static. If you follow that rule blindly, you can understand Listing 8-3 without knowing what static means.

But, if you want to know what static means, consider this tiny bit of code from Chapter 7:

```
... => _MyHomePageState();

// ... and later ...

class _MyHomePageState extends State<MyHomePage> {
  bool _ageSwitchValue = false;
```

In the first line, a constructor call creates an instance of the _MyHomePageState class. A bit later on, the code gives _MyHomePageState an instance variable named _ageSwitchValue. The code doesn't have any other _MyHomePageState constructor calls, so you have only one _MyHomePageState instance, and only one _ageSwitchValue variable.

In some programs, you may have occasion to call the _MyHomePageState constructor twice. If you do, you'll have two instances of _MyHomePageState, each with its own _ageSwitchValue variable. If you make an assignment such as _ageSwitchValue = true in one of the instances, it has no effect on the _ageSwitchValue variable in the other instance. That's the way instance variables work, but . . .

. . . that's not the way static variables work. In Listing 8-3, the _isFavorite variable is static. If you happen to declare two instances of MovieTitlePageState, both instances share one _isFavorite variable. If you make an assignment such as _isFavorite = true in one of the instances, it sets the _isFavorite value for both instances.

In a RouteSettings constructor call, the parameter name arguments is a bit misleading. That parameter can have only one value at a time — a value such as _isFavorite. So why is the parameter name plural (arguments) instead of singular (argument)? It's plural because the single thing that you pass to another page can have several parts. For example, you can pass many values by making the one and only arguments value be a list:

```
settings: RouteSettings(
  arguments: [_isFavorite, _isInTheaters, _isAComedy,],
),
```

Passing Data Back to the Source

In the previous section, the code uses Navigator.push to send a value from a source to a destination. That's cool, but how can the destination send values back to the source? Listing 8-4 has an answer.

LISTING 8-4: **From Detail Page to Movie Title Page**

```
// App0804.dart

import 'package:flutter/material.dart';

import 'App08Main.dart';

extension MoreMovieTitlePage on MovieTitlePageState {
  static bool _isFavorite;

  goToDetailPage() async {
    _isFavorite = await Navigator.push(
        context,
        MaterialPageRoute(
          builder: (context) => DetailPage(),
        ),
    ) ??
        _isFavorite;
  }

  Widget buildTitlePageCore() {
    return Column(
      crossAxisAlignment: CrossAxisAlignment.center,
      children: <Widget>[
```

(continued)

LISTING 8-4:   *(continued)*

```
      Row(
        mainAxisAlignment: MainAxisAlignment.center,
        children: <Widget>[
          Text(
            'Being John Malkovich',
            textScaleFactor: 1.5,
          ),
          Visibility(
            visible: _isFavorite ?? false,
            child: Icon(Icons.favorite),
          ),
        ],
      ),
      SizedBox(height: 16.0),
      RaisedButton.icon(
        icon: Icon(Icons.arrow_forward),
        label: Text('Details'),
        onPressed: goToDetailPage,
      ),
    ],
  );
}
}


extension MoreDetailPage on DetailPage {
  Widget buildDetailPageCore(context) {
    return Column(
      crossAxisAlignment: CrossAxisAlignment.center,
      children: <Widget>[
        Text(
          overview,
        ),
        SizedBox(height: 16.0),
        RaisedButton(
          child: Text(
            'Make it a Favorite!',
          ),
          onPressed: () {
            Navigator.pop(context, true);
          },
        ),
      ],
    );
  }
}
```

Figure 8-5 illustrates the action that takes place during a run of this section's example.

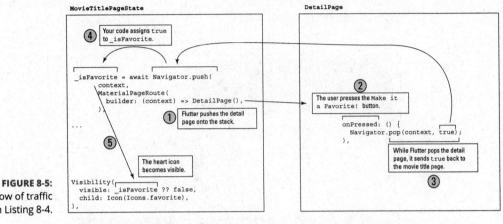

FIGURE 8-5:
The flow of traffic
in Listing 8-4.

The code in Listing 8-4 creates the `DetailPage` that you see in Figure 8-6.

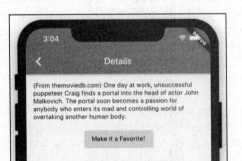

FIGURE 8-6:
A button on the
detail page offers
an option.

The `DetailPage` has two buttons — one on the app bar (a Back button) and one beneath the movie's overview (the *Make it a Favorite!* button). If the user presses the app bar's Back button, nothing exciting happens. The app returns to a `MovieTitlePage` like the one in Figure 8-1. But, if the user presses the *Make it a Favorite!* button, Flutter executes the following statement:

```
Navigator.pop(context, true);
```

Flutter pops the `DetailPage` off of its stack and sends the value `true` back to the `MovieTitlePage`. In the `MovieTitlePage`, an assignment with a mysterious looking `await` word sets `_isFavorite` to `true`:

```
_isFavorite = await Navigator.push(
    // ... Etc.
```

Finally, with `_isFavorite` set to `true`, the `MovieTitlePage` displays a little heart icon, as you see in Figure 8-7.

FIGURE 8-7:
A Favorite icon on the movie title page.

Dart's async and await keywords

A user launches the app in Listing 8-4, navigates from the `MovieTitlePage` to the `DetailPage`, and then pauses to have a cup of coffee. This user insists on having only the best coffee. With a smartphone displaying the `DetailPage`, this user takes an airplane to Vietnam, buys a fresh cup of Kopi Luwak (coming from a palm civet's digestive tract), and then flies home. Finally, three days after having launched this section's app, the user presses the *Make it a Favorite!* button, which returns `true` to the app's `MovieTitlePage`.

You never know how long a user will linger on the app's `DetailPage`. That's why Flutter's `Navigator.push` method doesn't really get `true` back from the `DetailPage`. Instead, a call to `Navigator.push` returns an object of type `Future`.

A `Future` object is a callback of sorts. It's a box that may or may not contain a value like `true`. While our coffee-loving user is visiting Vietnam, the `Future` box has nothing inside of it. But later, when the user returns home and clicks the *Make it a Favorite!* button, the `Future` box contains the value `true`. This is how Flutter manages a "don't know when" navigation problem.

What would happen with the following code?

```
// Bad code because await is missing:
static bool _isFavorite;

// And elsewhere, ...

_isFavorite = Navigator.push(
    // ... Etc.
```

In this erroneous code, the call to `Navigator.push` tries to hand a `Future` object to the `_isFavorite` variable. But the `_isFavorite` variable will have none of it because the `_isFavorite` variable's type is `bool`, not `Future`. What's a developer to do?

Listing 8-4 solves this problem using Dart's `await` keyword. An `await` keyword does two things:

» The `await` keyword tells Dart not to continue executing the current line until the `Future` box has something useful inside it.

   In Listing 8-4, Dart doesn't assign anything to `_isFavorite` until the `DetailPage` has been popped.

» When the `DetailPage` has been popped, the `await` keyword retrieves the useful value from the `Future` box.

   In Listing 8-4, the call to `Navigator.push` is a `Future` value, but the expression `await Navigator.push( // ... etc` is a `bool` value. (See Figure 8-8.) Your code assigns this `bool` value to `_isFavorite`, which, appropriately enough, is a `bool` variable.

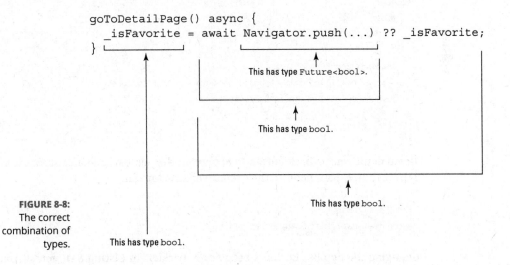

```
static bool _isFavorite;

goToDetailPage() async {
  _isFavorite = await Navigator.push(...) ?? _isFavorite;
}
```

This has type `Future<bool>`.

This has type `bool`.

This has type `bool`.

This has type `bool`.

FIGURE 8-8: The correct combination of types.

A function that contains the `await` keyword may take a long time to finish executing. If you're not careful, the entire app may come to a screeching halt while `await` does its awaiting. So, in addition to the `await` keyword, Dart has an `async` keyword and a rule to go along with this keyword:

> If a function declaration contains the `await` keyword, that declaration must also include the `async` keyword.

(Refer to Listing 8-4.) The `async` keyword tells Dart that it's okay to execute some other code while this function sits there, doing nothing, executing its `await` keyword. That way, the app may continue whatever else it's doing while our friend, the Kopi Luwak coffee lover, visits Vietnam.

Taking control of the app bar's Back button

The app bar button in Figure 8-6 is a backward-pointing arrow. When the user clicks this button, your app returns to its source page. These two facts are true by default. But what if you don't like the defaults? Can you change them? Of course, you can.

For example, you can change the button's appearance from a backward arrow to a red backspace button. To do so, add a `leading` parameter to an `AppBar` constructor call in Listing 8-1.

```
appBar: AppBar(
  title: Text(
    'Details',
  ),
  leading: IconButton(
    icon: new Icon(Icons.keyboard_backspace, color: Colors.red),
    onPressed: () => Navigator.pop(context),
  ),
)
```

If you don't want a back button to appear on the app bar, add an `automatically ImplyLeading` parameter to the `AppBar` constructor call.

```
appBar: AppBar(
  automaticallyImplyLeading: false,
```

Changing the app bar button's behavior is trickier. In Listing 8-1, you surround the `Scaffold` constructor call with a `WillPopScope` call:

```
@override
Widget build(BuildContext context) {
  return WillPopScope(
```

```
    onWillPop: () => _onPop(context),
    child: Scaffold(
```

In the WillPopScope constructor call, the onWillPop parameter is a function and, in keeping with the word Will in onWillPop, that function returns a Future. Here's a small example:

```
Future<bool> _onPop(BuildContext context) async {
    return await showDialog(
        context: context,
        child: AlertDialog(
            title: Text("The back button doesn't work"),
            content: Text('Sorry about that, Chief.'),
            actions: <Widget>[
              new FlatButton(
                onPressed: () => Navigator.pop(context, false),
                child: Text('OK'),
              ),
            ],
          ),
      ) ??
      false;
}
```

When the user clicks the back button on the DetailPage app bar, Flutter displays a dialog box containing a FlatButton labeled OK. (See Figure 8-9.) When the user clicks the FlatButton, Flutter dismisses the dialog box.

The back button doesn't work

Sorry about that, Chief.

OK

FIGURE 8-9:
*You Can't Go
Home Again*
(Thomas Wolfe).

Passing Data in Both Directions

This section's example is a bit more realistic than examples in the previous sections. In this section, the source and destination pages pass information back and forth. The code is in Listing 8-5.

LISTING 8-5: **From Title Page to Detail Page and Back Again**

```dart
// App0805.dart

import 'package:flutter/material.dart';

import 'App08Main.dart';

extension MoreMovieTitlePage on MovieTitlePageState {
  static bool _isFavorite;

  goToDetailPage() async {
    _isFavorite = await Navigator.push(
        context,
        MaterialPageRoute(
          builder: (context) => DetailPage(),
          settings: RouteSettings(
            arguments: _isFavorite,
          ),
        ),
      ) ??
      _isFavorite;
  }

  Widget buildTitlePageCore() {
    return Column(
      crossAxisAlignment: CrossAxisAlignment.center,
      children: <Widget>[
        Row(
          mainAxisAlignment: MainAxisAlignment.center,
          children: <Widget>[
            Text(
              'Being John Malkovich',
              textScaleFactor: 1.5,
            ),
            Visibility(
              visible: _isFavorite ?? false,
              child: Icon(Icons.favorite),
            ),
          ],
        ),
        SizedBox(height: 16.0),
        RaisedButton.icon(
          icon: Icon(Icons.arrow_forward),
          label: Text('Details'),
          onPressed: goToDetailPage,
        ),
```

```
        ],
      );
    }
  }

extension MoreDetailPage on DetailPage {
  Widget buildDetailPageCore(context) {
    final _isFavoriteArgument =
        ModalRoute.of(context).settings.arguments ?? false;
    return Column(
      crossAxisAlignment: CrossAxisAlignment.center,
      children: <Widget>[
        Text(
          overview,
        ),
        SizedBox(height: 16.0),
        RaisedButton(
          child: Text(
            _isFavoriteArgument ? 'Unfavorite this' : 'Make it a Favorite!',
          ),
          onPressed: () {
            Navigator.pop(context, !_isFavoriteArgument);
          },
        ),
      ],
    );
  }
}
```

In this section's app, the MainTitlePage and DetailPage share the responsibility for the movie's "favorite" status. When the Favorite icon appears, it appears on the MainTitlePage, but the DetailPage has the button that switches between "favorite" and "not favorite."

Figure 8-10 describes the action of this section's app. In the next several paragraphs, I guide you through the numbered bullets in that figure.

1. When you launch this section's app, the value of _isFavorite becomes false. You see a page with a movie title and a Details button, but no Heart icon. To see that page as it appears on your phone, refer to Figure 8-1.

When you press the Details button, the goToDetailPage method sends the value of _isFavorite to the DetailPage:

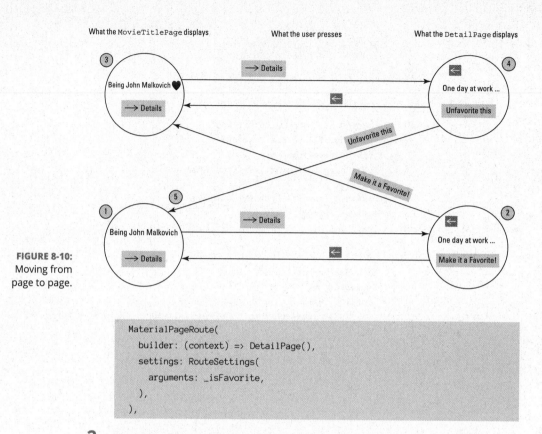

FIGURE 8-10:
Moving from
page to page.

```
MaterialPageRoute(
    builder: (context) => DetailPage(),
    settings: RouteSettings(
      arguments: _isFavorite,
    ),
),
```

2. The `DetailPage` receives the value coming from the `MovieTitlePage`. The `DetailPage` stores that value in its own `_isFavoriteArgument` variable:

```
final _isFavoriteArgument =
    ModalRoute.of(context).settings.arguments ?? false;
```

Using this variable's value, the `DetailPage` decides what to display on the face of a button:

```
RaisedButton(
  child: Text(
    _isFavoriteArgument ? 'Unfavorite this' : 'Make it a Favorite!',
  ),
```

At this point in the app's run, `_isFavoriteArgument` is `false`. So the raised button displays the sentence *Make it a favorite!* Figure 8-11 shows you the `DetailPage` that appears on your phone.

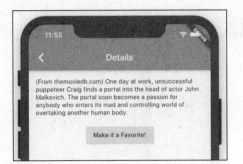

FIGURE 8-11:
You can make
this movie a
favorite.

If you press the Make It a Favorite! button, Dart's exclamation point operator
(!) prepares the opposite of _isFavoriteArgument to be sent back to the
MovieTitlePage:

```
onPressed: () {
  Navigator.pop(context, !_isFavoriteArgument);
},
```

Because _isFavoriteArgument is false, the DetailPage sends its opposite
(true) back to the MovieTitlePage.

3. Upon receipt of the value true, the MovieTitlePage displays the Heart icon.
Figure 8-12 shows you the MovieTitlePage that appears on your phone.

FIGURE 8-12:
This movie is a
favorite.

When you press the Details button, the MovieTitlePage sends true to the
DetailPage.

4. This time, the line

```
_isFavoriteArgument ? 'Unfavorite this' : 'Make it a Favorite!'
```

tells the DetailPage to display the Unfavorite This button. Figure 8-13 shows
you the DetailPage that appears on your phone.

FIGURE 8-13:
You can
unfavorite
this movie.

If you press the Unfavorite This button, Dart's exclamation point operator prepares the opposite of _isFavoriteArgument to be sent back to the MovieTitlePage. Because _isFavoriteArgument is true, the DetailPage sends its opposite (false) back to the MovieTitlePage.

5. Upon receipt of the value false, the MovieTitlePage doesn't display the Heart icon.

TECHNICAL STUFF

The drawing in Figure 8-10 is what is known as a *finite state machine* diagram. Diagrams of this kind help a lot when you want to organize your thoughts about an app's page transitions.

Creating Named Routes

Navigation can be complicated. Here's an example:

> "Go where the user wants to go unless the user isn't logged in, in which case, go to the login page (but remember where the user wanted to go). If the user logs in correctly, go where the user wanted to go. Otherwise, go to the 'invalid login' page, where the user has the option to go to the 'forgot password' page. From the 'forget password' page . . ." And so on.

In Flutter, screens and pages are called *routes*, and Flutter lets you assign a name to each of your routes. This Named Routes feature makes your code a bit more concise. More importantly, the feature keeps you from going crazy, keeping track of the user's paths and detours. The code in Listing 8-6 doesn't display any movie data — only app bars and buttons. Even so, the listing shows you how named routes work.

LISTING 8-6: **Let's All Play "Name That Route"**

```dart
// App0806.dart

import 'package:flutter/material.dart';

void main() => runApp(App0806());

class App0806 extends StatelessWidget {
  @override
  Widget build(BuildContext context) {
    return MaterialApp(
      routes: {
        '/': (context) => MovieTitlePage(),
        '/details': (context) => DetailPage(),
        '/details/cast': (context) => CastPage(),
        '/details/reviews': (context) => ReviewsPage(),
      },
    );
  }
}

class MovieTitlePage extends StatelessWidget {
  @override
  Widget build(BuildContext context) {
    return _buildEasyScaffold(
      appBarTitle: 'Movie Title Page',
      body: _buildEasyButton(
        context,
        label: 'Go to Detail Page',
        whichRoute: '/details',
      ),
    );
  }
}

class DetailPage extends StatelessWidget {
  @override
  Widget build(BuildContext context) {
    return _buildEasyScaffold(
      appBarTitle: 'Detail Page',
      body: Column(
        children: <Widget>[
          _buildEasyButton(
            context,
            label: 'Go to Cast Page',
            whichRoute: '/details/cast',
          ),
```

(continued)

LISTING 8-6:   *(continued)*

```
              _buildEasyButton(
                context,
                label: 'Go to Reviews Page',
                whichRoute: '/details/reviews',
              ),
          ],
        ),
      );
    }
  }

  class CastPage extends StatelessWidget {
    @override
    Widget build(BuildContext context) {
      return _buildEasyScaffold(
        appBarTitle: 'Cast Page',
        body: Container(),
      );
    }
  }

  class ReviewsPage extends StatelessWidget {
    @override
    Widget build(BuildContext context) {
      return _buildEasyScaffold(
        appBarTitle: 'Reviews Page',
        body: Container(),
      );
    }
  }

  Widget _buildEasyScaffold({String appBarTitle, Widget body}) {
    return Scaffold(
      appBar: AppBar(
        title: Text(appBarTitle),
      ),
      body: body,
    );
  }

  Widget _buildEasyButton(
    BuildContext context, {
    String label,
    String whichRoute,
  }) {
    return RaisedButton(
      child: Text(label),
```

```
    onPressed: () {
      Navigator.pushNamed(
        context,
        whichRoute,
      );
    },
  );
}
```

The code in Listing 8-6 doesn't depend on any other listing's code. Simply place this section's code in a .dart file, and then run it.

Figure 8-14 shows the tops of the pages for the app in Listing 8-6.

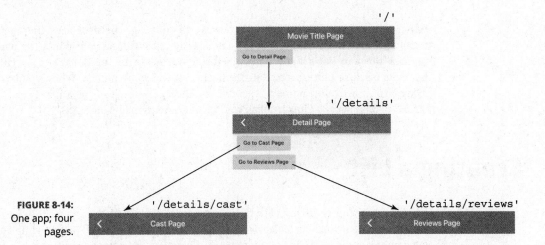

FIGURE 8-14:
One app; four
pages.

Other listings in this chapter scatter their routing information willy-nilly throughout the code. But Listing 8-6 summarizes its routing information in the MaterialApp constructor's routes parameter. Notice the hierarchical naming of the routes in Figure 8-14. The more subordinate the route, the more slash characters (/) in the route's name.

As an added bonus, the Navigator class's pushedNamed method is a bit simpler than the class's plain old push method. With simpler code comes less anguish for you, the developer, and a better chance that the code is correct.

In Listing 8-6, the MaterialApp constructor call has no home parameter. That's okay because the constructor's routes parameter takes up the slack. By default, a route named '/' is the starting point for your app.

If you decide not to have a route named '/', or if you want to override the default, you can add the initialRoute parameter. For example, you can add one line to the code in Listing 8-6, like so:

```
Widget build(BuildContext context) {
  return MaterialApp(
    routes: {
      '/': (context) => MovieTitlePage(),
      '/details': (context) => DetailPage(),
      '/details/cast': (context) => CastPage(),
      '/details/reviews': (context) => ReviewsPage(),
    },
    initialRoute: '/details/cast',
  );
}
```

When the app with this modified code starts running, the user sees the app's CastPage, and what happens next may or may not surprise you. When the user presses the app bar's Back button, Flutter navigates to the DetailPage. This happens because Flutter looks at the slashes in the route names. When you back away from a route named '/details/cast', '/details/reviews', or '/details/*whatever*', Flutter takes you to the route named '/details'.

Creating a List

Imagine this. You're sitting with friends at a local diner. Someone says, "Remember that movie *Being John Malkovich?* I wonder what it was about." So you whip out your phone and say, "What a coincidence! I have an app whose sole purpose is to show me an overview of that movie's plot."

After you read the overview to your friends, one of them says, "That's great! What about Charlie Kaufman's next movie? I think it's called *Adaptation.*" And you say, "We're out of luck. My app has info on only one movie."

At this point, one of your friends says, "How much did you pay for that app?" And you reply, "I didn't pay for it. Barry Burd paid me to install it."

The beginning of this chapter describes the master-detail interface. It says, "The first page [in a master-detail interface] displays a *list* of items." You can't cram information about every item on the list into one page. So, for details about a particular item, the user clicks that item and navigates to a separate page.

This section shows you how to navigate between a list of items and a detail page. The new example is much more useful than the chapter's *Being John Malkovich* examples. The app in Listing 8-7 lists all 25 films in Sylvester Stallone's *Rocky* franchise.

LISTING 8-7: **A Rather Long List**

```dart
// App0807.dart

import 'package:flutter/material.dart';

import 'App08Main.dart';

extension MoreMovieTitlePage on MovieTitlePageState {
  goToDetailPage(int index) {
    Navigator.push(
      context,
      MaterialPageRoute(
        builder: (context) => DetailPage(),
        settings: RouteSettings(
          arguments: index,
        ),
      ),
    );
  }

  Widget buildTitlePageCore() {
    return ListView.builder(
      itemCount: 25,
      itemBuilder: (context, index) => ListTile(
        title: Text('Rocky ${index + 1}'),
        onTap: () => goToDetailPage(index + 1),
      ),
    );
  }
}

extension MoreDetailPage on DetailPage {
  Widget buildDetailPageCore(context) {
    final sequelNumber = ModalRoute.of(context).settings.arguments;
    final overview =
        'For the $sequelNumber${getSuffix(sequelNumber)} time, palooka '
        'Rocky Balboa fights to be the world heavyweight boxing champion.';
    return Column(
      crossAxisAlignment: CrossAxisAlignment.center,
      children: <Widget>[
        Text(overview),
```

(continued)

LISTING 8-7: *(continued)*

```
      ],
    );
  }

  String getSuffix(int sequelNumber) {
    String suffix;
    switch (sequelNumber) {
      case 1:
      case 21:
        suffix = 'st';
        break;
      case 2:
      case 22:
        suffix = 'nd';
        break;
      case 3:
      case 23:
        suffix = 'rd';
        break;
      default:
        suffix = 'th';
    }
    return suffix;
  }
}
```

REMEMBER

To run the app in Listing 8-7, your project must have at least two .dart files — one containing the code in Listing 8-7 and another containing the code in Listing 8-1.

When you run the code in Listing 8-7, you get two pages — a front page with a list of movie titles and, as usual, a detail page. Figure 8-15 shows you the page with the list of movie titles, and Figure 8-16 shows you a detail page.

FIGURE 8-15:
The start of a
long list.

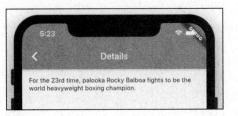

FIGURE 8-16:
The user taps
the 23rd item
in the list.

The ListView widget

The essence of Listing 8-7 is a call to Flutter's ListView.builder constructor. The constructor takes two parameters: an itemCount and an itemBuilder.

The itemCount parameter

To no one's surprise, the itemCount tells Flutter how many items to display in the list. With the code in Listing 8-7, the list's last item is *Rocky 25*. But if you omit the itemCount parameter, the list never ends. The user can scroll for hours to see list items named *Rocky 1000* and *Rocky 10000*. (At least, that's what I think will happen. To be honest, I've never tried scrolling beyond *Rocky 1200*. When I try, my hand gets tired.)

The secret behind ListView with its itemCount is the ability to scroll. In theory, the list has more items than the user sees on the device's screen. In reality, Flutter juggles list items and keeps only enough to fill the user's screen. When an item disappears off the edge of the screen, Flutter recycles that item by giving it a new *Rocky* number and displaying it at the other end of the screen. By recycling list items, Flutter saves memory space and processing time. So the scrolling of the list goes smoothly.

The itemBuilder parameter

An itemBuilder parameter's value is a function. In Listing 8-7, to create 25 items, Flutter starts by creating 25 indices with values 0, 1, 2, and so on, up to and including 24. Flutter plugs these values into the itemBuilder function, like so:

```
// This isn't real code. It's the way itemBuilder behaves.

         (context, 0) => ListTile(
  title: Text('Rocky ${0 + 1}'),
  onTap: () => goToDetailPage(0 + 1),
)

         (context, 1) => ListTile(
  title: Text('Rocky ${1 + 1}'),
```

```
    onTap: () => goToDetailPage(1 + 1),
  )

            (context, 2) => ListTile(
  title: Text('Rocky ${2 + 1}'),
  onTap: () => goToDetailPage(2 + 1),
  )

// ... and so on.
```

The result is a list containing 25 items. The *Rocky* number on each item's Text widget is one more than the index value. That way, the list doesn't start with a movie named *Rocky 0*. (*Rocky: The Prequel?*)

REMEMBER

In Dart, anything that counts automatically starts with 0, not 1. This includes things like the index of an itemBuilder, the position of a character in a String, and the default for the minimum value of a Slider.

In addition to its Text widget, each item has an onTap function. Each onTap function sends its own value (a number from 1 to 25) to the goToDetailPage function. If you keep following the trail, you find that the goToDetailPage function sends the number value onward as an argument to the app's DetailPage. And, in turn, the DetailPage uses that value to decide what information to display. In a real-life app, the DetailPage might use the value to look up the overview of a movie — maybe one of several thousand movies. But in Listing 8-7, the DetailPage simply composes a fake overview.

CROSS REFERENCE

To see a way of getting real movie info, visit the later section "Fetching Data from the Internet."

By the way, you may notice that Listings 8-1 and 8-7 both have overview variables, and both of these variables live in the same DetailPage class. (The overview in Listing 8-1 is in the original DetailPage declaration. The overview in Listing 8-7 is an extension of the DetailPage class.) This double-use of a variable name is okay. The overview in Listing 8-1 is an instance variable, and the overview in Listing 8-7 is local to the buildDetailPageCore method. So, when you run the code in Listing 8-7, the name overview stands for a sentence about Rocky Balboa. It's all good.

CROSS REFERENCE

Are you unsure about the difference between instance variables and local variables? If so, refer to Chapter 5.

HOW TO PUT A ListView INSIDE A COLUMN

Some layouts — ones that you might think are okay — send Flutter into an unending, tail-chasing game. Chapter 6 has a section about it. The game is especially frustrating when you try to put a list view inside a column. Here's some bad code:

```
// Don't do this:
Widget buildTitlePageCore() {
  return Column(
    children: <Widget>[
      Text('Rocky Movies'),
      ListView.builder(
        itemCount: 25,
        itemBuilder: (context, index) => ListTile(
          title: Text('Rocky ${index + 1}'),
          onTap: () => goToDetailPage(index + 1),
        ),
      ),
    ],
  );
}
```

When you run this code, no list view appears. Among dozens of lines of diagnostics, Android Studio's Run tool window reports that Vertical viewport was given unbounded height. As it is in Chapter 6, one widget (the Column widget) is sending an unbounded height constraint to its children, and one of the children (the ListView widget) can't handle all that freedom. The result is an impasse in which the ListView can't be displayed. To fix the problem, do the same thing that helps in Chapter 6 — add an Expanded widget:

```
// Do this instead
return Column(
  children: <Widget>[
    Text('Rocky Movies'),
    Expanded(
      child: ListView.builder(
      // ... etc.
```

The Expanded widget says, "Hey, Column. Figure out how tall the Text widget is and tell the ListView how much vertical space is left over." When the Column hands this information to the ListView, the ListView says, "Thanks. I'll use all of the leftover space." The app displays itself correctly, and everyone's happy.

Dart's switch statement

In my first draft of Listing 8-7, the overview of *Rocky 3* reads:

> For the **3th** time, palooka Rocky Balboa fights to be the world heavyweight boxing champion.

I couldn't live with that, so I solicited the help of my friend — the switch statement. A switch statement is like an if statement except that switch statements lend themselves to multiway branching.

The switch statement in Listing 8-7 says:

```
Look at the value of sequelNumber.
  If that value is 1 or 21,
    assign 'st' to suffix,
    and then break out of the entire switch statement.
  If you've reached this point and that value is 2 or 22,
    assign 'nd' to suffix,
    and then break out of the entire switch statement.
  If you've reached this point and that value is 3 or 23,
    assign 'rd' to suffix,
    and then break out of the entire switch statement.
  If you've reached this point,
    assign 'th' to suffix.
```

Each break statement sends you out of the switch statement and onward to whatever code comes after the switch statement. What happens if you try to omit the break statements?

```
// Dart doesn't tolerate this ...
switch (sequelNumber) {
  case 1:
  case 21:
    suffix = 'st';
  case 2:
  // ... and so on.
```

In Dart, this is a no-no. If you type this code in Android Studio's Dart editor, Android Studio complains immediately. Android Studio refuses to run your program.

TIP

If you're not fond of break statements, you can rewrite the getSuffix function using return statements:

```
String getSuffix(int sequelNumber) {
  switch (sequelNumber) {
    case 1:
    case 21:
      return 'st';
    case 2:
    case 22:
      return 'nd';
    case 3:
    case 23:
      return 'rd';
  }
  return 'th';
}
```

This new version of getSuffix is much more concise than the one in Listing 8-7. In this version of getSuffix, each return statement jumps you entirely out of the getSuffix function. You don't even need a default clause, because you reach the return 'th' statement when none of the case clauses applies.

Even this new-and-improved getSuffix function falters if Sylvester Stallone makes *Rocky 31*. The movie's overview will be, "For the **31th** time, palooka Rocky Balboa . . ." That doesn't sound good.

There are dozens of ways to create more versatile versions of getSuffix, and it's fun to try to create one of your own. One of my personal favorites looks like this:

```
String getSuffix(int sequelNumber) {
  int onesDigit = sequelNumber % 10;
  int tensDigit = sequelNumber ~/ 10 % 10;
  Map<int, String> suffixes = {1: 'st', 2: 'nd', 3: 'rd'};
  String suffix = suffixes[onesDigit] ?? 'th';
  if (tensDigit == 1) suffix = 'th';
  return suffix;
}
```

SOME NEWS ABOUT SCROLLING

You don't need a `ListView` to create a scrolling screen. You can enclose all kinds of stuff inside a `SingleChildScrollView`. Here's some code:

```
return MaterialApp(
  home: Material(
    child: Column(
      children: <Widget>[
        SizedBox(height: 200, child: Text("You've")),
        SizedBox(height: 200, child: Text("read")),
        SizedBox(height: 200, child: Text("many")),
        SizedBox(height: 200, child: Text("chapters")),
        SizedBox(height: 200, child: Text("of")),
        Icon(Icons.book),
        SizedBox(height: 100, child: Text("Flutter For Dummies")),
        Icon(Icons.thumb_up),
      ],
    ),
  ),
);
```

My phone doesn't have enough room for all this stuff. So if I don't add some sort of scrolling, I see the dreaded black-and-yellow stripes along the bottom of the screen. To avoid seeing these stripes, I enclose the widgets in a `SingleChildScrollView`:

```
return MaterialApp(
  home: Material(
    child: SingleChildScrollView(
      child: Column(
        children: <Widget>[
          SizedBox(height: 200, child: Text("You've")),
          // ... etc.
        ],
      ),
    ),
  ),
);
```

When I rerun the code, I see the topmost few widgets with the option to scroll and see others.

Creating list items one-by-one

From one row to another, the items in Figure 8-15 have no surprises. Each item displays the name *Rocky* and a number. Each item exhibits the same behavior when you tap on it. Because of this uniformity, I can create one `itemBuilder` that describes all 25 of the list's items.

What do you do if there's little or no uniformity? What if there's some uniformity among the items, but so few items that creating an `itemBuilder` isn't worth the effort?

In such cases, you describe the items one-by-one using Flutter's `ListView` constructor. Listing 8-8 has the code; Figures 8-17 and 8-18 show you some of the results.

LISTING 8-8: **A Small List**

```
// App0808.dart

import 'package:flutter/material.dart';

import 'App08Main.dart';

const Map<String, String> synopses = {
  'Casablanca':
      'In Casablanca, Morocco in December 1941, a cynical American expatriate '
          'meets a former lover, with unforeseen complications.',
  'Citizen Kane':
      '... Charles Foster Kane is taken from his mother as a boy ... '
          'As a result, every well-meaning, tyrannical or '
          'self-destructive move he makes for the rest of his life appears '
          'in some way to be a reaction to that deeply wounding event.',
  'Lawrence of Arabia':
      "The story of British officer T.E. Lawrence's mission to aid the Arab "
          "tribes in their revolt against the Ottoman Empire during the "
          "First World War.",
};

extension MoreMovieTitlePage on MovieTitlePageState {
  goToDetailPage(String movieName) {
    Navigator.push(
      context,
      MaterialPageRoute(
        builder: (context) => DetailPage(),
        settings: RouteSettings(
          arguments: movieName,
```

(continued)

LISTING 8-8:   *(continued)*

```
        ),
       ),
     );
   }

   Widget buildTitlePageCore() {
     return ListView(
       children: [
         ListTile(
           title: Text('Casablanca'),
           onTap: () => goToDetailPage('Casablanca'),
         ),
         ListTile(
           title: Text('Citizen Kane'),
           onTap: () => goToDetailPage('Citizen Kane'),
         ),
         ListTile(
           title: Text('Lawrence of Arabia'),
           onTap: () => goToDetailPage('Lawrence of Arabia'),
         ),
       ],
     );
   }
 }

 extension MoreDetailPage on DetailPage {
   Widget buildDetailPageCore(context) {
     final movieName = ModalRoute.of(context).settings.arguments;
     final overview = '(From themoviedb.com) ${synopses[movieName]}';
     return Column(
       crossAxisAlignment: CrossAxisAlignment.center,
       children: <Widget>[
         Text(overview),
       ],
     );
   }
 }
```

If you visit https://api.flutter.dev/flutter/widgets/ListView-class.html, you see the documentation for Flutter's ListView class. In the page's upper right corner, you see the class's constructors, which include ListView and ListView. builder. Listing 8-7 calls the named ListView.builder constructor. But in the same place in Listing 8-8, you find the unnamed ListView constructor call.

FIGURE 8-17:
Three movies.

FIGURE 8-18:
"Play it
again, Sam"
(misquoted).

**CROSS
REFERENCE**

To read about Dart's named and unnamed constructors, refer to Chapter 3.

Flutter's unnamed `ListView` constructor has a `children` parameter, and that `children` parameter's value is . . . wait for it . . . a Dart language `List`. A Dart language `List` is a bunch of objects inside a pair of square brackets, like this:

```
// A Dart language List:

        [
    ListTile(...),
    ListTile(...),
    ListTile(...),
    ]
```

**CROSS
REFERENCE**

To read about Dart's `List` type, refer to Chapter 4.

In Listing 8-8, the Dart `List` is actually a bunch of `ListTile` widgets. (They're like bathroom tiles with no grout between them.) But Flutter's `ListView` is versatile. The children don't have to be `ListTile` widgets. The children of a `ListView` may be a mixture of `Text` widgets, `SizedBox` widgets, `Image.asset` widgets, and any other kinds of widgets. It can be a big grab bag.

(If you're keeping score, *Listing* 8-8 contains a `ListView` which contains a Dart language `List` of `ListTile` widgets.)

Another new Dart language feature

One evening, after working on this chapter for 14 hours straight, I was exhausted and became delirious. I thought about the app in Listing 8-7 with its 25 `ListView` items. I imagined a little person inside a user's phone creating the *Rocky 1* item, and then the *Rocky 2* item, and then *Rocky 3*, and so on. Maybe I can take that vision, silly as it is, and compose a list view with instructions such as "Build the first item, build the second item, build the third item, . . ." and more.

Most programming languages have statements that perform repetitive tasks. For example, languages such as Java, C/C++, and Dart have a thing called a `for` statement, also known as a `for` loop. Figure 8-19 shows you a tiny example.

FIGURE 8-19: Dart's for statement in action.

The example in Figure 8-19 is a Dart program, but it's not a Flutter program. To run this program, I didn't bother creating a Flutter project. Instead, I visited `https://dartpad.dev`, typed the code in the page's big editor window, and then pressed Run.

In Figure 8-19, the program's output is a column containing the numbers 1 through 5. That's because a `for` statement tells the device to repeat things over and over again. Figure 8-20 shows you an English language paraphrase of the `for` statement in Figure 8-19.

The fact that Dart has a `for` statement isn't newsworthy. Dart's `for` statement is almost exactly the same as the C language `for` statement, which was created in the early 1970s by Dennis Ritchie at Bell Labs. And the C language `for` statement is a direct descendant of FORTRAN's `DO` statement from the early 1960s. What's new and exciting in Dart is the idea that you can put a `for` construct inside a Dart language list. Listing 8-9 has an enlightening code snippet.

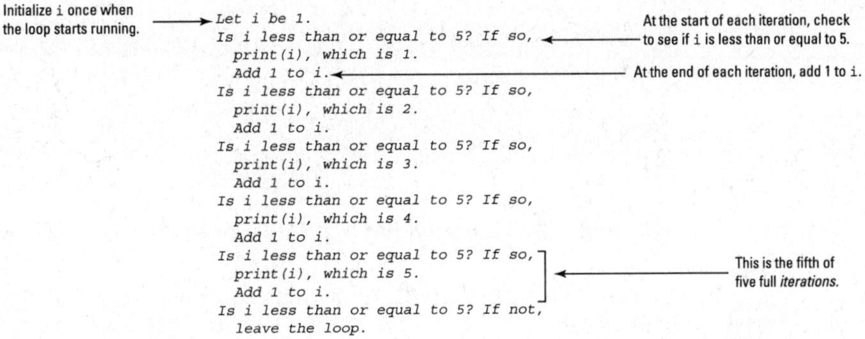

FIGURE 8-20:
Anatomy of a for
statement.

Initialize i once when the loop starts running. → Let i be 1.

At the start of each iteration, check to see if i is less than or equal to 5.

At the end of each iteration, add 1 to i.

```
Is i less than or equal to 5? If so,
  print(i), which is 1.
  Add 1 to i.
Is i less than or equal to 5? If so,
  print(i), which is 2.
  Add 1 to i.
Is i less than or equal to 5? If so,
  print(i), which is 3.
  Add 1 to i.
Is i less than or equal to 5? If so,
  print(i), which is 4.
  Add 1 to i.
Is i less than or equal to 5? If so,
  print(i), which is 5.
  Add 1 to i.
Is i less than or equal to 5? If not,
  leave the loop.
```

This is the fifth of five full *iterations*.

LISTING 8-9:

Interesting Code!

```
Widget buildTitlePageCore() {
  return ListView(
    children: <Widget>[
      for (int index = 0; index < 25; index++)
        ListTile(
          title: Text('Rocky ${index + 1}'),
          onTap: () => goToDetailPage(index + 1),
        ),
    ],
  );
}
```

If you replace the buildTitlePageCore method in Listing 8-7 with the code in Listing 8-9, your app behaves exactly the same way. When Flutter encounters the code in Listing 8-9, it starts creating 25 ListTile widgets.

Listings 8-7 and 8-9 give you two ways to create a 25-item ListView. Which way is better? You can decide by asking, "Which way makes the code easier to read and understand?" In my opinion, the new code (the code in Listing 8-9) is much clearer.

The stuff in Listing 8-9 looks like a for statement, but it's not really a for state-ment. It's a *collection for*. The name *collection for* comes from the fact that a List is one of Dart's collection types. (See Table 4-2, over in Chapter 4, for more on col-lection types.) You can put a collection for inside any kind of collection — a List, a Set, or a Map. The following code does all three of these things:

```
main() {
  List<int> myList = [for (int i = 1; i <= 5; i++) i];
  Set<int> mySet = {for (int i = 1; i <= 5; i++) i};
```

```
    Map<int, int> myMap = {for (int i = 1; i <= 5; i++) i: i + 100};
    print(myList);
    print(mySet);
    print(myMap);
}
```

For some rollicking good fun, run this code at `https://dartpad.dev`.

CROSS
REFERENCE
Compare Dart's collection for with its collection if. The collection if appears in Chapter 7.

TECHNICAL
STUFF
The collection for and collection if features work with Dart versions 2.3 and higher. With earlier versions of Dart, you're out of luck.

Dart's collection for is interesting because it's a new kind of programming language construct. The two pillars of programming languages are *statements* and *expressions*, but the collection for is neither a statement nor an expression. If you want to do some reading about all this geeky stuff, visit `https://medium.com/dartlang/making-dart-a-better-language-for-ui-f1ccaf9f546c`.

Fetching Data from the Internet

Do this chapter's examples remind you of movies that you've enjoyed? Would you like an app that displays facts about these movies? If so, look no further than Listing 8-10.

LISTING 8-10: **Accessing Online Data**

```dart
// App0810.dart

import 'dart:convert';

import 'package:flutter/material.dart';
import 'package:http/http.dart';

import 'App08Main.dart';

extension MoreMovieTitlePage on MovieTitlePageState {
  goToDetailPage(String movieTitle) {
    Navigator.push(
      context,
      MaterialPageRoute(
```

```
          builder: (context) => DetailPage(),
          settings: RouteSettings(
            arguments: movieTitle,
          ),
        ),
      );
  }

  Widget buildTitlePageCore() {
    TextEditingController _controller = TextEditingController();
    return Column(
      crossAxisAlignment: CrossAxisAlignment.center,
      children: <Widget>[
        TextField(
          decoration: InputDecoration(labelText: 'Movie title:'),
          controller: _controller,
        ),
        SizedBox(height: 16.0),
        RaisedButton.icon(
          icon: Icon(Icons.arrow_forward),
          label: Text('Details'),
          onPressed: () => goToDetailPage(_controller.text),
        ),
      ],
    );
  }
}

extension MoreDetailPage on DetailPage {
  Future<String> _getMovieData(String movieTitle) {
    return updateOverview(
      movieTitle: movieTitle,
      api_key: "Parents: Don't let your sons and "
          "daughters put api keys in their code.",
    );
  }

  Widget buildDetailPageCore(context) {
    final _movieTitle = ModalRoute.of(context).settings.arguments ?? '';
    return Column(
      crossAxisAlignment: CrossAxisAlignment.center,
      children: <Widget>[
        FutureBuilder<String>(
          future: _getMovieData(_movieTitle),
          builder: (context, snapshot) {
            if (snapshot.hasData) {
```

(continued)

LISTING 8-10: *(continued)*

```
                    return Text(snapshot.data);
                }
                return CircularProgressIndicator();
            },
        ),
      ],
    );
}


Future<String> updateOverview({String api_key, String movieTitle}) async {
  final response = await get(
      'https://api.themoviedb.org/3/search/movie?api_key=' +
          '$api_key&query="$movieTitle"');
  return json.decode(response.body)['results'][0]['overview'];
}
}
```

Figures 8-21 and 8-22 show a run of the code in Listing 8-10.

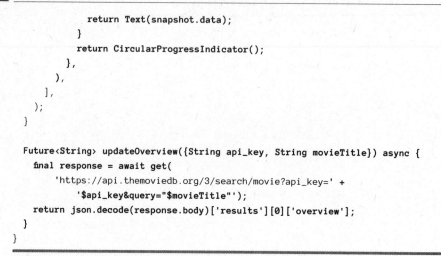

FIGURE 8-21:
The user types a
movie's name.

FIGURE 8-22:
The app displays
info from The
Movie Database.

There's a lot to unpack in Listing 8-10, so I divide it into parts.

Using a public API

Before creating Listing 8-10, I searched the web for a site that provides free access to movie information. Among the sites I found, the one I liked best was The Movie Database (https://www.themoviedb.org). Like many such sites, The Movie Database provides access through its own *application programming interface* (API). When you use the prescribed API code to send a query to themoviedb.org, the site spits back information about one or more movies.

For example, to get information about the movie *THX 1138*, you can try typing the following URL in a browser's address bar:

```
https://api.themoviedb.org/3/search/movie?api_key=XYZ&query="THX 1138"
```

When you do, the following message appears in your browser window:

```
Invalid API key: You must be granted a valid key.
```

Oops! Instead of typing XYZ, you should have typed a valid API key — a string of characters you get when you sign up on The Movie Database website. Everyone who signs up gets their own API key.

So get your own API key, replace XYZ with the API key, and type the new URL into a web browser's address bar:

```
// Not a real API key ...
https://api.themoviedb.org/3/search/movie?api_key=4c23b2f8f&query="THX 1138"
```

When you do, you don't see an error message, and you don't get a fancy-looking web page, either. Instead, you get code that looks something like the stuff in Listing 8-11.

LISTING 8-11: **JSON Code**

```
{
  "page": 1,
  "total_results": 4,
  "total_pages": 1,
  "results": [
    {
      "popularity": 8.126,
      .
      .
      .
```

(continued)

LISTING 8-11: *(continued)*

```
            "title": "THX 1138",
            "vote_average": 6.6,
            "overview": "People in the future live in a totalitarian ...",
            "release_date": "1971-03-11"
        },
        {
            "popularity": 3.11,
            "id": 140979,

            . . . and more . . .
```

The text in Listing 8-11 isn't Dart code. It's JSON code. The acronym JSON stands for JavaScript Object Notation. The best way to understand JSON code is to realize that it describes a tree. Compare the code in Listing 8-11 with the upside-down tree in Figure 8-23.

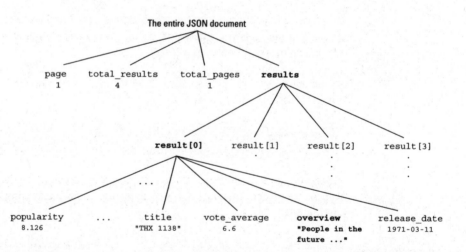

FIGURE 8-23:
A JSON document describes a tree.

TECHNICAL STUFF

Sending a URL to a server and getting JSON code in return is an example of Representational State Transfer, also known as REST.

As an app developer, your job is to make your app do two things:

» Send a URL to The Movie Database.

» Make sense of the JSON code that comes back from The Movie Database.

Sending a URL to a server

One way to enable web server communication is to import Dart's http package. An import line near the top of Listing 8-10 does the trick. The only "gotcha" is that if you fail to add a line to your project's pubspec.yaml file, Flutter can't do the importing:

```
dependencies:
  flutter:
    sdk: flutter
  http: ^0.12.0+4
```

Of course, the strange looking version number ^0.12.0+4 is sure to be obsolete by the time you read this book. To find out what number you should be using, visit https://pub.dev/packages/http.

REMEMBER

In a .yaml file, indentation matters. So, in your project's pubspec.yaml file, be sure to indent the http line the way you see it here.

CROSS REFERENCE

To find out about your project's pubspec.yaml file, refer to Chapter 3.

In your app's Dart code, you use the package's get function to send a URL out onto the web:

```
final response = await get(
    'https://api.themoviedb.org/3/search/movie?api_key=' +
        '$api_key&query="$movieTitle"');
```

TIP

A simple function name like get doesn't scream out at you, "I'm part of the http package." To make your code more readable, do two things: Add some extra words to the http package's import declaration

```
import 'package:http/http.dart' as http;
```

and add a prefix to your get function call:

```
final response = await http.get(     // ... etc.
```

The need for await, async, and Future in Listing 8-10 comes from one undeniable fact: If you send a request to a web server, you don't know when you'll get back a response. You don't want your Flutter app to freeze up while it waits for a response from who-knows-where. You want to entertain the user while a response makes its way along the Internet. That's why, in Listing 8-10, you display a Circular-ProgressIndicator widget until the response has arrived.

Making sense of a JSON response

In Listing 8-10, the `updateOverview` method awaits a response from The Movie Database. When a response arrives, the method assigns that response to its own variable named `response`. (How clever!) The `response` variable contains all kinds of information about HTTP headers and status codes, but it also contains a body, and that body looks like the JSON code in Listing 8-11.

But wait! How do you sift information out of all that JSON code? I'll tell you how. You call the `json.decode` function — one of the many functions in Dart's `convert` package. (Refer to code near the top and bottom of Listing 8-10.) The `json.decode` function turns the code in Listing 8-11 into a big Dart `Map` structure. Like all of Dart's maps, this map has keys and values, and some of the values can be lists. You use square brackets to get the values from maps and lists. (Refer to Chapter 7.) So, to pull a movie's overview out of the code in Listing 8-11, you write the following line:

```
return json.decode(response.body)['results'][0]['overview'];
```

Each pair of square brackets brings you closer to the bottom of the tree in Figure 8-23.

What's Next?

```
Navigator.push(
  context,
  MaterialPageRoute(
    builder: (context) => Chapter_9(),
  ),
);
```

Chapter **9**

Moving Right Along . . .

I f you've read other material in this book, you're probably tired of my long chapter introductions, with all their personal stories and bad jokes. That's why, for this chapter, I skip the preliminaries and get straight to the point.

This chapter is about animation — making things change right before the user's eyes. When I think about animation, I immediately think of movement, but Flutter provides a much broader definition of animation. With Flutter, you can change almost any property of a widget on almost any time scale.

Setting the Stage for Flutter Animation

This chapter's first listing has a bunch of reusable code. Subsequent listings contain code that works cooperatively with the code in the first listing. Thanks to Dart's extensions feature, each new listing can create methods belonging to the first listing's classes. You can read all about Dart extensions in Chapter 8.

The code in Listing 9-1 can't do anything on its own. Instead, this code relies on declarations in the chapter's other listings.

LISTING 9-1: **Reuse This Code**

```
// App09Main.dart

import 'package:flutter/material.dart';

import 'App0902.dart';  // Change to App0903, App0904, and so on.

void main() => runApp(App09Main());

class App09Main extends StatelessWidget {
  @override
  Widget build(BuildContext context) {
    return MaterialApp(
      home: MyHomePage(),
    );
  }
}

class MyHomePage extends StatefulWidget {
  @override
  MyHomePageState createState() => MyHomePageState();
}

class MyHomePageState extends State<MyHomePage>
    with SingleTickerProviderStateMixin {
  Animation<double> animation;
  AnimationController controller;

  @override
  void initState() {
    super.initState();
    controller =
        AnimationController(duration: const Duration(seconds: 3), vsync: this);
    animation = getAnimation(controller);
  }

  @override
  Widget build(BuildContext context) {
    return Material(
      child: SafeArea(
        child: Padding(
          padding: const EdgeInsets.all(8.0),
          child: Column(
            children: <Widget>[
              Expanded(
                child: Stack(
                  children: <Widget>[
                    buildPositionedWidget(),
```

```
            ],
          ),
        ),
        buildRowOfButtons(),
      ],
    ),
  ),
);
}

Widget buildRowOfButtons() {
  return Row(
    mainAxisAlignment: MainAxisAlignment.center,
    children: <Widget>[
      RaisedButton(
        onPressed: () => controller.forward(),
        child: Text('Forward'),
      ),
      SizedBox(
        width: 8.0,
      ),
      RaisedButton(
        onPressed: () => controller.animateBack(0.0),
        child: Text('Backward'),
      ),
      SizedBox(
        width: 8.0,
      ),
      RaisedButton(
        onPressed: () => controller.reset(),
        child: Text('Reset'),
      ),
    ],
  );
}

@override
void dispose() {
  controller.dispose();
  super.dispose();
}
}
```

Figure 9-1 illustrates the concepts that come together to make Flutter animation.

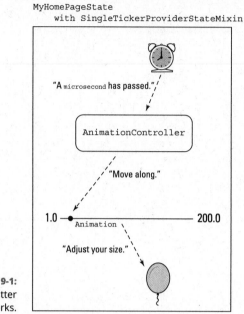

MyHomePageState
with SingleTickerProviderStateMixin

"A microsecond has passed."

AnimationController

"Move along."

1.0 •————————— 200.0
Animation

"Adjust your size."

FIGURE 9-1:
How Flutter
animation works.

You want something to change as the user looks on. To do this, you need four things: an Animation, an AnimationController, a ticker, and a feature of the app that changes. Here's how it all works:

> » **An Animation is a plan for changing a value.**
>
> In Listing 9-1, the words Animation<double> indicate that the changing value is a number with digits beyond the decimal point — a number like 0.0, 0.5, or 0.75. The plan in Figure 9-1 is to change a value in the range from 1.0 to 200.0.
>
> The Animation itself isn't about movement of any kind. The value that goes from 1.0 to 200.0 may be a position, but it may also be a size, an amount of transparency, a degree of rotation, or whatever. For the animation variable in Listing 9-1, values like 1.0 and 200.0 are only numbers. Nothing else.
>
> By the way, if you're looking in Listing 9-1 for a reference to an animation's double value, stop looking. The code in Listing 9-1 makes no reference to such a value. If you peek ahead to the next section's listing, you see animation.value. That's your tangible evidence that an Animation instance holds a value of some kind.
>
> Flutter's Animation class is nice, but an Animation can't do much without an AnimationController. Here's why:

>> **An** AnimationController **makes the animation start, stop, go forward, go backward, repeat, and so on.**

Calls such as controller.forward(), controller.animateBack(0.0), and controller.reset() push the animation in one direction or another.

In Listing 9-1, the AnimationController constructor call says that the animation lasts for 3 seconds. If seconds aren't good enough, you can use other parameters, such as microseconds, milliseconds, minutes, hours, and days. Each of the following constructors describes 51 hours:

```
Duration(hours: 51)

Duration(days: 1, hours: 27)

Duration(days: 2, hours: 3)

Duration(minutes: 3060)
```

In addition to its duration, the AnimationController in Listing 9-1 has a vsync property. If you're wondering what that is, keep reading.

>> **A** *ticker* **notifies the** AnimationController **when each time interval passes.**

The words with SingleTickerProviderStateMixin in Listing 9-1 make MyHomePageState into a ticker. The ticker wakes up repeatedly and says, "It's time to change a value."

But which value gets changed? What part of the code hears the ticker's announcement? Making MyHomePageState be a ticker doesn't connect MyHomePageState with a particular AnimationController.

To make that connection, the AnimationController in Listing 9-1 has a vsync: this parameter. That parameter tells Flutter that "this instance of MyHomePageState is the ticker for the newly constructed Animation Controller."

TIP

I've carefully worded my explanation of tickers and vsync: this so that the explanation doesn't offend anyone who knows all the details. The trouble is, precise explanations can be difficult to understand. If you don't comprehend all the stuff about vsync: this, simply add those words to your own code, and then move on. None of this book's examples requires an in-depth understanding of tickers and vsync.

CROSS
REFERENCE

In Listing 9-1, the name SingleTickerProviderStateMixin suggests that the Dart programming language has something called a mixin. A *mixin* is something like an extension, except that it's not the same as an extension. For a comparison, see the later sidebar "Another way to reuse code."

Here's the final ingredient in a Flutter animation:

» **Some feature changes as a result of the change in the** Animation **value.**

In Figure 9-1, a balloon's size changes with an Animation instance's double value. But the code in Listing 9-1 makes no reference to a balloon's size, or to any other use of the animation variable's value. On this count, Listing 9-1 is somewhat lacking.

The code to make things change is in the buildPositionedWidget function, and that function's body is in Listings 9-2 through 9-6. Each of those listings does something different with the Animation object's double values.

Listing 9-1 has one more interesting feature: It has a place where widgets can move freely. Imagine making an icon the child of a Center widget. The Center widget determines the icon's position, and that's the end of the story. A Center widget's constructor has no parameters that let you wiggle its child in one direction or another. Don't bother trying to make a Center widget's child move. You have no vocabulary for moving it.

What you need is a widget that lets you mark its children's exact coordinates within the available space. For that, Flutter has a Stack.

A Stack is like a Row or a Column, but a Stack doesn't place its children in a straight line. Instead, a Stack has two kinds of children — Positioned widgets and all other kinds of widgets. Each Positioned widget can have top, bottom, left, and right properties, which determine the exact location of the Positioned widget's child. The other widgets (the ones that aren't Positioned) get stuffed into some default location.

Have a look at the following code:

```
Stack(
  children: <Widget>[
    Positioned(
      top: 100.0,
      left: 100.0,
      child: Container(
        width: 50.0,
        height: 50.0,
        color: Colors.black,
      ),
    ),
    Positioned(
      top: 120.0,
      left: 120.0,
```

```
        child: Container(
          width: 25.0,
          height: 25.0,
          color: Colors.white,
        ),
      ),
    ],
  )
```

This code creates the drawing shown in Figure 9-2.

FIGURE 9-2:
Two containers
on a stack.

The drawing consists of two `Container` rectangles — one black and the other white. The white rectangle's width and height are half those of the black rectangle. But notice this: The two rectangles overlap because the rectangles' top and left edges are almost the same.

TIP

A `Stack` constructor has a `children` parameter, and that parameter's value is a list. The order of the widgets in the list matters. If two widgets overlap one another, the widget that comes later in the list appears to be on top. In the code accompanying Figure 9-2, you don't want to change the order of the two `Positioned` widgets in the list. If you do, the white rectangle becomes completely hidden behind the bigger black rectangle.

ON THE
WEB

You can download and run the little `Stack` app shown in Figure 9-2. It's the project named `app0900` in the files that you download from this book's website.

Moving Along a Straight Line

"A meal without wine is like a day without sunshine."
— AUTHOR UNKNOWN (AT LEAST, NOT KNOWN BY ME)

"Listing 9-1 without an extension is like a day without dessert."
— AUTHOR KNOWN (KNOWN TO BE ME)

Listing 9-2 contains an extension for the code in Listing 9-1.

Going Downward

```
// App0902.dart

import 'package:flutter/material.dart';

import 'App09Main.dart';

extension MyHomePageStateExtension on MyHomePageState {
  Animation getAnimation(AnimationController controller) {
    Tween tween = Tween<double>(begin: 100.0, end: 500.0);
    Animation animation = tween.animate(controller);
    animation.addListener(() {
      setState(() {});
    });
    return animation;
  }

  Widget buildPositionedWidget() {
    return Positioned(
      left: 150.0,
      top: animation.value,
      child: Icon(
        Icons.music_note,
        size: 70.0,
      ),
    );
  }
}
```

Taken together, Listings 9-1 and 9-2 form a complete Flutter app. Figure 9-3 shows you what the app looks like when it starts running. The dotted line is my way of illustrating the movement of the app's Musical Note icon. (The dotted line doesn't actually appear as part of the app.)

Listing 9-2 has the buildPositionedWidget method declaration that's missing from Listing 9-1. In the method's body, a Positioned widget tells Flutter where its child (the Musical Note icon) should appear. When the app starts running, the numbers

```
left: 150,
top: animation.value,
```

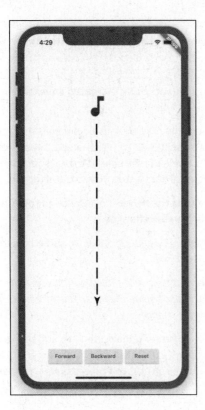

FIGURE 9-3:
Drop me a note.

place the icon 150.0 dps from the left edge of the `Stack`, and 100.0 dps from the top of the `Stack`. The number 100.0 comes from the animation's `begin` value, which is declared near the start of Listing 9-2. As `animation.value` increases, the Musical Note icon moves downward.

**CROSS
REFERENCE**

To find out what *dps* means, refer to Chapter 3.

Listing 9-2 also has a `getAnimation` method — a method that's called in Listing 9-1 but not declared in Listing 9-1. The `getAnimation` method in Listing 9-2 creates a `Tween` — a thing that comes from the world of animated cartoons. Imagine a cartoon character moving an arm from left to right. A cartoonist draws the arm's starting position and end position, and a computer creates the arm's "between" images. In the same way, an instance of Flutter's `Tween` class has `begin` and `end` values. When the animation moves forward, Flutter changes these values gradually from the `begin` value to the end `value`.

The rest of the `getAnimation` method's code connects the `Tween` with all the other puzzle pieces:

>> **The call to** `tween.animate(controller)` **creates an actual** `Animation` **instance.**

The way I describe a Tween, you may think that a Tween is the same as an Animation. But it's not. Fortunately, if you've created a Tween, you can make an Animation from it. In Listing 9-2, the `tween.animate(controller)` call creates an Animation object. That's a step in the right direction.

>> **The call to** `addListener` **tells the** `MyHomePageState` **to rebuild itself whenever the animation's value changes.**

In app development, a *listener* is a generic name for something that listens for events. The code in Listing 9-2 says,

Create a function that redraws the screen by calling setState. Make that function listen for changes in the animation's value. That way, Flutter redraws the screen whenever the animation's value changes.

Each call to `setState` makes Flutter update the `left` and `top` values of the `Positioned` widget in Listing 9-2. Because `left` is always 150.0, the icon doesn't move sideways. But the `animation` object's `value` property changes from moment to moment, so the icon moves up and down along the screen.

The `AnimationController` in Listing 9-1 determines the icon's movement:

>> **When the user presses the app's Forward button, Listing 9-1 calls the** `controller.forward` **method.**

The icon moves downward if it's not already at the bottom of its trajectory.

>> **When the user presses the app's Backward button, Listing 9-1 calls** `controller.animateBack(0.0)`.

The icon moves upward if it's not already at the top.

In the world of animations, numbers from 0.0 to 1.0 are very useful. In an `animateBack` call, the number `0.0` means "roll the animation backward until it reaches its `begin` value." To make the animation reach its midpoint, you'd call `controller.animateBack(0.5)`.

>> **When the user presses the app's Reset button, Listing 9-1 calls** `controller.reset()`.

The icon jumps to its starting position. (If it's already at the starting position, it stays there.)

TECHNICAL STUFF

You may never see the code in Listing 9-2 in any other book. This book's version of the getAnimation method avoids a trick that Flutter developers commonly use. They summarize the entire method body in one statement:

```
return Tween<double>(begin: 100.0, end: 500.0).animate(controller)
  ..addListener(() {
    setState(() {});
  });
```

In this code, the pair of dots in front of addListener is Dart's *cascade* operator. The operator calls addListener on the Animation instance that's about to be returned. The use of this operator makes the code much more concise.

ANOTHER WAY TO REUSE CODE

Listing 9-2 has an extension, and Listing 9-1 has a mixin. Both extensions and mixins are ways to make use of code from outside sources. How do mixins differ from extensions?

When you create an extension, you name the class that you intend to extend.

```
extension MyHomePageStateExtension on MyHomePageState
```

This code from Listing 9-2 adds functionality to only one class — the MyHomePageState class in Listing 9-1. You can't use this extension in any other context.

On the other hand, you can add a mixin to almost any class. Here's the SingleTickerProviderStateMixin declaration from Flutter's API:

```
mixin SingleTickerProviderStateMixin<T extends StatefulWidget> on State<T>
    implements TickerProvider
```

The declaration says nothing about the MyHomePageState class or about any other such class, so any class can use this mixin. (Well, any class that's already a StatefulWidget can use this mixin.)

The good thing about mixins is that they spread the wealth. The stewards of Flutter write 75 lines of SingleTickerProviderStateMixin code and, as a result, anyone's StatefulWidget can become a ticker. How convenient!

Bouncing Around

My big disappointment in writing this chapter is that the figures don't do justice to the apps they're supposed to illustrate. Figure 9-3 has a dotted line instead of real motion. Figure 9-4 is even worse because the dotted line isn't really accurate.

In this section's app, the Cake icon doesn't move sideways. The dotted line in Figure 9-4 moves to the right only to show some up-and-down motion near the end of the animation. Even so, Flutter's API calls this motion a *curve*. The code for Figure 9-4 is in Listing 9-3.

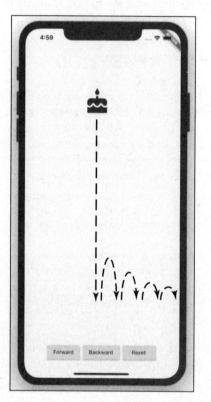

FIGURE 9-4:
A cake made of rubber?

LISTING 9-3:	Changing the Animation's Velocity

```
// App0903.dart

import 'package:flutter/material.dart';

import 'App09Main.dart';
```

```
extension MyHomePageStateExtension on MyHomePageState {
  Animation getAnimation(AnimationController controller) {
    return Tween<double>(begin: 100.0, end: 500.0).animate(
      CurvedAnimation(
        parent: controller,
        curve: Curves.bounceOut,
      ),
    )..addListener(() {
        setState(() {});
      });
  }

  Widget buildPositionedWidget() {
    return Positioned(
      left: 150.0,
      top: animation.value,
      child: Icon(
        Icons.cake,
        size: 70.0,
      ),
    );
  }
}
```

Once again, to change the properties of an object, you enclose that object inside of another object. It's a pattern that occurs over and over again in Flutter app development. Rather than call animate(controller) the way you do in Listing 9-2, you call

```
animate(
  CurvedAnimation(
    parent: controller,
    curve: Curves.bounceOut,
  )
```

You wrap the controller inside a CurvedAnimation object. In Listing 9-2, the object's curve property is Curves.bounce.Out, which means "bounce as the animation ends." Table 9-1 lists some alternative curve values.

The Flutter API has many more curve values. Each value comes from a precise equation and describes its own, special pattern for timing the animation. You can see the whole list of ready-made curve values by visiting https://api.flutter.dev/flutter/animation/Curves-class.html.

TABLE 9-1 **Some Constants of the Curves Class**

Value	What It Does
Curves.bounceIn	Bounces as the animation begins
Curves.decelerate	Slows down as the animation progresses
Curves.slowMiddle	Moves normally, and then slowly, and then normally
Curves.fastOutSlowIn	(Can you guess?)
Curve.ease	Speeds up quickly but ends slowly
Curve.elasticOut	Rushes in quickly enough to overshoot the end value and then settles in on the end value
Curve.linear	Doesn't change anything (used whenever you must use CurvedAnimation for some reason, but you don't want to apply a curve)

Animating Size and Color Changes

With Flutter's Animation class, you're not restricted to moving things. You can control the change of any value you think needs changing. This section's example changes an icon's size and color. The code is in Listing 9-4.

LISTING 9-4: **Changing a Few Values**

```dart
// App0904.dart

import 'package:flutter/material.dart';

import 'App09Main.dart';

extension MyHomePageStateExtension on MyHomePageState {
  Animation getAnimation(AnimationController controller) {
    return Tween<double>(begin: 50.0, end: 250.0).animate(controller)
      ..addListener(() {
        setState(() {});
      });
  }

  Widget buildPositionedWidget() {
    int intValue = animation.value.toInt();
    return Center(
      child: Icon(
        Icons.child_care,
```

```
        size: animation.value,
        color: Color.fromRGBO(
          intValue,
          0,
          255 - intValue,
          1.0,
        ),
      ),
    );
  }
}
```

When the app in Listing 9-4 starts running, a small, blue-colored baby face appears on the screen. (See Figure 9-5. If you're reading the printed version of this book, ignore the fact that you don't see the color.) When the user presses Forward, the baby face grows and turns color from blue to red. (See Figure 9-6. If you really care, find a crayon and paint the face yourself.)

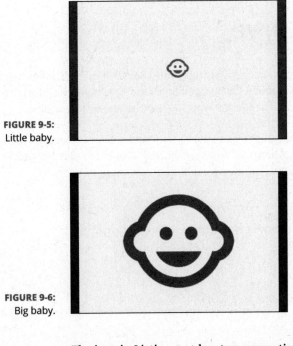

The icon in Listing 9-4 has two properties whose values can change.

>> **The** size **property changes along with** animation.value.

The icon grows from 50.0 dps to 250.0 dps.

> » **As the animation progresses, the** color **property's redness shrinks and its blueness grows.**
>
> Chapter 6 introduces Flutter's Color.fromRGBO constructor. The constructor's parameters are int values representing amounts of red, green, and blue and a double value that represents opacity. In Listing 9-4, the amount of red increases from 50 to 250, and the amount of blue decreases from 205 to 5.

This section is almost at an end. The moral of this section is, an Animation instance's value can mean anything you want it to mean. In Listings 9-2 and 9-3, the animation's value controls an icon's position. But in Listing 9-4, the animation's value controls an icon's size and color.

What value would you like to animate? Rotation? Sound volume? Speed? Curvature? Shadow? Background color? Border shape? Mood? The price of a *For Dummies* book?

Be creative.

Moving Along a Curve

Life doesn't always move along a straight line. Sometimes, fate takes bends and turns. To make this happen in Flutter, you don't have to change anything about an animation. Instead, you change the way you use the animation's value.

The Tween constructor call in this section's example is almost identical to the calls in this chapter's other listings. What's different about this section's example is the Positioned widget's parameters. It's all in Listing 9-5.

LISTING 9-5: **Fancy Parabolic Motion**

```
// App0905.dart

import 'dart:math';

import 'package:flutter/material.dart';

import 'App09Main.dart';

extension MyHomePageStateExtension on MyHomePageState {
  Animation getAnimation(AnimationController controller) {
    return Tween<double>(begin: 0.0, end: 400.0).animate(controller)
```

```
    ..addListener(() {
      setState(() {});
    });
}

Widget buildPositionedWidget() {
  double newValue = animation.value;
  return Positioned(
    left: 15 * sqrt(newValue),
    top: newValue,
    child: Icon(
      Icons.hot_tub,
      size: 70,
    ),
  );
}
}
```

In Figure 9-7, the dotted line shows the path taken by the Hot Tub icon when the animation moves forward.

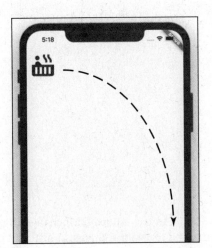

Have a look at the code in Listing 9-5. As the animation's value increases, both the icon's left and top parameter values change. The top parameter is the same as the animation's value, but the left parameter is 15 times the square root of the animation's value. How do I come up with the idea of taking 15 times the square root of the animation's value? It's partly knowing the math and partly trial-and-error.

You can use Dart's `sqrt` function only if you import `dart.math`. When you forget to import `dart.math`, Android Studio says, "Method 'sqrt' isn't defined."

As I prepared this section's example, I added some code to make the app print the values of `left` and `top`. Here's what I got:

```
left:   top:
  0.0    0.0
  7.4   40.7
 22.1   70.5
 29.4   81.4
 41.2   96.2
 65.0  120.9
 71.8  127.1
 86.5  139.5
101.5  151.1
119.7  164.1
147.4  182.1
165.4  192.9
174.3  198.0
197.9  211.0
206.8  215.7
222.7  223.9
238.3  231.6
266.8  245.0
290.0  255.5
312.6  265.2
335.1  274.6
352.3  281.5
367.2  287.4
384.6  294.2
399.0  299.6
400.0  300.0
```

The `Positioned` widget's `left` and `top` values both change. But, because of the square root formula, the `left` and `top` values change at different rates. That's why the icon's movement forms a curve.

Dragging Things Around

In this section's app, the user drags a widget all around the screen. I'd like to create a figure to show you what happens, but I simply can't do it. Maybe my next Flutter book will be a pop-up book with cardboard pieces that you can slide from place to place. Until then, you have to use your imagination. Picture an icon that looks like the infinity symbol (∞). As the user moves a finger, the icon changes position.

But wait! Rather than imagine a user dragging an icon, you can run the code in Listing 9-6 and see it in action.

LISTING 9-6: **Exercise for a User's Index Finger**

```
// App0906.dart

import 'package:flutter/material.dart';

import 'App09Main.dart';

double distanceFromLeft = 100;
double distanceFromTop = 100;

extension MyHomePageStateExtension on MyHomePageState {
  Animation getAnimation(AnimationController controller) {
    return null;
  }

  Widget buildPositionedWidget() {
    return Positioned(
      top: distanceFromTop,
      left: distanceFromLeft,
      child: GestureDetector(
        onPanUpdate: (details) {
          setState(() {
            distanceFromLeft += details.delta.dx;
            distanceFromTop += details.delta.dy;
          });
        },
        child: Icon(
          Icons.all_inclusive,
          size: 70,
        ),
      ),
    );
  }
```

Like other listings in this chapter, Listing 9-6 relies on the code in Listing 9-1. Because of that, the app that's generated by Listing 9-6 has Forward, Backward, and Reset buttons. Even so, pressing these buttons has no effect.

In the same way, Listing 9-6 has a getAnimation method. That's necessary because the code in Listing 9-1 calls a getAnimation method. But to make a widget move along with the user's finger, you don't need an Animation instance. In a sense, the user is the app's AnimationController, and the Animation instance is somewhere inside the user's mind. So, in Listing 9-6, the getAnimation method returns null. In Dart, null stands for "nothing," "nada," "zip," "goose egg," "zilch," "diddly," "bupkis."

Listing 9-6 has no Animation instance, so what part of the code makes the all_inclusive icon move? The icon lives inside of a GestureDetector — a widget that senses touches on the screen. A GestureDetector has tons of properties such as onTap, onDoubleTap, onTapUp, onTapDown, onLongPress, onLongPressStart, and onLongPressEnd. Other methods belonging to the GestureDetector class have names with less-than-obvious meanings. The following list has a few (somewhat oversimplified) examples:

» onSecondaryTapDown: While holding one finger on the screen, the user places a second finger on the screen.

» onScaleUpdate: With two fingers, the user pinches in or out.

» onHorizontalDragUpdate: The user moves something sideways — a common gesture for dismissing an item.

» onPanUpdate: The user moves a finger in one direction or another.

The onPanUpdate parameter's value is a method, and that method's parameter is a DragUpdateDetails object. In Listing 9-6, the DragUpdateDetails object goes by the name details:

```
onPanUpdate: (details) {
  setState(() {
    distanceFromLeft += details.delta.dx;
    distanceFromTop += details.delta.dy;
  });
```

When the user moves a finger along the screen, Flutter fills details with information about the movement and calls the onPanUpdate parameter's method.

The details variable contains some useful pieces of information:

>> details.globalPosition: The distance from the upper left corner of the app screen to the current position of the user's finger

>> details.localPosition: The distance from the place where the user's finger first landed on the screen to the current position of the user's finger

>> details.delta: The distance from a finger's previous position to its current position

Each piece of information has two parts: dx (the horizontal distance) and dy (the vertical distance). The Positioned widget in Listing 9-6 places the app's all_inclusive icon at the points distanceFromLeft and distanceFromTop. When Flutter detects finger movement, the code changes the values of distanceFromLeft and distanceFromTop by adding the details.delta parameter's dx and dy values. That's what makes the icon move around. It's pretty clever!

TECHNICAL STUFF

The GestureDectector in Listing 9-6 has a child. But, for any old GestureDectector constructor call, the child parameter is optional. A GestureDetector with no child grows to be as large as its parent widget. In contrast, a GestureDetector with a child shrinks to fit tightly around the child. With the app in Listing 9-6, the GestureDetector is about the same size as its child — the all_inclusive icon. To make the icon move, the user's finger must start right on the icon. Otherwise, nothing happens.

You're near the end of this book, so maybe it's time to relax and have some raucous, carefree fun. Can destroying something be fun? Here are some ways to break Listing 9-6:

>> **Remove the** setState **call.**

```
// Bad code:
onPanUpdate: (details) {
  distanceFromLeft += details.delta.dx;
  distanceFromTop += details.delta.dy;
}
```

Removing a setState call is almost never a good idea. If you remove the call in Listing 9-6, the values of distanceFromLeft and distanceFromTop change, but Flutter doesn't redraw the screen. As a result, the icon doesn't budge.

» **Move the** distanceFromLeft **and** distanceFromTop **declarations so that they're immediately before the** buildPositionedWidget **method.**

```
// More bad code:
Animation getAnimation(AnimationController controller) {
  return null;
}

double distanceFromLeft = 100;
double distanceFromTop = 100;

Widget buildPositionedWidget() {
// ... etc.
```

If you do this, you can't even run the app. Dart's rules include one about declaring top-level variables inside of extensions. You're simply not allowed to do it.

Chapter 5 has some information about top-level variables.

CROSS
REFERENCE

» **Move the** distanceFromLeft **and** distanceFromTop **declarations so that they're inside the** buildPositionedWidget **method.**

```
// Even more bad code:
Widget buildPositionedWidget() {
  double distanceFromLeft = 100;
  double distanceFromTop = 100;
  return Positioned(
  // ... etc.
```

The program runs, but the icon never moves. This happens because the code sets distanceFromLeft and distanceFromTop to 100 whenever Flutter redraws the screen. (Actually, the icon moves a tiny bit but not enough for you to notice. You get a tiny bit of movement from the details.delta values, but not the kind of movement you want.)

» **Rather than add to the** distanceFromLeft **and** distanceFromTop **values, set them equal to the position of the user's finger:**

```
// You guessed it! Bad code!
onPanUpdate: (details) {
  setState(() {
    distanceFromLeft = details.globalPosition.dx;
    distanceFromTop = details.globalPosition.dy;
  });
}
```

The app runs, but the icon jumps when the user's finger starts moving. Throughout the dragging gesture, the icon stays half an inch away from the user's finger. This happens because Flutter doesn't use the middle of the icon as the Positioned widget's top and left points.

Similar things happen if you try to use details.localPosition.

Flutter's animation features don't end with simple movements and basic size changes. If you're interested in making objects move, be sure to check Flutter's physics.dart package. With that package, you can simulate springs, gravity, friction, and much more. You can get information about the package by visiting https://api.flutter.dev/flutter/physics/physics-library.html.

Where To Go From Here

Learning doesn't end with the last page of a book. Keep coding and asking questions, and — by all means — keep in touch. My email is flutter@allmycode.com. Send me a note, and let me know what you're up to.

4

The Part of Tens

Chapter **10**

Ten Ways to Avoid Mistakes

Put Capital Letters Where They Belong

The Dart language is case-sensitive. Don't type `Class` when you mean to type `class`. Don't type `Runapp` when you mean to type `runApp`.

Use Parentheses When (and Only When) They're Appropriate

Remember the difference between `_incrementCounter` with parentheses:

```
void _incrementCounter() {
  setState(() {
    _counter++;
  });
}
```

and _incrementCounter without parentheses:

```
floatingActionButton: FloatingActionButton(
  onPressed: _incrementCounter,
  tooltip: 'Increment',
  child: Icon(Icons.add),
)
```

For details, refer to Chapter 5.

Limit Access to Variables

Wherever you can, avoid declaring top-level variables. To keep other files from changing your file's variables, start variable names with an underscore. (Refer to Chapter 5.)

Call setState

If you press a widget and nothing happens, look for a method with a missing setState call. (Refer to Chapter 5.)

Make Adjustments for Indices Starting at Zero

To make values start with 1, you have to add 1 (Refer to Chapter 8.):

```
return ListView.builder(
  itemCount: 25,
  itemBuilder: (context, index) => ListTile(
    title: Text('Rocky ${index + 1}'),
    onTap: () => goToDetailPage(index + 1),
  ),
);
```

Use the Expanded Widget

When your test device displays black-and-yellow stripes or an empty screen, the layout you've coded is causing trouble. Consider wrapping one or more widgets inside Expanded widgets. Sometimes, it works wonders. (Refer to Chapters 6 and 8.)

Add itemCount to Your ListView.builder

Without an itemCount parameter, the list of items never ends. (Refer to Chapter 8.)

Add Imports When They're Required

For example, if you want to use Dart's math library, start your file with

```
import 'dart:math';
```

If your app pulls data from the Internet, add this line to the top of your file:

```
import 'package:http/http.dart';
```

For details, refer to Chapters 8 and 9.

Declare Assets and Dependencies in pubspec.yaml

To display brokenheart.jpg and heart.jpg on the screen, add some lines to your project's pubspec.yaml file:

```
assets:
  - brokenheart.jpeg
  - heart.jpeg
```

To get data from the Internet, add `http` to the file's list of dependencies:

```
dependencies:
  flutter:
    sdk: flutter
  http: ^0.12.0+4
```

For details, refer to Chapters 3 and 8. And remember, in a `pubspec.yaml` file, indentation matters.

Indent Your Code According to Dart Language Guidelines

Code that's not properly indented is difficult to read and difficult to maintain. Format your code by selecting Code➪Reformat Code from Android Studio's main menu.

Chapter **11**

Ten Ways to Enhance Your App Development Career

With my email address in many of my books, readers often ask me for career advice: "What should I do next? How can I find a job? How can I prepare for work in the software industry?" In this chapter, I offer some of my best hints.

Practice! Practice!

Write as much code as you can. Find problems on the web or make up problems that interest you. If you get stuck on a problem, look for help on developer forums or set the problem aside for a while.

When you've finished solving a problem, look for ways to add features to your solution. The more practice you have writing programs, the better your developer skills will be.

Critique Your Own Code

Don't be satisfied with code that merely works. Good code does more than that. Good code is readable and maintainable. Good code complies with published style guidelines. Good code runs efficiently. No matter what kind of code you write, there's always room for improvement.

Have Others Review Your Code

Other developers can find flaws that you're too entrenched in the code to notice. Expect reviewers to be critical but respectful. Respond to reviews with an open mind. Think carefully about each comment, and decide whether the suggestion makes sense to you.

Find Out Which Technologies Your Nearby Companies Use

If local companies use MySQL, learn something about MySQL. If local companies program in Haskell, learn something about Haskell. What's trendy throughout the industry may have little demand in the town where you live.

Attend User Group Meetings

When you hang out with programming professionals, three very nice things happen.

>> **You learn about things that you might not discover on your own.**

As a novice at a user group meeting, you don't choose the topic. That's a good thing because it exposes you to ideas on the periphery of your range of knowledge.

>> **You find out what issues are at the forefront of today's technology.**

A few years ago, I heard the word *microservices* at a small session in New York City. When I looked it up the next day, I found several blog posts calling microservices "the next big thing." The blog posts were right.

> **» You network with professionals in your chosen field.**
>
> Who knows? Maybe one of them can help you find work!

When you attend a meeting and listen to the discussion, you may not understand what people are saying. That's okay. If nothing else, you're learning by osmosis.

Ask Questions

In my college classes, students apologize for asking what they think are stupid questions. "Don't apologize," I say. "The stupid questions are the ones I'm sure I can answer."

Ask Yourself Whether You Truly Understand

Sometimes, I ignore a gap in my grasp of a particular concept. When I do, it's because I'm either too busy, too embarrassed, or too lazy to stop and think in-depth about the concept. Eventually, my lack of understanding comes back to haunt me. Even if it doesn't, I carry around the nagging feeling that I'm deceiving myself and sometimes deceiving others.

If you don't understand something that's useful for you to know, stop and try to figure it out. The effort always pays off.

Learn Things That You May Never Need to Know

You may never need to run 13 miles, but you sign up for a half-marathon anyway. You may never need to paint a stunning landscape, but you visit art museums anyway. Exercise your mind. Nothing you learn ever goes to waste.

Do What You Love to Do

If you love your work, you love your life.

You may need to earn money in a job you don't enjoy. If so, make a mental note to yourself: "For now, I'll do what I have to do to support myself and my family. When I can, I'll find work that I look forward to every day."

Get Plenty of Sleep

That extra hour you spend trying to be an overachiever won't help you when you're too tired to think clearly. To misquote Ben Franklin: "Early to bed and late to rise puts a sparkle in your eyes."

» A celebration of having ten chapters in this book

» Perhaps a waste of two pages

Chapter **12**

Ten Chapters about Flutter App Development

Introduction

Remarks about this book

What Is Flutter?

A bunch of vocabulary (some interesting and some not-so-interesting), all of it useful

Setting Up Your Computer for Mobile App Development

Downloading and installing stuff

'Hello' from Flutter

Examining a simple Flutter app

Hello Again

Digging deeper into the simple Flutter app

Making Things Happen

Responding to button presses and other such events

Laying Things Out

Making widgets be where you want them to be

Interacting with the User

Doris's dating app

Navigation, Lists, and Other Goodies

Taking your app from one page to another and, as a special bonus, fetching information from the Internet

Moving Right Along . . .

Adding animation to your app

5 Appendices

Appendix A

Doris's Dating App

Taken together, the examples in Chapter 7 form a dating app with several questions for the user. As real-world apps go, the dating app isn't very large — only 340 lines of code. But the app is too large to squeeze into Chapter 7. So, instead of forcing the app on you in Chapter 7, I put the app's full text here in Appendix A.

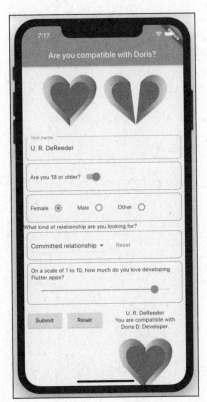

Doris's stunning
achievement.

```dart
import 'package:flutter/material.dart';

void main() => runApp(App0707());

class App0707 extends StatelessWidget {
  @override
  Widget build(BuildContext context) {
    return MaterialApp(
      home: MyHomePage(),
    );
  }
}


class MyHomePage extends StatefulWidget {
  @override
  _MyHomePageState createState() => _MyHomePageState();
}


const _youAre = 'You are';
const _compatible = 'compatible with\nDoris D. Developer.';

enum Gender { Female, Male, Other }

String show(Gender gender) => gender.toString().replaceAll("Gender.", "");

enum Relationship {
  Friend,
  OneDate,
  Ongoing,
  Committed,
  Marriage,
}

Map<Relationship, String> nice = {
  Relationship.Friend: "Friend",
  Relationship.OneDate: "One date",
  Relationship.Ongoing: "Ongoing relationship",
  Relationship.Committed: "Committed relationship",
  Relationship.Marriage: "Marriage",
};

List<DropdownMenuItem<Relationship>> _relationshipsList = [
  DropdownMenuItem(
    value: Relationship.Friend,
```

```
        child: Text(nice[Relationship.Friend]),
      ),
    DropdownMenuItem(
      value: Relationship.OneDate,
        child: Text(nice[Relationship.OneDate]),
      ),
    DropdownMenuItem(
      value: Relationship.Ongoing,
        child: Text(nice[Relationship.Ongoing]),
      ),
    DropdownMenuItem(
      value: Relationship.Committed,
        child: Text(nice[Relationship.Committed]),
      ),
    DropdownMenuItem(
      value: Relationship.Marriage,
        child: Text(nice[Relationship.Marriage]),
      ),
];

class _MyHomePageState extends State<MyHomePage> {
  TextEditingController _nameFieldController;
  bool _ageSwitchValue;
  Gender _genderRadioValue;
  Relationship _relationshipDropdownValue;
  double _loveFlutterSliderValue;
  String _messageToUser;
  Image _resultImage;

  /// State

  @override
  void initState() {
    super.initState();
    _nameFieldController = TextEditingController();
    _reset();
  }

  @override
  void dispose() {
    _nameFieldController.dispose();
    super.dispose();
  }
```

```
@override
Widget build(BuildContext context) {
  return Scaffold(
    appBar: AppBar(
      title: Text("Are you compatible with Doris?"),
    ),
    body: GestureDetector(
      onTap: () {
        FocusScope.of(context).requestFocus(FocusNode());
      },
      child: SingleChildScrollView(
        child: Column(
          crossAxisAlignment: CrossAxisAlignment.stretch,
          children: <Widget>[
            _buildTitleImage(),
            _buildNameTextField(),
            _buildAgeSwitch(),
            _buildGenderRadio(),
            _buildRelationshipDropdown(),
            _buildLoveFlutterSlider(),
            _buildSubmitRow(),
          ],
        ),
      ),
    ),
  );
}


/// Build

Widget _buildTitleImage() {
  return Row(
    mainAxisAlignment: MainAxisAlignment.center,
    children: <Widget>[
      Image.asset("Heart.png"),
      Image.asset("BrokenHeart.png"),
    ],
  );
}


Widget _buildNameTextField() {
  return Container(
    padding: EdgeInsets.symmetric(vertical: 4.0, horizontal: 8.0),
    child: TextField(
```

```
        controller: _nameFieldController,
        decoration: InputDecoration(
          labelText: "Your name:",
          border: OutlineInputBorder(
            borderRadius: BorderRadius.all(Radius.circular(10.0)),
          ),
        ),
      ),
    ),
  );
}

Widget _buildCommonBorder({Widget child}) {
  return Container(
    padding: EdgeInsets.symmetric(vertical: 10.0, horizontal: 10.0),
    margin: EdgeInsets.symmetric(vertical: 4.0, horizontal: 8.0),
    decoration: BoxDecoration(
      border: Border.all(width: 0.5),
      borderRadius: BorderRadius.all(
        Radius.circular(10.0),
      ),
    ),
    child: child,
  );
}

Widget _buildAgeSwitch() {
  return _buildCommonBorder(
    child: Row(
      children: <Widget>[
        Text("Are you 18 or older?"),
        Switch(
          value: _ageSwitchValue,
          onChanged: _updateAgeSwitch,
        ),
      ],
    ),
  );
}

Widget _buildGenderRadio() {
  return _buildCommonBorder(
    child: Row(
      children: <Widget>[
        Text(show(Gender.Female)),
```

```
          Radio(
            value: Gender.Female,
            groupValue: _genderRadioValue,
            onChanged: _updateGenderRatio,
          ),
          SizedBox(width: 25.0),
          Text(show(Gender.Male)),
          Radio(
            value: Gender.Male,
            groupValue: _genderRadioValue,
            onChanged: _updateGenderRatio,
          ),
          SizedBox(width: 25.0),
          Text(show(Gender.Other)),
          Radio(
            value: Gender.Other,
            groupValue: _genderRadioValue,
            onChanged: _updateGenderRatio,
          ),
      ],
    ),
  );
}


Widget _buildRelationshipDropdown() {
  return Column(
    crossAxisAlignment: CrossAxisAlignment.start,
    children: <Widget>[
      Text("What kind of relationship are you looking for?"),
      _buildDropdownButtonRow(),
    ],
  );
}


Widget _buildDropdownButtonRow() {
  return _buildCommonBorder(
    child: Row(
      mainAxisAlignment: MainAxisAlignment.start,
      children: <Widget>[
        DropdownButton<Relationship>(
          items: _relationshipsList,
          onChanged: _updateRelationshipDropdown,
          value: _relationshipDropdownValue,
          hint: Text("Select One"),
        ),
```

```
          if (_relationshipDropdownValue != null)
            FlatButton(
              child: Text(
                "Reset",
                style: TextStyle(color: Colors.blue),
              ),
              onPressed: _resetDropdown,
            ),
      ],
    ),
  );
}


Widget _buildLoveFlutterSlider() {
  return _buildCommonBorder(
    child: Column(
      children: <Widget>[
        Text("On a scale of 1 to 10, "
            "how much do you love developing Flutter apps?"),
        Slider(
          min: 1.0,
          max: 10.0,
          divisions: 9,
          value: _loveFlutterSliderValue,
          onChanged: _updateLoveFlutterSlider,
          label: '${_loveFlutterSliderValue.toInt()}',
        ),
      ],
    ),
  );
}


Widget _buildSubmitRow() {
  return Container(
    padding: const EdgeInsets.symmetric(vertical: 12.0, horizontal: 8.0),
    child: Row(
      crossAxisAlignment: CrossAxisAlignment.start,
      children: <Widget>[
        RaisedButton(
          child: Text("Submit"),
          onPressed: _updateResults,
        ),
        SizedBox(
          width: 15.0,
        ),
```

```
            RaisedButton(
              child: Text("Reset"),
              onPressed: () => setState(_reset),
            ),
            SizedBox(
              width: 15.0,
            ),
            Expanded(
              child: Column(
                children: <Widget>[
                  Text(_messageToUser, textAlign: TextAlign.center),
                  _resultImage ?? SizedBox(),
                ],
              ),
            ),
      ],
    ),
  );
}


/// Actions

void _reset() {
  _nameFieldController.text = "";
  _ageSwitchValue = false;
  _genderRadioValue = null;
  _relationshipDropdownValue = null;
  _loveFlutterSliderValue = 1.0;
  _messageToUser = "";
  _resultImage = null;
}

void _updateAgeSwitch(bool newValue) {
  setState(() {
    _ageSwitchValue = newValue;
  });
}

void _updateGenderRatio(Gender newValue) {
  setState(() {
    _genderRadioValue = newValue;
  });
}
```

```
void _updateRelationshipDropdown(Relationship newValue) {
  setState(() {
    _relationshipDropdownValue = newValue;
  });
}

void _resetDropdown() {
  setState(() {
    _relationshipDropdownValue = null;
  });
}

void _updateLoveFlutterSlider(double newValue) {
  setState(() {
    _loveFlutterSliderValue = newValue;
  });
}

void _updateResults() {
  bool isCompatible = _ageSwitchValue && _loveFlutterSliderValue >= 8;
  setState(() {
    _resultImage =
        Image.asset(isCompatible ? "Heart.png" : "BrokenHeart.png");
    _messageToUser = _nameFieldController.text +
        "\n" +
        _youAre +
        (isCompatible ? " " : " NOT ") +
        _compatible;
  });
}
}
```

Index

Symbols

Run icon, 85
Run tool window (Android Studio), 62
Runes type, 122
running
  apps, 36–42
  apps on Android devices, 52–53
  sample programs from book, 63–66
runtime, 12

S

SafeArea widget, 181
Scaffold widget, 87
scaffolds, creating, 86–87
scrolling, 284
SDK (Software Development Kit), 30
SEARCH ON WIDGETS IN FIRST 100 PAGES
sending URLs to servers, 295
servers, sending URLs to, 295
Set type, 122
setState function, 143–145, 153, 154, 155, 306, 317, 324
setup, computer for mobile app development, 332
shorten method, 238–239
showing
  images, 100–104
  user choice, 235–236
  widgets, 194–195
simulator, 31
single quotation marks, 93
SingleChildScrollView, 284
size
  animation and, 310–312
  of devices, 199–203
size property, 311
SizedBox widget, 175
slash character (/), 275
slashes (//), 77, 120
sleep, importance of, 330
slider app, 217–220
software
  about, 10–15
  compatibility and, 16

downloading, 31
installing, 32–34
obtaining, 32–34
operating system (OS), 11
Software Development Kit (SDK), 30
source code, 10
source page, 255
sources
  passing data back to, 261–267
  passing data to destinations from, 256–261
split method, 228
sqrt function, 314
square brackets, 296
Stack, 302, 303
stacks, 255–256
Stanley's Swell Shaving Cream/Superior Shaving Cream, 131–132
starting
  Android Studio, 44, 59–60
  AVD Manager, 48–50
state, 134
State object, 223
stateful widgets, 134–135
StatefulWidget class, 307
stateless widgets, 134–135
StatelessWidget class, 80, 151–152
statements
  for, 288–290
  about, 289
  assignment, 115
  break, 282–283
  Dart programming language, 112–113
  defined, 116
  DO, 288
  if, 200–201, 213–214, 244
  import, 160–161
  return, 110, 112, 283
  switch, 282–283
static members, 229
static variables, 260
status bar (Android Studio), 63
straight lines, animation along, 303–307
String instance, 114, 122, 228

About the Author

Barry Burd received an MS degree in computer science at Rutgers University and a PhD in mathematics at the University of Illinois. As a teaching assistant in Champaign-Urbana, Illinois, he was elected five times to the university-wide List of Teachers Ranked as Excellent by Their Students.

Since 1980, Barry has been a professor in the department of mathematics and computer science at Drew University in Madison, New Jersey. He has spoken at conferences in the United States, Europe, Australia, and Asia. He is the author of several articles and books, including *Java For Dummies*, *Beginning Programming with Java For Dummies*, and *Java Programming for Android Developers For Dummies*, all from Wiley.

Barry lives in Madison, New Jersey, with his wife of 40 years. In his spare time, he enjoys eating chocolate and avoiding exercise. You can reach him at `flutter@ allmycode.com`.

Dedication

For Abram and Katie, Benjamin and Jennie, Sam and Ruth, Harriet, Sam, and Jennie,

Author's Acknowledgments

I heartily and sincerely thank Paul Levesque, for his work on so many of my books in this series. Thanks also to Katie Mohr and Steve Hayes, for their patience and support. Thanks to Martin Rybak, for his technical advice and his ongoing encouragement. Thanks to Becky Whitney, for keeping my grammar and punctuation in check. Thanks to the staff at Wiley, for helping to bring this book to bookshelves.

Thanks to Frank Greco and the leaders of the New York JavaSIG — Jeanne Boyarsky, Rodrigo Graciano, Chandra Guntur, Justin Lee, Sai Sharan Donthi, Lily Luo, and Vinay Karle. Thanks to Michael Redlich of the ACGNJ Java User Group. Thanks to my colleagues, the faculty members in the mathematics and computer science department at Drew University — Sarah Abramowitz, Chris Apelian, Ferdi Eruysal, Seth Harris, Emily Hill, Steve Kass, Yi Lu, Ziyuan Meng, Ellie Small, and Steve Surace. Finally, a special thanks to Richard Bonacci, Peter Lubbers, and Cameron McKenzie, for their long-term help and support.

Publisher's Acknowledgments

Acquisitions Editor: Steve Hayes

Senior Project Editor: Paul Levesque

Copy Editor: Becky Whitney

Editorial Assistant: Matthew Lowe

Sr. Editorial Assistant: Cherie Case

Production Editor: Magesh Elangovan

Cover Image: andresr/Getty Images, screen image courtesy of Barry Burd

Take dummies with you everywhere you go!

Whether you are excited about e-books, want more from the web, must have your mobile apps, or are swept up in social media, dummies makes everything easier.

Find us online!

dummies.com

dummies
A Wiley Brand

Leverage the power

Dummies is the global leader in the reference category and one of the most trusted and highly regarded brands in the world. No longer just focused on books, customers now have access to the dummies content they need in the format they want. Together we'll craft a solution that engages your customers, stands out from the competition, and helps you meet your goals.

Advertising & Sponsorships

Connect with an engaged audience on a powerful multimedia site, and position your message alongside expert how-to content. Dummies.com is a one-stop shop for free, online information and know-how curated by a team of experts.

- Targeted ads
- Video
- Email Marketing
- Microsites
- Sweepstakes sponsorship

20 MILLION PAGE VIEWS EVERY SINGLE MONTH

15 MILLION UNIQUE VISITORS PER MONTH

43% OF ALL VISITORS ACCESS THE SITE VIA THEIR MOBILE DEVICES

700,000 NEWSLETTER SUBSCRIPTIONS TO THE INBOXES OF
300,000 UNIQUE INDIVIDUALS EVERY WEEK

# of dummies

Custom Publishing

Reach a global audience in any language by creating a solution that will differentiate you from competitors, amplify your message, and encourage customers to make a buying decision.

- Apps
- Books
- eBooks
- Video
- Audio
- Webinars

Brand Licensing & Content

Leverage the strength of the world's most popular reference brand to reach new audiences and channels of distribution.

For more information, visit dummies.com/biz

PERSONAL ENRICHMENT

Staying Sharp
9781119187790
USA $26.00
CAN $31.99
UK £19.99

Facebook
9781119179030
USA $21.99
CAN $25.99
UK £16.99

Guitar
9781119293354
USA $24.99
CAN $29.99
UK £17.99

Investing
9781119293347
USA $22.99
CAN $27.99
UK £16.99

Beekeeping
9781119310068
USA $22.99
CAN $27.99
UK £16.99

Digital Photography
9781119235606
USA $24.99
CAN $29.99
UK £17.99

Meditation
9781119251163
USA $24.99
CAN $29.99
UK £17.99

Pregnancy
9781119235491
USA $26.99
CAN $31.99
UK £19.99

Samsung Galaxy S7
9781119279952
USA $24.99
CAN $29.99
UK £17.99

iPhone
9781119283133
USA $24.99
CAN $29.99
UK £17.99

Crocheting
9781119287117
USA $24.99
CAN $29.99
UK £16.99

Nutrition
9781119130246
USA $22.99
CAN $27.99
UK £16.99

PROFESSIONAL DEVELOPMENT

Windows 10
9781119311041
USA $24.99
CAN $29.99
UK £17.99

AutoCAD
9781119255796
USA $39.99
CAN $47.99
UK £27.99

Excel 2016
9781119293439
USA $26.99
CAN $31.99
UK £19.99

QuickBooks 2017
9781119281467
USA $26.99
CAN $31.99
UK £19.99

macOS Sierra
9781119280651
USA $29.99
CAN $35.99
UK £21.99

LinkedIn
9781119251132
USA $24.99
CAN $29.99
UK £17.99

Windows 10 All-in-One
9781119310563
USA $34.00
CAN $41.99
UK £24.99

SharePoint 2016
9781119181705
USA $29.99
CAN $35.99
UK £21.99

Fundamental Analysis
9781119263593
USA $26.99
CAN $31.99
UK £19.99

Networking
9781119257769
USA $29.99
CAN $35.99
UK £21.99

Office 2016
9781119293477
USA $26.99
CAN $31.99
UK £19.99

Office 365
9781119265313
USA $24.99
CAN $29.99
UK £17.99

Salesforce.com
9781119239314
USA $29.99
CAN $35.99
UK £21.99

Coding
9781119293323
USA $29.99
CAN $35.99
UK £21.99

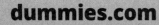
dummies.com

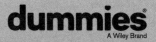
dummies®
A Wiley Brand

Learning Made Easy

ACADEMIC

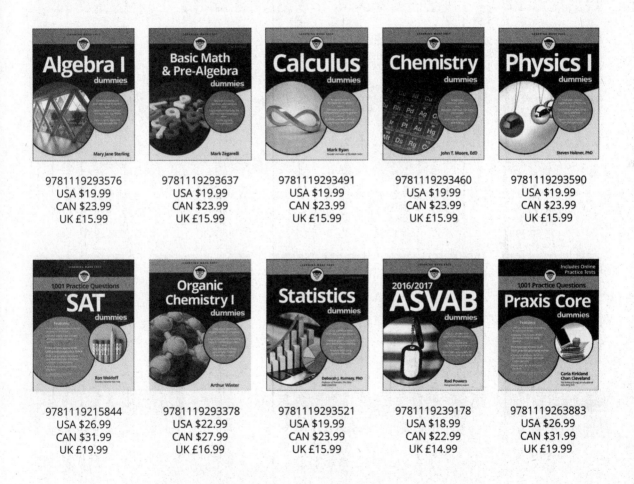

Algebra I dummies
Mary Jane Sterling

9781119293576
USA $19.99
CAN $23.99
UK £15.99

Basic Math & Pre-Algebra dummies
Mark Zegarelli

9781119293637
USA $19.99
CAN $23.99
UK £15.99

Calculus dummies
Mark Ryan

9781119293491
USA $19.99
CAN $23.99
UK £15.99

Chemistry dummies
John T. Moore, EdD

9781119293460
USA $19.99
CAN $23.99
UK £15.99

Physics I dummies
Steven Holzner, PhD

9781119293590
USA $19.99
CAN $23.99
UK £15.99

1,001 Practice Questions
SAT dummies
Ron Woldoff

9781119215844
USA $26.99
CAN $31.99
UK £19.99

Organic Chemistry I dummies
Arthur Winter

9781119293378
USA $22.99
CAN $27.99
UK £16.99

Statistics dummies
Deborah J. Rumsey, PhD

9781119293521
USA $19.99
CAN $23.99
UK £15.99

2016/2017
ASVAB dummies
Rod Powers

9781119239178
USA $18.99
CAN $22.99
UK £14.99

Includes Online Practice Tests
1,001 Practice Questions
Praxis Core dummies
Carla Kirkland, Chan Cleveland

9781119263883
USA $26.99
CAN $31.99
UK £19.99

Available Everywhere Books Are Sold

dummies.com

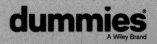

dummies
A Wiley Brand

Small books for big imaginations

9781119177173
USA $9.99
CAN $9.99
UK £8.99

9781119177272
USA $9.99
CAN $9.99
UK £8.99

9781119177241
USA $9.99
CAN $9.99
UK £8.99

9781119177210
USA $9.99
CAN $9.99
UK £8.99

9781119262657
USA $9.99
CAN $9.99
UK £6.99

9781119291336
USA $9.99
CAN $9.99
UK £6.99

9781119233527
USA $9.99
CAN $9.99
UK £6.99

9781119291220
USA $9.99
CAN $9.99
UK £6.99

9781119177302
USA $9.99
CAN $9.99
UK £8.99

Unleash Their Creativity

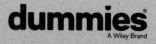